Two Crows Denies It

R. H. Barnes

Two Crows Denies It

A History
of Controversy
in Omaha
Sociology

University of Nebraska Press

Lincoln and London

Portions of chapter 4
have previously been published,
in different form,
as "Personal Names and Social
Classification," in
Semantic Anthropology, edited
by David Parkin
(London: Academic Press, 1982),
211-26; and of chapter 10
as "Dispersed Alliance and the
Prohibition of Marriage:
Reconsideration of McKinley's
Explanation of Crow-
Omaha Terminologies," *Man* 11
(1976):384-99.

The paper in this book meets
the guidelines for
permanence and durability
of the Committee on
Production Guidelines for
Book Longevity of the
Council on Library Resources.

Library of Congress
Cataloging in Publication Data

Barnes, R. H., 1944-
Two Crows denies it.

Bibliography: p.
Includes indexes.
1. Omaha Indians – Kinship.
2. Omaha Indians – Social
life and customs.
3. Indians of North America –
Nebraska – Kinship.
4. Indians of North America –
Nebraska – Social life
and customs.   I. Title.
E99.O4B37   1984
306.8'008997   84-2276
ISBN 0-8032-1182-1

To the Omahas and Their Ethnographers

Contents

Plates

Acknowledgments

For students of descent, alliance, and relationship systems, many paths lead to the Omahas. My first two teachers of anthropology, David French and Gail Kelly of Reed College, introduced me to the early Omaha ethnographies by James Owen Dorsey and by Alice Fletcher and Francis La Flesche. As an undergraduate I was impressed, as others have been, by the wealth of information they presented, but largely at a loss for what to make of it. Like other readers I was also startled by Dorsey's bland chronicle of the many disagreements among his informants. Two Crows in particular seemed continually to introduce doubt with his brusque dismissals of other Omaha opinion. Later, as a postgraduate student of Rodney Needham, I studied an Indonesian society with a positive form of marriage alliance. Others before me, notably Claude Lévi-Strauss, have sensed and argued that there are systematic ties—characterized by similarities, but, just as important, also by contrasts—between the analysis of alliance systems and the issues raised by the Omahas. Lévi-Strauss's publications in particular drew me to look again at the Omahas.

Inspecting the Omaha ethnographies, I felt that they contained gaps at just those points at which Lévi-Strauss's speculations might usefully be tested. The texts, however, suggested in several ways that the needed information might well exist in unpublished form. I turned to expert Americanists, several of whom provided useful tips. It was Raymond J. DeMallie who told me that what I needed might be found in the papers of Dorsey and Fletcher at the National

Anthropological Archives, Smithsonian Institution, in Washington, D.C. Most important among several useful manuscripts were Dorsey's complete handwritten Omaha genealogies and the notebooks and records relating to Omaha families deriving from Alice Fletcher's allotment of Omaha lands. A small grant from the Faculty Board of Anthropology and Geography, University of Oxford, permitted me to purchase photocopies of this material. From this point the present project acquired momentum and direction. A grant-in-aid from the American Council of Learned Societies permitted me to visit the archives in 1980. Grants from the Faculty Board of Anthropology and Geography, University of Oxford, and from the American Philosophical Society permitted me to conduct further searches in 1982 at the Library of Congress, Washington, D.C., and the Nebraska State Historical Society, Lincoln, Nebraska. I also had the very good fortune to discuss these matters to some extent with Lévi-Strauss and Françoise Héritier when they invited me to take the position for two months of Directeur d'Etudes Associé at L'Ecole des Hautes Etudes en Sciences Sociales at Paris in 1980.

Good fortune also came my way in the person of Paul E. Brill of Terre Haute, Indiana, who, without knowledge of Dorsey's genealogies, carried out research into Omaha family lines in 1961–63 for the Bureau of Indian Affairs. Brill had access to persons and court records either no longer living or not available to the public, and his extensive record, which he has selflessly made available to me, is a valuable independent source, often superior to Dorsey's.

I should like to express my gratitude to the persons mentioned above for their various forms of assistance or instruction and also to the staff of the following institutions or libraries: the American Council of Learned Societies; American Philosophical Society; Faculty Board of Anthropology and Geography, University of Oxford; Library of Congress, National Anthropological Archives, and National Archives, Washington, D.C.; the Anthropological Library of the Smithsonian Institution, Washington; the Library and Archives of the Nebraska State Historical Society, Lincoln, Nebraska; the Balfour, Bodleian, Law, Radcliffe Science, Rhodes House, and Tylor libraries, University of Oxford.

Portions of two chapters have been published elsewhere. Thanks are due to Academic Press for sections of "Personal Names and Social Classification," in *Semantic Anthropology*, ed. David Parkin (1982), included in chapter 4, and to *Man: The Journal of the Royal Anthropological Institute*, for "Dispersed Alliance and the Prohibition of Marriage" (1976), now chapter 10.

NOTE ON THE SPELLING OF OMAHA WORDS

Fletcher and La Flesche use an orthography quite different from Dorsey's when recording Omaha words. Since this book is a commentary on these authors and does not offer original ethnographic or linguistic material, I have avoided introducing yet another spelling method. That adopted by Fletcher and La Flesche (1911) is by far the easiest to print, and this book follows them. Their "Phonetic Guide" (p. 28) describes their conventions as follows:

All vowels have the Continental values.

Superior $n^{(n)}$ gives a nasal modification to the vowel immediately preceding.

x represents the rough sound of h in the German *hoch*.

th has the sound of the *th* in *the*.

ç has the sound of *th* in *thin*.

Every syllable ends in a vowel or in nasal $n^{(n)}$.

Introduction

It is sometimes forgotten that
the social anthropologist relies
on direct observation only in
his rôle of ethnographer and that
when he starts to make comparative
studies he has to rely on documents, just as the historian does.

EVANS-PRITCHARD 1962, 50

The Omahas, a small community of American Indians now situated on a reservation in northern Nebraska, have had a long-continued and significant influence on anthropology. At one time or another most leaders of the profession have had something to say about theoretical issues conventionally associated with the tribe's name, and some have written books or articles about the Omahas. Among the tribe's ethnographers have been James Owen Dorsey, Alice Fletcher, Francis La Flesche, Margaret Mead, and Reo Fortune—all of whom have established for themselves substantial positions in the history of anthropology. "Omaha" has so long served as a by-word for patrilineal descent that anthropologists often seem to take it for granted that what is true of the Omahas is true of any other patrilineal society. Recently their name has threatened to become attached to another topic. Unless this book accomplishes its purpose, anthropologists will soon be speaking of "Omaha alliance" as a kind of institution discoverable in places as remote from Nebraska as Africa and New Guinea. Lévi-Strauss (1969, xxxvi) has even asserted, implausibly, that the complexities of Omaha society are beyond the capacities of mere anthropologists and can be explained only by mathematicians.

The attention the Omahas have attracted is due in large measure to the early classic reports about them published by the Bureau of American Ethnology. The first of these, Dorsey's *Omaha Sociology* (1884), is known principally for its descriptions of Omaha kinship and clan organization. In these respects it was superior to what was generally available in its day. European writers, such as Josef Kohler, professor of jurisprudence at the University of Berlin, or the modern founder of French sociology, Emile Durkheim, seized on Dorsey's material while making pioneering and fundamental contributions to anthropological theory. They received with equal interest the second classic Omaha ethnography, Alice Fletcher and Francis La Flesche's *The Omaha Tribe* (1911). This book supplements Dorsey's, in many respects surpassing it in scope and quality of information, though in other ways it is inferior. There are also numerous discrepancies and implicit disagreements between the two books.

Evans-Pritchard (1962, 50) has said that "anthropologists have tended to be uncritical in the use of documentary sources," directing this charge particularly at Durkheim, who lavished remorseless criticism upon theorists of religion but not on the writers about Australian aboriginals whose work he used in *The Elementary Forms of the Religious Life*. Perhaps this comment is not so true of modern authors, but there are many examples in recent literature of inaccurate or inapt adumbrations of the facts of Omaha life, and more than one famous scholar has created a theory about their social organization that does not fit the evidence. For various reasons the ethnographic facts do not simply speak for themselves, and an assessment of analytic claims about the Omahas requires treating the published writings about them as the historian does documents and subjecting them to the historical criticism that Evans-Pritchard recommends. There is also the point made by Raymond Firth (1975, 20), that "the significance of anthropological field material as historical record seems to me to be often undervalued."

The starting point for this project has been an interest in a set of analytic issues, mostly having to do with descent, relationship terminologies, naming systems, and group formation. As one generation of anthropologists after another has attempted to advance our understanding of these matters, they have relied greatly on the early Omaha monographs—of course among many other works—so that a patina of theoretical speculation attaches now to their reputation.

A British myth (Evans-Pritchard 1973) holds that intensive professional research using the language spoken in the field situation began with Malinowski, Radcliffe-Brown, and Evans-Pritchard. Respect is due the advances made by these men, but they did have predecessors—in the United States especially among those whose contributions to the Bureau of American Ethnology established its tradition of direct observation. Lienhardt has commented of the Bureau's ethnographers (1964, 19) that their "orderly and detailed observations are far superior to most of the records of travellers and missionaries on which the anthropology of European possessions largely relied until this century." He even affirms that "the accounts of custom and culture published by the Bureau compare in thoroughness and quality of reporting with modern ethnographic studies." Conversely, their various admitted faults also have parallels in modern publications. That company of researchers that John Wesley Powell gathered at the Bureau faced field conditions in which the similarities with twentieth-century routine are undoubtedly greater than the differences. Lévi-Strauss (1966c, 124) commends the Bureau for having instituted (no doubt not alone) standards that still serve as guides and may not always be met. He also envisions a day when scholars deprived of opportunities for direct observation will gratefully devote themselves to reanalyzing and commenting on the Bureau's publications. Evans-Pritchard asserted (1960, 24) that "It is a fact, which none can deny, that the theoretical capital on which anthropologists today live is mainly the writings of people whose research was entirely literary," referring particularly to Durkheim and his associates. He was answered in advance by Durkheim's testimony (1915, 8) that ethnologists' observations "have frequently been veritable revelations, which have renewed the study of human institutions." The intricate web of intellectual debts between ethnographic reporters (be they missionaries, government officers, or academic professionals) and speculative generalizers like Durkheim deserves more consideration than it has so far been given: "Nothing is more unjust than the disdain with which too many historians still regard the work of ethnographers. Indeed, it is certain that ethnology has frequently brought about the most fruitful revolutions in the different branches of sociology" (Durkheim 1915, 9).

An adequate characterization of the present book may be that it constitutes a criticism of sources insofar as the documents are pertinent to specific analytic questions. The initial interest still determines the approach and selection of topics. The factual evidence must be weighed and, to an extent, sifted. This process necessitates considering aspects of Omaha history as well as looking closely at the history of the ethnographies themselves, the ethnographers, and where possible their informants. This study is *not*, however, a history of the Omahas—though that is intrinsically fascinating and sufficient information exists to invite the labors of someone well placed to take up the task. The following chapters keep rather close to social organization and do not attempt a comprehensive treatment of all aspects of Omaha culture. In particular they leave aside for the most part religion, ritual, myth, oral literature, and music—subjects that demand competence in the Omaha language. Dorsey and Fletcher both published widely on the Omahas as well as on other peoples, and of course they were not alone. The two monographs mentioned above do not stand by themselves, and the other sources will therefore not be neglected.

Looking again at how the story of the Omahas was put together permits us to reassess in certain regards the present state of anthropology. Of greater interest, it involves confrontation with the Omaha people. Most of those who figure here lived in the nineteenth century. To an extent still not matched by some contemporary communities, the Omahas represent a historical culture. Ludwickson (n.d., 4) believes the Omahas were situated on the Ohio River in the seventeenth century (see also Ludwickson, Blakeslee, and O'Shea 1981, 49). The first historical notice of them occurs on maps deriving from the explorations of Louis Joliet and Father Jacques Marquette in 1673–74, where their name is spelled Maha, as often occurs subsequently (Smith 1974, 43). Ludwickson presumes that by this time they were already farther west, near present southwestern Minnesota and northwestern Iowa. By 1702 they seem to have settled near the Little Sioux River, east of the Missouri in Iowa, not far from their present reservation. Already at this date there were Frenchmen living among them (Wedel 1981, 7, 9). Contacts with white traders became increasingly frequent throughout the eighteenth century. As Smith (1974, 49) observes, by 1854 (the date of an important treaty) the Omahas had experienced direct white influence for more than a century and a half.

Only during the last years of the eighteenth century do records begin to provide circumstantial information about Omaha institutions and individuals. These documents have been collected and published by Nasatir (1952). At this time the Omahas were living on the Missouri, where they held a commanding position and were able to exact tribute from St. Louis traders trying to reach the tribes farther upriver. Around the turn of the century a series of partially interconnected events seriously weakened their position. Among these were a devastating smallpox epidemic during the winter of 1800–1801, the sale of Louisiana to the United States in 1803, and the beginning about 1804–6 of a series of attacks by hostile tribes, principally the various bands of the Sioux, against which they defended themselves only with difficulty and at the cost of many lives.

There are several summaries of the influences on the Omahas in the historical period and of the resulting events and changes. In addition to those already cited, the appendix in Fletcher and La Flesche (1911, 611–42) is conveniently available, though subsequent authors have had to correct and amend it. Until 1763 the Missouri region belonged to France. In that year France officially transferred the colony of Louisiana to Spain to compensate it for the loss of Florida, but it was still mostly the French who came in touch with the tribes along the river. In 1800 Napoleon compelled Spain to return Louisiana, the exchange not becoming effective until 1802. In April 1803 the United States purchased Louisiana Territory from France. The Omahas called the French by a term that suggested they were not strangers but mingled with the tribal peoples, unlike the British and later the white Americans. The British they called Big Knives, a sobriquet borrowed from another tribe.

After 1758, when Chevalier de Kerlerce prepared a report on the peoples of the Mississippi and Missouri valleys, information about the nature of these contacts increases, but only from the 1790s and later are there reliable eyewitness accounts giving the circumstances of trade and naming individuals. Long before then the Omahas had European trade goods, including metal knives, scrapers, hoes, axes, and traps as well as glass beads and silver or brass bangles and finger rings. They purchased paint and heavy woolen cloth, and Truteau (in Nasatir 1952, 1:283) bartered scarlet cloth, china, unwrought silver, brandy, guns, kettles, and powder and balls in exchange for the hides of beaver, otter, deer, and other animals.

In the 1790s the French agents presented prominent Omaha men with medals, goods, and other favors (Truteau and Mackay in Nasatir 1952, 1:284, 359). Chapter 1 considers these and other white intrusions into Omaha political structure. The first treaty with the United States was made at Portage des Sioux on 20 July 1815 in the aftermath of the War of 1812. The treaty reestablished peace with the Omahas, who had become dependent on British trade (Peters 1848, 129; Smith 1974, 74–75). In a treaty of 6 October 1825 between Henry Atkinson, Benjamin O'Fallon, and the Omahas the tribe acknowledged the supremacy of the United States, which in turn promised protection (Peters 1848, 282–84; Smith 1974, 82). In a treaty of 15 July 1830 between William Clark, Willoughby Morgan, and several tribes, the Omahas made their first land cession, giving up all claims east of the Missouri in the present state of Iowa, a region where they had often lived and hunted. The treaty also provided for the Nemaha "half-breed" reservation, to cope with a number of offspring of unions between women of the Omahas or other tribes and white men. For the first time the Omahas became eligible for annuity payments (Peters 1848, 328–32; Smith 1974, 87–88).

On 15 October 1836 John Dougherty concluded a treaty with several tribes, including the Omahas, in which they ceded any claim to lands between the state of Missouri and the Missouri River (Peters 1848, 524–26; Smith 1974, 93). The treaty made provision for a village near the town of Bellevue, south of the city of Omaha, where they lived until 1854. On 21 June of that year Commissioner of Indian Affairs George W. Manypenny and representatives of the tribe concluded a treaty by which the Omahas ceded all their hunting lands in Nebraska except for a tract of 300,000 acres along the Missouri River in the north of the state. Save for a strip sold to the United States in March 1865 to provide a reservation for the destitute Winnebagos and some later sales, this tract constitutes the present Omaha reservation. The United States promised to survey the land and apportion a certain section for individuals who wanted permanent homes. It also agreed to erect a sawmill and a gristmill and to make annual payments for forty years from the money paid for the ceded land. The 1854 treaty is naturally of the greatest importance for the subsequent history of the tribe, and it provided the basis of successful litigation in the 1950s before the

Indian Claims Commission to recover the difference between what was paid for the land given up in 1854 and its value at that time (Minot 1855, 1043–47; Sanger 1868, 667–69; Smith 1974, 142).

The agent carried out an allotment of lands in 1871, but this step was largely nullified by the transfer of some of the allotted holdings to the Winnebagos. A new allotment was provided for by an act of 7 August 1882 (*U.S. Statutes at Large* 1883, 341–43). Alice Fletcher completed the allotment in July 1884.

The events dryly cataloged above would not have taken place but for the special circumstances of the frontier after 1800. The Omahas under their famous chief Blackbird were generally successful at intimidating rival tribes (James 1905, 15:87–91), but a smallpox epidemic during the winter of 1800–1801 (Smith, 1974, 94), which carried off Blackbird and several hundred others, broke their strength. Thereafter they became especially vulnerable to assault by various bands of Sioux. Smith (1974, 218–19) lists no fewer than twelve attacks by Sioux or Sauks between 1804 and 1848 in which the Omahas were worsted, losing as many as seventy-three persons each time. These encounters forced several changes of the village site, until the Omahas finally moved to their reservation in 1855 (Dorsey 1884, 213–14; Fletcher and La Flesche 1911, 85–89; Ludwickson, n.d.; Smith 1974, 181–87).

The effects of warfare and disease on the Omaha population are of great significance when we assess the later ethnographic descriptions. Perhaps of most concern are the reports about the epidemic of 1800–1801. According to Mooney (1928, 12), smallpox swept the whole of the plains from the Gulf of Mexico to Dakota, being especially destructive in Texas and among the Omahas. Clark (in Thwaites 1904–5, 1:109–10) wrote that it had carried off 400 men and women and children in proportion, reducing the number of men to 300. This ambiguous phrasing may be interpreted as meaning that 400 men had died, as well as a proportional number of women and children, for a total of about sixteen hundred persons. It can also be read to say that only 400 persons had died, proportionally divided among men, women, and children. The second interpretation corresponds with the record of Lewis and Clark's Sergeant John Ordway, who visited the deserted Omaha camp. "Near half the Nation died with the Small pox, which was as I was informed about 400" (Quaife 1916, 110). At the same time Sergeant Charles Floyd wrote that Blackbird and 300 of his men had died (Thwaites 1904–5, 7:25). Clark's statement has frequently been interpreted to mean that the total population fell to 300 persons (see the sources quoted in Smith 1974, 210, 213, 215) in conformity with another ambiguous claim (Thwaites 1904–5, 6:88) that their numbers were reduced to "something less than 300." On the preceding page (p. 87), however, Lewis and Clark report 60 tents or lodges, 150 warriors, and 600 total population. As Mooney (1928) remarks, "Both of these estimates are probably too low." In 1802 Vilemont (in Nasatir 1952, 2:694) wrote that there were 180 men bearing arms, and Chouteau (in Nasatir 1952, 2:760) mentioned 300 *hombres*. Appraisals pertaining to the period immediately preceding the epidemic are 600 men in 1798 (Truteau in Nasatir 1952, 2:539), 600 men using arms (Perrin du Lac in Nasatir 1952, 2:710), and 700 warriors (Thwaites 1904–5, 88). Mooney judged their size in the 1780s as about 2,800. On the basis of D'Iberville's assertion (Margry 1876–86, 4:598, 601) that the Omahas consisted of 1,200 families in 1702, Mooney supposed they may have numbered 4,800 early in the eighteenth century.

The discrepancy in Mooney's two estimates is not explained by known historical events and may be due to faulty guesswork. Assessments made in the nineteenth century, when there was better control of the facts, also are often widely out of line with each other. Bradbury (1904–7, 5:90) attributed 200 warriors to the Omahas in 1811, whereas three years later Clark (Smith 1974, 199) credited them with 400 men—2,000 souls—an astonishing increase over the supposed 300 persons of fourteen years before. Estimates for later years invariably place them at well over 1,000 persons until the 1850s, when their numbers declined toward the 1,179 registered by the 1884 allotment (Smith 1974, 200–201; Fletcher and La Flesche 1911, 33–34). Mooney's claim that "They suffered again from smallpox in 1837, and lost heavily by the cholera in 1849" (Ubelaker 1976, 276) is not clearly borne out by the reports of the agent Miller and others who were in touch with them at this time (1,400 in 1834, 1,301 in 1844, 1,300 in 1846, 1,349 in 1851). Fletcher and La Flesche (1911, 622) appear to be right that the government's program after the treaty of 1815 of vaccinating them against smallpox was instrumental in saving them in 1837.

Had there really been a drastic decline from 2,800 to 300 in 1800, leaving a rump of little over 10 percent, there should have been an equally catastrophic disruption of the social organization; yet the camping circle remained intact (see below), and all the clans and almost all the subclans were still represented when Dorsey collected genealogies of the tribe in 1889. Even a decline to somewhat under a thousand, which seems more likely, would be severe. Although the doubts on these matters are beyond resolution, they must be kept in mind, for they impose significant limits to the confidence with which we can draw conclusions about tribal life before 1800 based on information deriving from the nineteenth century.

Before 1849 the Bureau of Indian Affairs was in the War Department and officials dealing with the tribes were normally under military authority, but the principal impulse for contact was largely commercial (Smith 1974, 100). In 1810 the American Fur Company set up a trading post at Bellevue. The successive Indian traders were Francis Deroin, Joseph Roubideux, John Cabanne, and Peter A. Sarpy. The Council Bluffs Indian agency moved to Bellevue in 1823 and assumed responsibility for the Omahas, Otos, Pawnees, and Potawatomis. In 1846 the Presbyterian Board of Foreign Missions established a mission at Bellevue. In 1848 the mission established a school for Otos and Omahas, which took on a handful of students. In 1847 the first group of Mormons under Brigham Young appeared on the Missouri, and in 1849 Sarpy's ferry at Bellevue transported across the river the gold hunters bound for California (Bangs 1887, 293–95). In 1854 the Omahas moved north from Bellevue to their newly defined reservation, and from 1856 the United States government operated a specific Omaha Agency.

The Omahas continued their seminomadic pattern of subsistence, resisting pressure from government agents to abandon their annual communal hunt until after 1877, when the buffalo completely disappeared (Milner 1982, chap. 6). This event was the culmination of a long process of white incursion leading to the depletion of game the Omahas depended on. Already in 1828 Chief Big Elk wrote, "The white people who have been in the habit of coming into my village have had great influence with us and have consequently kept us scouring the country in search of skins until the animals themselves have left us" (quoted in Smith 1974, 85).

An act of Congress in 1871 declared that Indian societies were no longer regarded as independent nations and that dealings with them therefore did not require formal treaties. On the advice of his former aide-de-camp and new commissioner of Indian affairs, the Seneca chief General Ely S. Parker, President Grant decided to remove the agencies from the military officers who had previously controlled them and to place them in the charge of missionaries from various denominations. Hicksite Quakers took responsibility for the Northern Superintendency. They gradually withdrew during the 1880s under pressure of a change in government policy, the last Quaker agent to the Omahas resigning in 1880. Milner (1982) has published a history of the largely unsuccessful Quaker efforts at administering the tribes; his chapter 6 is devoted to the Omahas.

Beginning in 1848 the Presbyterians ran a boarding school for the Omahas, funded in part from the Omaha annuity. In 1868 it provided education to sixty students. It was unpopular with members of the tribe, partly because of domestic misbehavior by one of the missionaries. When the first Quaker agent arrived in 1869, the chiefs asked that the funds be withdrawn from the boarding school and used to establish two day schools. These were more successful and at less cost accommodated as many as 160 pupils. The Quakers closed these schools when they left, and the boarding school reopened in 1881. By 1879, 155 Omahas could read. In that year only a few Omahas associated with Joseph La Flesche owned houses; the rest camped on their allotments in the summer and lived in the woods in the winter. (This paragraph is a summary of Milner's chap. 6.)

During the tenure of the next-to-last Quaker agent, Jacob Vore, the Reverend James Owen Dorsey arrived at the reservation. The Omahas had frequently been mentioned by travelers of various kinds; by no means were they ethnographically unknown. In particular, in 1823 Edwin James had published a good deal of substantial information on their life and social organization, derived from S. H. Long's expedition to the Rocky Mountains. Lewis Henry Morgan visited them in 1860 and subsequently (1870) published a version of their relationship system. These early writers therefore had already sketched in the general lines for investigation when Major John Wesley Powell deputized Dorsey to acquire linguistic and anthropological material on the Omahas for the Smithsonian Institution. When the Bureau of Ethnology (later Bureau of American Ethnology) was instituted under Powell's direction in 1879, Dorsey was formally attached to it and remained so for the rest of his life.

Powell picked Dorsey because of Dorsey's acquaintance with the Poncas, whose langauge, with minor differences, is the same as that of the Omahas. Dorsey was born in Baltimore 31 October 1848. By age ten he could read Hebrew. He studied the classics in high school and later entered the Theological Seminary of Virginia. On Easter Day 1871, at the age of twenty-three, he was ordained a deacon of the Protestant Episcopal church. In May of the same year he went to Dakota Territory as missionary to the Poncas. Said to have had a natural gift for languages, Dorsey proceeded to study that spoken by the Poncas. After two years illness interrupted his mission work, and in August 1873 he returned to Maryland; but by then he could converse with the Poncas without an interpreter. He took up parish work until the opportunity arose to revert to his scholarly interests. He lived with the Omahas from July 1878 until April 1880. Thereafter he maintained his ties with the Omahas by letter, and various of his informants visited him in Washington. He made several field trips to gather information on other tribes. He concentrated in particular on gathering comparative linguistic information about the various Siouan groups, which include the Omahas and Poncas, but he also made investigations into the Athapascan, Kusan, Takilman, and Yakonan stocks. His linguistic work was principally descriptive and was done at a time when the discipline itself was at a pioneering stage, but it was conscientious and methodical and remains of great value. W. J. McGee (in Dorsey 1897, 207) wrote that "His publications were many yet the greater part of the material amassed during his years of labor remains for elaboration by others." The holdings of the National Anthropological Archives attest that he was still in the midst of a fertile scholarly career when on 4 February 1895, at the age of forty-seven, he died of typhoid fever (Hewitt 1895, 180–83; Powell 1894, xliii; Hinsley 1981).

On 1 September 1881 Alice Fletcher arrived at Omaha, Nebraska, as the guest of Thomas Henry Tibbles and his wife, Susette "Bright Eyes" La Flesche. Forty-three years old, Fletcher had been born in Cuba, the daughter of a New York lawyer and a Boston lady (La Flesche 1923; Hough 1923; Green 1969, 203; Hoxie and Mark 1981, xxvii; Mark 1980), and had been a private student of Frederic Putnam, director of the Peabody Museum of Harvard University in 1879 when Tibbles and Susette La Flesche toured the East seeking support for the Poncas who had been forcibly removed to Oklahoma. Alice Fletcher persuaded a reluctant and doubtful Tibbles of her desire to visit Indian tribes and live as they did so as to observe Indian ways firsthand.

Her hosts took her to the Omaha reservation, then, after a short stay, they all departed for a wagon tour of the Winnebago, Ponca, and Santee Sioux reservations, accompanied by an Omaha relative of the La Flesche family—Wajepa, or Samuel Freemont (ca. 1835–1906). Tibbles relates the events of this trip in his book *Buckskin and Blanket Days* (1957; summarized in Lurie 1966), but Fletcher's own diary of the journey survives[1] and tells much about her attitudes before she embarked on the ethnographic enterprises that would occupy the rest of her life. During their first dinner on the trail Wajepa told her, "I believe all of the white men tell lies." She reponded:

I looked up as he spoke and found him looking at me with a seriousness and concentration of gaze that I can never forget. In it it had memory, judgment, based on hard facts. There was seemingly no appeal—Two races confronted each other, and mine preeminently guilty. I said, thro Susette, "Not all white men are bad, there are some good ones." He replied, "Perhaps so, a few." I responded, "I don't wonder that you think them all bad, your people have been wronged by white men."

Later Wajepa returned to the topic.

Wajapa says it seems as though after the white men came in two years the buffalos were gone.

Wajapa says that the Indians call the bluejoint, Red Grass. It comes where the white people are . . . the other fine grass follows the buffalo. He thinks the white race may have sprung from Red grass, there is such an affinity—believes the white people are this grass.

Fletcher did not know Wajepa or Omaha history well enough at this time to realize he was not being entirely candid, though of course there were many specific grounds for complaint. Although he squarely allied himself with La Flesche's "Citizens'" or Progressive party, Fletcher was inclined to see him as the idealized Indian only recently converted to white men's clothing.

His mind is alert and of a statesmanlike character, tho he is rather restless, made so by the uncertainty of Indian tenure of land. . . . Wajapa rides ahead, when the road is good he will sometimes make short cuts. When a distance off he will sing in the expressive Indian fashion. At every high hill he gallops to the top and then stands, he and his horse silhouetted against the clear blue sky.

Later on the trip, suffering from exhaustion and illness, she turned pensive.

Wajapa tucked me up finely and I slept better than usual. The ground was softer on account of the long grass which made it like hay under our beds.
The hot soup and the blazing fire gave me a little warmth at last and I got on better. . . .
Wajapa was up at daylight and out gathering wood, moving a dim robed shadow against the eastern sky. Soon he came in, arms filled with sticks and long boughs with twigs and threw them in the tent door, then kneeling, he turned over last night's logs and stirred the ashes and blew the little embers. He then broke off all the little twigs, got his hands full and broke them short like little slips, and dropped these on the fire, soon [there was] a leaping blaze some two or three feet high—then came the logs laid on like the spokes of a wheel. I lay and watched the flames and Wajapa's profile, and listened to the snoring of the others and wondered at it all—life included.

Alice Fletcher also appreciated his flattery.

Privacy is impossible, he watched me furtively clean my teeth. I fancy he must think white women spend much time in adornment that hardly pays. He was really moved to speech by the sight of my hair. When Susette asked him to look at it as she sat by the fire cooking breakfast and he was by the wagon, I was off at a distance. He said it was the longest he had ever seen and that nothing was so beautiful on a woman. Susette said he paid me a great compliment but I could not understand it. . . .

We all take names—Wajapa names me, Ma-she-ha-the. It means, The motion of eagle as he sweeps high in the air. He gives me the names of his family and band. He belongs to the eagle family. . . .

Talked of a white farmer who thought all Indians thieves, told him some white men were not good, said he had but one white man for a friend—Mr. Dorsey—and he thought as much of me as of Mr. D.

Shortly thereafter, however, the party overheard Wajepa giving more equivocal expression of his esteem while speaking to a strange group of Indians encountered on the trail.

Wajapa said, "she is a christian woman, I hear she is one of the very good ones but I have not known her long enough yet to tell myself."

We all heartily enjoyed this recital and voted it to be put upon the minutes.

The members of the party, both Indian and white, had their moods too.

Wajapa got angry with me when I essayed a little jest and will not speak. I asked a question and he failed to answer. Am much disappointed that he is such a baby.

Before the expedition was at an end, Fletcher was instructing Wajepa in arithmetic and telling him how to make a checkerboard so that she could teach him that game.

With a touch of irony, Tibbles rendered Fletcher's Omaha name as "High Flyer." She was strong-willed and even capricious. When they arrived at their destination, she refused to meet the Santee agent in his office on the grounds that a lady should be received at home (Lurie 1966, 80). Paul Radin, who had crossed swords with her in his youth, described her to Lurie (p. 33) as a "dreadfully opinionated woman." Jane Gay, her companion during her allot-ment work among the Nez Percés (1889–92), continually referred to her as "Her Majesty" because of a supposed resemblance to Queen Victoria (Gay 1981).

The Omahas had been disappointed in the results of the allot-ment of 1871, a portion of which was later sold to the Winnebagos. Having recently been forced to abandon the hunt and many other of their means of gaining subsistence, they were worried about their survival and under threat of forced removal. The government's promise of an adequate allotment remained unfulfilled, and the La Flesche faction in particular was anxious for a resolution. Fletcher returned to the Omahas for the last half of November 1881 and visited in Omaha homes. She intended to study tribal organization and customs, but the Omahas' more pressing preoccupations soon came up in conversation. Several of them wanted written entitlements to their land that would prevent their being driven to Oklahoma. Fletcher helped them draw up a petition to Congress, which they then sent to Senator John T. Morgan of Alabama.

Fletcher returned to Washington and took up the cause with a characteristically single-minded zeal. The upshot was an act of 7 August 1882 granting the Omahas their land in severalty. This act became the model for the Dawes Severalty Act of 7 February 1887, which made allotments the standard provision for Indian peoples. By the 1887 act, the Omahas became citizens of the United States. Fletcher was appointed special agent to perform the Omaha allotment, which she carried out from May 1883 until July 1884. Each head of family received 160 acres, orphans and single persons eighteen years or over were granted 80 acres, and those under eighteen received 40 acres. Of special importance for the present study is that she prepared and indexed "a full registry of the tribes by families, giving the name of each member and their relationship, and also the number of each allotment of each individual" (Fletcher 1884c, 661).[2]

When she was ready to begin the allotment, the older members of the tribe performed the calumet ceremony for her. As the ritual ended, they told her she was free to study that or any other tribal rite (La Flesche 1923, 115). While she was allotting the land, she contracted inflammatory rheumatism, which caused her to walk with a limp and use a cane for the rest of her life. Frank La Flesche, who was serving as her interpreter, lifted her into a wagon and drove her to the mission (Green 1969, 85), where she made herself an uninvited guest of the Presbyterian missionary Homer W. Partch. While she was convalescing, Omahas visited daily and sang to her, so that she began working on their music (Hough 1923, 255). A somewhat exasperated Partch applied to her a remark the chief justice of Great Britain had made while in St. Louis: "In order to do much mischief in the world a person must be very talented and rather good."[3]

She returned to Washington in July 1884 and began publishing portions of her Omaha material, but other projects distracted her. In 1886 she prepared a report on Indian civilization and education for the United States Bureau of Education, then traveled to Alaska and the Aleutian Islands for the United States commissioner of education (Putnam 1887, 565). Between July 1887 and April 1889 she conducted the Winnebago allotment, then performed a similar service for the Nez Percés in 1889–92. She devoted herself to this work in the certainty that the best way to prepare Indians for the future was to teach them to live like whites. "Chiefs oppose because land in severalty breaks up completely their tribal power and substitutes civilization. . . . It is hugging a delusion to suppose that any distinct Indian nation or nations can exist within the limits of the United States; that question has been settled for men of all colors and races" (Fletcher 1884c, 663).

After a brief visit to the Omahas in 1910 she wrote (Fletcher and La Flesche 1911, 640), "The act has not been altogether evil nor has it been wholly good for the people." In fact the allotments' eventual effects on the tribes were catastrophic, leading to large-scale loss of land and livelihood (Mead 1932, 46–47; Lurie 1966, 80–81). The postallotment tribulations are outside the scope of this study, but Fletcher's ethnographic writings are much affected by her crusading spirit.

In 1891 Mary Copley Thaw, widow of a Pittsburgh railroad and steel magnate, endowed a lifetime fellowship for Alice Fletcher in connection with the Peabody Museum. Its terms permitted her to reside in Washington, and Mary Thaw helped her purchase a duplex apartment at 214 First Street, SE. In 1892 she moved in with Jane Gay and Francis La Flesche (Hoxie and Mark 1981, xxxiv–v). She and Francis La Flesche engaged in a lifetime's scholarly collaboration. Green (1969, 182) remarks that their close association and frequent travel together gave rise to gossip, especially in view of Francis's unfortunate marital record.[4] In the foreword to their joint monograph, she acknowledges more than twenty-five years of cooperation. In fact, she in effect adopted Francis in 1891, not doing so formally only because he did not wish to change his family name

(Green 1969, 184). He was her principal heir when she died at the age of eighty-five on 6 April 1923.

Alexander (1933, 329) wrote of *The Omaha Tribe* that, while the text is from Fletcher's pen, the rich materials assembled for it are due more to Francis La Flesche. Fletcher herself makes this more or less clear (Fletcher and La Flesche 1911, 30); there is little evidence that she acquired any practical ability in the Omaha language. From the beginning her contacts with the Omaha tribe and culture were through the La Flesche family. Although she interviewed and became acquainted with most of the adults of the tribe while allotting their land, her perpetual dependency on the La Flesches gives a distinctive cast to her monograph. Only in a qualified way did she succeed in making "the Omaha his own interpreter."

Alexander (1933, 328) gives Francis La Flesche's birthdate as Christmas Day 1857. The day is improbable, and estimates of the year vary between 1855 and 1862. He was the son of To^n $'i^nthi^n$, Elizabeth Esau (d. 1883), of the Flashing Eyes Pipe subclan, third of his father's four wives. His father, Joseph La Flesche, Jr., or Iron Eye, had been a head chief of the Omahas. Although born after the Omahas moved to their present reservation, he still participated in his youth in three buffalo hunts (Dorsey 1890a, 467) and in some ceremonies. He was among Dorsey's informants. Dorsey said of him (p. 2) that he had a fair knowledge of English and was the only Omaha who could write his native dialect. "I have had many opportunities of testing his skill as interpreter, and I did not find him wanting." He attended the Presbyterian Mission School at Bellevue and later wrote of these experiences in his autobiographical book *The Middle Five* (1900). When Tibbles took the Ponca chief Standing Bear on an eastern tour in 1879, Francis went with them as an interpreter. Senator Samuel J. Kirkwood of Iowa came to know of him and in 1881, as secretary of the interior, appointed him a copyist in the Indian Office.

La Flesche kept up his ties with both Dorsey and Fletcher, and during the following decade he published one or two short ethnographic notes. After being adopted by Fletcher in 1891, he attended the National University while continuing to work at the Indian Office, earning the LL.B. in 1892 and the LL.M. in 1893. In

1910 F. W. Hodge arranged his transfer to the Bureau of American Ethnology (BAE), which sent him to Pawhuska, Oklahoma. From 1920 the Bureau permanently employed him as "ethnologist," a position he held until his retirement on 26 December 1929. Apart from *The Omaha Tribe,* his main anthropological productions consisted of a series of articles and monographs (including four annual reports of the BAE) on the Osages. An early essay (1916) on right and left in Osage ceremonies was of sufficient merit to be reprinted in a recent collection on lateral symbolism (Needham 1973*a*). The National Anthropological Archives contain the manuscripts of many of his short stories, mostly on Indian themes. He was coauthor of the libretto for C. W. Cadman's never-performed opera *Da-o-ma.* The University of Nebraska awarded him an honorary LL.D. in 1926. He died in his brother's home on the reservation 5 September 1932 (Alexander 1933; Green 1969, 41, 50–55, 175–206).

Emile Durkheim and Marcel Mauss thought highly enough of *The Omaha Tribe* to devote separate reviews to it in the same volume of *L'Année Sociologique.* Durkheim (1913) praised its attempt to grasp the internal principles of Omaha life and make visible both its unity and its complexity. He contrasted it favorably with Dorsey's fragmentary, dry, and superficial attempts at analysis. Mauss (1913) was more critical, finding in it doubtful etymologies and a mystical manner of expression. The authors salt their monograph with numerous oblique criticisms of Dorsey. Even their claim at the beginning (p. 30) that "nothing has been borrowed from other observers" is aimed principally at him. In fact, their failure to explicitly come to terms with their colleague is one of the most distracting features of their work. Mauss objected to it. We know, he said, that historians, working directly from archives, preoccupy themselves with facts and take little account of the ideas of their predecessors. "But there are works which are themselves documents." Francis La Flesche had after all been one of Dorsey's own sources, and Dorsey frequently mentions him. Although relations between Dorsey and Fletcher, which publicly remained cordial, may have been strained by professional rivalry, something else appears to have come between Dorsey and La Flesche.

The National Anthropological Archives contain a startling exchange of letters between these two men in the year before Dorsey's death.[5] Dorsey was then working on his monograph on the personal names of the Siouan tribes, which he never completed. There were some last-minute details he wished to check, particularly concerning the deposition of rights in children in the event of divorce. Tactlessly, he phrased his questions in terms of several examples from La Flesche's family. La Flesche responded rather sharply.

> My dear Mr. Dorsey.
> I have looked over the questions you submitted to me, and after thinking over them I decline to answer them in the way they are put.
>
> I think that too much of the private affairs of many of the Omahas has already been published in the Bureau of Ethnology reports without their consent and I do not wish to add more, or have it done with my assistance.
>
> Some things you have published about me which I did not wish published but you took the liberty to do it.
> Yours truly.
> F. La Flesche

There is ample internal evidence in *Omaha Sociology* to permit an idea of the grounds for La Flesche's displeasure, but as it happens the authors made them plain in a letter provoked by a hostile review (Anonymous 1912). The reviewer alleged that *The Omaha Tribe* is virtually an elaboration of *Omaha Sociology*. He accused them of persisting in family emphasis and trying to enhance the tribal importance of the La Flesche family. In particular he brings up the old charge that Joseph La Flesche was not an Omaha at all but a Ponca. Fletcher and La Flesche (1912) responded with a comprehensive assault on Dorsey and his work. His numerous inaccuracies arose, they averred, from his "lack of a clear understanding of the Omaha language which he persistently used while carrying on his inquiries" and to "his inability to distinguish between information honestly given him by serious-minded persons and misleading information given in jest by mischief-loving individuals."

Their (i.e., Fletcher's) disapproval of Dorsey's attempt to employ the Omaha language as an instrument of investigation strikes an odd note today, now that Dorsey's method is commonly accepted as essential to good ethnography. Furthermore, Dorsey was by no means given to arrogance or slapdash attitudes. He scrupulously published vernacular texts with interlinear translations, and he carefully recorded the divergent views of his informants.

It is just these divergent viewpoints that Fletcher and La Flesche did not think worth a hearing. Something should therefore be said about some of the informants to whom they were hostile. Among them were Gahi´ge, or Chief, Garner Wood (ca. 1820–82). He was a leader of the Black Shoulder Pipe subclan and one of the last keepers of the two sacred pipes. Gahi´ge was son and successor of Gahi´gezhiⁿga (Little Chief) Ish´kadabi or Waxaga, Thomas Wood, who had been third peace chief and the one the whites thought the most recalcitrant of Omaha leaders. Some of Gahi´ge's information serves to enhance the tribal standing of his own clan. Another was Disobedient or Lion, Oliver Lyon (b. ca. 1816), of the Deer Head Pipe subclan. In March 1880 he gave Dorsey a good deal of information about clan division later disputed by Joseph La Flesche and Two Crows. During a visit to Washington, a government official gave him the name Lion. Though he was not a chief by Omaha tradition, the government made him one of the "paper chiefs" in 1869. Together with White Horse, Ellis Blackbird (b. ca. 1835), of the "Sacred" Earth Maker subclan and He is Known, Benjamin Hallowell (ca. 1833–1884), of the Flashing Eyes Pipe subclan, he formed a swing group between the Chief's party and the Young Men's or Progressive party (Dorsey 1884, 358). He was keeper of his clan's sacred pipe. Dorsey wrote (1890a, 4), "The Omaha do not put much confidence in him, and he is regarded by some as a mischief-maker." Another man the La Flesches often disagreed with was Not Afraid of Pawnee, Jordon Stabler (b. ca. 1831); he, however, was a member of Joseph La Flesche's party and was said by Dorsey (1890a, 2) to be one of his best informants.

Edward Sapir (1938, 7) wrote of the shock he received as a student in coming across statements such as "Two Crows denies this" in *Omaha Sociology*. From this comment Sapir went on to some speculations about the relation between anthropology and psychology that are not relevant here. Frederica de Laguna (1957) later referred to Two Crows's doubts as the starting point for some considerations about anthropological objectivity. Neither writer bothered to look more closely at the implications that the disagreements among Dorsey's informants have for our knowledge of Omaha facts. Dorsey's book is laced with comments that Two Crows, usually in conjunction with Joseph La Flesche, disagrees with other sources, often on routine points that should be beyond dispute. The impression they leave on the reader is indeed disconcerting, and if we are to rely only on the evidence in the book there is little we can make of them.

A clue to understanding the problem lies in how Dorsey put the final version together. In the summer of 1882 Dorsey was revising the text of *Omaha Sociology* for publication. Two Crows and Joseph La Flesche visited him in Washington to help (Dorsey 1894, 362; 1884, 297). To judge by the results, they went through the manuscript with him page by page while Dorsey registered their responses. Sometimes they supplemented what he already had, sometimes they disagreed, and sometimes they offered conflicting descriptions. The important chapter 4, in which Dorsey published his original and voluminous account of Omaha relationship terminology and marriage rules, appears to have resulted almost entirely from this visit.

Although not a Christian, Two Crows, Lewis Morris (ca. 1826–94), was an active member of La Flesche's Progressive party. He was not one of the traditional chiefs, but he was elected one of the new-style seven equal chiefs in March 1880 (Dorsey 1884, 358). He was nevertheless well versed in traditional aspects of Omaha life. He had been a soldier or policeman on the buffalo hunt and had acted as captain of a war party against the Sioux in 1854. He had killed two Sioux in battle in 1847. It was he who searched for Logan Fontenelle and found his body after the fight with the Oglala Sioux in 1855 (see below). He was a leading man in the Leader Mottled Object subclan and a principal doctor in the Buffalo dance society. His character "commanded the respect of the tribe" (Fletcher and La Flesche 1911, 100–101, 211; Dorsey 1884, 347; 1890a, 426, 452–62, 688, 718; 1894, 362). "[Two Crows] has been a leader of the young men for several years, though he is a grand-parent. He was the leader of the tribe on the hunt and war-path, and is still feared even by the chiefs' party. He says just what he thinks, going directly to the point. He is regarded as the speaker of the purest Omaha, and one has no difficulty in understanding him" (Dorsey 1890a, 3).

Two Crows was therefore a knowledgeable and authentic Omaha informant. Fortune (1932, 73), however, thought that Two Crows had deliberately withheld from Dorsey all important information concerning the Buffalo society.

The principal defense Fletcher and La Flesche mounted against their hostile critic was a genealogy purporting to prove that Joseph La Flesche's mother was an Omaha. The historical relevance of this issue necessitates an extended explanation, but its ethnographic relevance is quickly demonstrated. In describing Omaha marriage laws (1884, 255–56), Dorsey stated that Joseph La Flesche's mother belonged to the Ponca Wasabe-hit´age clan, his mother's mother was a Ponca Wajaje, and his mother's mother's mother was a Ponca Maka^n. Joseph La Flesche was therefore prohibited from marrying women in any of these Ponca descent groups. Elsewhere (p. 215) Dorsey described Joseph La Flesche as "a Ponka by birth, who spent his boyhood with the tribe" and listed him (p. 268) among Poncas who had been incorporated into the Omaha tribe.

I regard [Joseph La Flesche] as my best authority. By birth he is a Ponka, but he has spent most of his life among the Pawnees, Otos, and Omahas. He has acquired a knowledge of several Indian languages, and he also speaks Canadian French. While Frank [not Francis], his younger brother, has remained with the Ponkas, and is now reckoned as a chief in that tribe, Mr. La Flèche has been counted as an Omaha for many years. Though debarred by Indian law from membership in any gens [clan], that did not prevent him from receiving the highest place in the Omaha governmental system. (Dorsey 1890a, 1)

Pardoxically, the value of La Flesche's evidence concerning the nature of Omaha marriage regulations comes into question if it turns out that Joseph's mother is an Omaha rather than a Ponca. If that evidence is undermined, then much theoretical scaffolding in anthropology begins to shake. Fletcher and La Flesche (1912, 855) say that the genealogy Dorsey gives in the relevant place (1884, 256) is actually that of Joseph's half-brother, the elder Frank La Flesche, who everyone agrees is a Ponca through his mother. If this assertion were true, it would mean that Frank La Flesche had violated the rules, for he married No^{n}çe´i^{n}the, Mary England, of the Ponca Wajaje clan.

Fletcher and La Flesche (1911, 631) give the year of Joseph La Flesche's birth as 1818. Other records such as the 1871 allotment show his birth year as 1822. He died 24 September 1888. His father, Joseph La Flesche, Sr., was a French Canadian in the employ of the American Fur Company. The elder Joseph La Flesche is only a shadowy figure in history, but he appears as an interpreter as early as 1817 and continued to act as one from time to time until 1840.[6] He married an Indian woman, the mother of Joseph, Jr., but she became tired of his long absences while on trading expeditions to other tribes. She left him and married the elder Doesn't Flee (Non´çondashi), of the Omaha Deer Head Pipe subclan. This union produced Joseph's half-brother Doesn't Flee, Dwight Sherman (b. ca. 1837), and his half-sister Solitary (Ezhnon´monhe), Lucy Sherman (ca. 1825–1912). The mother and her Omaha husband died in a Sioux attack near Tekamah, Nebraska, in 1847. The elder Joseph subsequently married another Indian woman, a Ponca, who bore White Swan, Frank La Flesche, Joseph's Ponca half-brother. According to an account given by Wajepa,[7] Joseph's mother's brother, the Ponca Standing Grizzly Bear, was taken captive in his youth by Sioux, grew up among them, and became a chief. He sent for Joseph, Jr., Wajepa's father, and Wajepa's father's sister and kept them with him for three years, and so Joseph learned to speak Dakota. Some years later Joseph's father took his son to Saint Louis, where he learned to speak French. He accompanied his father on trips and as a result learned Iowa, Pawnee, and Oto.

He spent much time with the Omaha chiefs, particularly the second Big Elk, who had succeeded his father, the first Big Elk, in 1843. The Jesuit priest Pierre-Jean De Smet baptized the second Big Elk on 18 August 1839, naming him James and giving his age as seventeen (Chittenden and Richardson 1905, 4:1532). He would therefore have been about the same age as Joseph, to whom he was related in some way through his own Ponca mother. Joseph began to make a number of gifts to Big Elk and the other Omaha chiefs, according to Omaha practice. In the end Big Elk asked him to join the council of chiefs. Fletcher and La Flesche (1911, 632) place the time between 1845 and 1850. Joseph's Omaha name Iron Eye (a name proper to Big Elk's We´zhinshte clan and given him by Big Elk) appears on the 1848 census. In the next year he was among the

24

signers of a petition of Omaha chiefs.[8] Big Elk died in 1853, but first he "pipe danced" Joseph and publicly declared him his son and successor as head chief, while entrusting his own young son to Joseph's care (Giffen 1898, 28–30).[9]

The Omahas performed their normal ritual for conferring head chieftainship upon Joseph. Dorsey (1884, 224) published this apparently verbatim comment from the young Francis La Flesche.

When my father was about to be installed a head chief, Mahi^n-zi [Yellow Knife of the Flashing Eyes Pipe subclan, d. 1853], whose duty it was to fill the pipes, let one of them fall to the ground, violating a law, and so preventing the continuation of the ceremony. So my father was not fully initiated. When the later fall was partly gone Mahi^n-zi died.

Fletcher and La Flesche (1911, 209) say that during the ceremony for the chiefs, the keeper of the pipes had to be careful not to let them fall, otherwise the meeting would be at an end and the keeper would be in danger. In 1912 (p. 886), they say that the passage Dorsey quoted from Francis is an example of Dorsey's lack of a clear understanding of Omaha language.

During the recital Mo^n'-hi^n-çi dropped the bowl of one of the sacred pipes accidentally. This meant death to the person being initiated and necessitated the discontinuance of the ceremony. Big Elk, who was present, became silent and showed much displeasure. Seeing this, Mo^n'-hi^n-çi said to La Flesche, "My son, this was an accident; whatever must follow I will take it upon myself." In the autumn of that year Mo^n-hi^n-çi died.

Actually there is no point of fact in which this account contradicts that given by Dorsey; so their charges about his misunderstanding are misplaced. Even their claim that the pipe was dropped accidentally does not entirely disprove the implication that it was done deliberately and therefore registered opposition from other chiefs. To his credit or otherwise, Dorsey does not himself make this inference.

Except for a brief period when he contended with Logan Fontenelle for the head chieftainship, Joseph served in this capacity until 1866. While there is no doubt that Joseph La Flesche was fluent in Omaha and intimately knowledgeable in Omaha culture and affairs, there are good reasons not to regard him as being an Indian personality pure and simple. As a young man he was employed as a clerk by the trader Sarpy. Later he and Logan Fontenelle ran a ferry across the Missouri. From the proceeds La Flesche established a store.[10] During his head chieftainship he continued to act as a trader to the tribe. That he could neither read, write, nor speak English (Giffen 1898, 27) doubtless increased the sense of cultural difference for some ethnographers, but he did speak French, and he participated in the French world of commerce that still survived along the Missouri in his youth. He was quite used to handling merchandise and cash worth thousands of dollars. He lent money to missionaries, provided at his own expense uniforms for the Omaha police, and contributed funds for the relief of the tribe when they suffered a poor hunt.

As a chief he established his own community, called by his opponents the "Make-Believe Whitemen's Village," where his followers erected frame houses and took up agriculture. He tried to discourage the annual hunt, and he severely and successfully suppressed the use of alcohol. He maintained an uneasy alliance with the Presbyterian missionaries and, with one threatened disruption, supported their school.

Opposition arose from other chiefs, who wished to keep the older patterns of subsistence, political ties, and tribal ceremonies. But Joseph did participate in Omaha ceremonies, followed the tribe's practices in other respects, and engaged with them in battle against other tribes. For a period he maintained three wives. Hamilton described him as "the only strictly honest and intelligent chief among them" and "the only one that cannot be made a tool of the traders and other designing men."[11]

In 1864 Colonel Robert W. Furnas, enjoying political connections with the Radical Republicans, was appointed agent to the Omahas. He was accustomed to command and to receive obedience. At the same time he held clear views on white supremacy. Within a short time he fell out with Joseph La Flesche. Among many grounds for their troubles was Furnas's desire to place his own nominee as official trader to the Omahas, a capacity exercised jointly by Henry Fontenelle and Joseph La Flesche. In several letters of the time Furnas indulged in unrestrained criticism of La Flesche.[12] Perhaps the most revealing charge is that La Flesche had been unwilling to be subordinate to the agent. Furnas repeatedly asserted that Joseph was not an Omaha but a Ponca. Finally, in 1866 La Flesche relinquished the chieftainship and left the agency (cf. Green 1969, 30–34).

The political nature of the charge was plain enough. His mother's tribal affiliation was obviously a vulnerable point. Fletcher and La Flesche state that Joseph's response to the Ponca suggestion was "That is impossible!" That she was a Ponca was widely accepted and frequently reported (Henry Fontenelle in MacMurphy 1893, 54; Morton and Watkins 1907, 2:153; Gilmore 1919, 68). Joseph's children were uncertain about it, which in itself suggests something was amiss. Fletcher and La Flesche base their case on a genealogy they took down from Wajepa in March 1906. This is one of several depositions on the subject by Wajepa and Joseph's wife Mary Gale, but it is the only one that explicitly says she was an Omaha. Moreover, it was recorded in the last year of Wajepa's life. Joseph's wife Mary, on the other hand, several times explicitly said his mother was a Ponca.[13] In 1962 the Office of Indian Affairs removed some of his descendants from the tribal roll on the grounds that they were not Omahas (see Green 1969, 3). The investigator privately communicated that they were later restored on the principle that Joseph's adoption was sufficient reason for admission, even though he was not Omaha by blood. The issue is still a living one.

An additional source of information, which provides the grounds for this study, is a complete set of Omaha genealogies by clan and subclan that Dorsey recorded in Washington with the assistance of Wajepa and George Miller.[14] In 1890 Dorsey (1890b, 263, 268) announced that he was preparing a monograph on Indian personal names that would end with several genealogical tables of Omahas and Poncas. They were to illustrate not only personal names but the kinship system and marriage laws as well. The table for the Poncas (which in fact covers only two of the clans) would have been forty feet long. The project was ended by Dorsey's early death. He may have begun working on Omaha genealogies while he was in the field, but it is plain that he had not finished the work by the time he published *Omaha Sociology*. Wajepa went to Washington in the fall of 1888 and dictated the material until February 1889 (Dorsey 1894, 362). In September 1889 Abandoned, George Miller (b. ca. 1852), of the Flashing Eyes Pipe subclan went to Washington to help him revise the genealogies but returned home at the end of November, when his wife wrote complaining about being alone (Dorsey 1891, 111, 113, 121; Powell 1894, xxxi–ii). Taken together with Fletcher's allotment papers, census records, and other materials, these genealogies provide a unique chance to reconstruct the personal background to many published generalizations about Omaha life.

Fletcher and La Flesche say that Joseph's mother was a member of the Black Shoulder clan, full sister of the father of Tahe´zhinga (Little Buffalo Horns), that is Xu´ga (Badger), Asa Lovejoy (ca. 1842–1912). Dorsey's genealogies curiously do not show such a sister, nor do they show who Badger's mother was, though they show that Badger's father was named I^{n}kedeshuga. Dr. Marguerite Picotte, daughter of Joseph La Flesche and Mary Gale, recorded in her journal (cited above) a statement, apparently from Mary, that described Badger as the son of Joseph's mother's sister (rather than mother's brother). If this is the case, she would not have belonged to the Black Shoulder clan and perhaps not to the Omaha tribe. More substantial is their assertion that "No^n´-ço^n-da-zhi, a full Omaha and a half-brother of La Flesche, both having had the same mother, still lives; a full sister of the former and a half-sister of the latter, named Eshno^n´-mo^n-he, died recently. These facts in no way bear out the statement of Mr. Dorsey."

These persons are Dwight and Lucy Sherman, mentioned above. The nature of their connection to Joseph La Flesche is not in doubt. However, Dorsey's genealogies, which after all derive from Wajepa too, do not confirm their mother's membership in the Black Shoulder clan. In the relevant section Dorsey penciled in, strangely enough, "Kanze gens?" There is no confirmation anywhere else for this suggestion. In a deposition given in the Court of Claims[15] in September 1912, six months after the writing of the Fletcher and La Flesche letter, Dwight Sherman plainly states that he is one-half Ponca, his mother being a Ponca, sister of a Ponca chief named Ubi´ska (a vulgar name).

Because membership in Omaha clans is derived through the father, the status of Joseph's mother is actually of no consequence for his position in the tribe. His adoption by Big Elk was sufficient to make him an Omaha and gives him a nominal association with the Elk clan. His fluency in the language and knowledge of the culture are far more important for his value as an informant than his bloodline. It seems a safe conclusion that, though his mother unquestionably had family ties to the Omahas, she was by patrilineal descent a Ponca. The same rule, disregarding adoption, made Joseph La Flesche a French Canadian. Dorsey thus comes out of this examination somewhat vindicated. This critical scrutiny of circumstances also gives further reason to take seriously those statements with which Two Crows and La Flesche disagree and to reflect on their implications.

Two less substantial monographs were produced by Margaret Mead (1932) and Reo Fortune (1932), who visited the Omahas briefly between June and October 1930. Both receive consideration below, though the main focus of their studies is outside the scope of this book. Perhaps no one today would have the brass to comment, as Fortune did (1932, 2), "Fortunately for my work on the secret societies I had some informants literally under the rack of extreme privation and want, and so I was able to penetrate into secrets that are not usually admitted." Nor would many show the breezy self-confidence of Margaret Mead, who explained (1932, 16), "English was used throughout, as there is not sufficient unrecorded cultural material to warrant the necessary expenditure of two or three months' time in learning the language."

1: Chieftainship

Omaha ethnographers have been unable to agree on the traditional way chieftainship was accorded. Doubt remains whether these offices were obtained by hereditary right or achieved through brave deeds and ostentatious gift giving. This uncertainty corresponds to conflicting views within the tribe both about who held rights to positions of leadership and about the effects on ancient institutions of contacts with whites in the historical period.

The recorded history of Omaha chieftainship begins with a usurpation. Fletcher and La Flesche (1911, 82) write that an Omaha "visited the trading post at St. Louis, and on his return assumed an air of importance, saying that he had been made a great chief by the white men." This man began to appoint "soldiers," among them a certain Blackbird, whom he took with him on a return to St. Louis. Blackbird's handsome bearing attracted more attention than his benefactor received, and when they returned to the tribe Blackbird announced that the white men had now made him a chief.

By this account neither of these early chiefs held offices sanctioned by tribal custom and hereditary right; they assumed unusual powers on the strength of their access to foreign traders. Fletcher and La Flesche describe Blackbird's companion only as "the great-grandfather of a chief who was living twenty-five years ago" (i.e., ca. 1880). In his brief "History of the Omaha Indians," Henry Fontenelle (1885, 78) records the names of the first remembered chiefs as Blackbird and Ta-ha-zhou-ka (Forked Horn), the father of "Big Elk the First," thus a man of the Elk clan. Fletcher and La Flesche may have intended the great-grandfather of the man called No Knife, who assumed importance in the latter part of the nineteenth century. If so, then according to Dorsey's genealogies the early chief would have been Big Elk's grandfather rather than his father, but in any case both sources imply a direct male line of succession and membership in the Elk clan. Forked Horn has left little impression in history. The name does not appear in the appropriate place in the genealogies, though it is known to belong to the Elk clan, and given that Omaha men often bore more than one name, this attribution may well be correct.

About Blackbird, contemporary and subsequent records have a great deal more to say. Cruzat listed El Pajaro Negro as the principal chief of the Omahas as early as 1777 (Houck 1909, 1:144; Smith 1974, 42). The journals from 1794 to 1795 of the French trader Jean-Baptiste Truteau (Nasatir 1952, 1:259–311) contain vivid descriptions of Blackbird and bitter complaints about him as well as most of the stories later repeated about him, including the allegation that he kept his tribe subordinated by means of poison (said to be arsenic given him by the traders).[1] Because the Omahas blocked the way up the Missouri, he was able to dictate terms of trade to the French and control their access to tribes farther up the river. He also shrewdly played the Louisiana French off against the British in Illinois. He held great power over the Omahas and neighboring tribes until his death during the great smallpox epidemic of the winter of 1800–1801 (see Smith 1974, 61, 66). His grave was a landmark on the Missouri for decades until the traveling artist George Catlin in 1832 allegedly removed Blackbird's skull, later reported to be in the United States National Museum (Catlin 1841, 2:5–7; Donaldson 1886, 2:262).

Truteau (Nasatir 1952, 283, 288) mentions a "chief of the second rank" named "Big Rabbit," obviously the same "Big Rabbit" or Mush-shinga whom Long (James 1905, 14:320) says succeeded Blackbird and possessed considerable authority, though he lived to enjoy it only a few years. Rabbit appears as a name in the Leader clan, and Dorsey (n.d.) indicates it for the Black Shoulder clan, but the individual in question cannot be identified. Long adds a further complication by describing White Cow (actually White Buffalo) as the hereditary successor to Big Rabbit, but White Buffalo was a member of yet a different descent group, the Small Birds section of On the Left Side clan.

Still another name appears in the early records, that of "Little Bow," who quarreled with Blackbird and established a separate village for his followers (Perrin du Lac in Nasatir 1952, 710). According to Lewis and Clark (Smith 1974, 63–64), this breakaway group reunited with the main Omaha band after Blackbird's death, but Perrin du Lac reported that they were too weak to resist the Sioux after the death of Little Bow and finally were absorbed into the Sioux. Little Bow does not appear in Dorsey's genealogies, and the name occurs in none of the available lists of clan-owned personal names; so there is no way of determining his affiliation.

If we assume for argument that the preceding reports are accurate, as far as they go, we can hypothesize the following succession of offices during the late eighteenth century.

> Forked Horn (Elk clan)
> Blackbird (Earth Maker clan), by 1777
> Big Rabbit (Leader clan), after 1800

Fletcher and La Flesche refer (1911, 201) to legends concerning an ancient reorganization of the tribe and the establishment of a governing council by seven old men who were visiting the Omahas. These men established a *nini'baton* (pipe-possessing) division in some of the clans, and each of these subdivisions furnished one member to the council, "which was to be the governing authority, exercising control over the people, maintaining peace in the tribe, but having no relation to offensive warfare." Two old men, one in the Leader clan and the other in the Black Shoulder clan, became keepers of the two "sacred pipes" and were charged with giving pipes to each Nini'baton division. In making the distribution they omitted the Red Dung, Elk, and Leader clans. No reason is known for the omission of the Red Dung group, but the Leader clan had the duty of calling the council together and the Elk clan already had control of war rites and could not participate, "for the duties of the council formed from the Nini'baton subdivisions were to be solely in the interests of peace." There are numerous discrepancies of detail among the various versions of this event, but the preceding list of pipe-receiving groups is the same as that given to Dorsey by Anbaheba (Dorsey 1884, 222–23). Of the ten clans, only seven received pipes and the right to send a member to the tribal council. Of these seven four belonged to the Sky moiety, or tribal half, and three to the Earth moiety.

Fletcher and La Flesche claim (1911, 202) that the council was "composed of hereditary chiefs."

How long the hereditary character was maintained and what had previously constituted leadership in the tribe are not known, nor is there any knowledge as to how the change from hereditary to competitive membership in the council came about. It may be that the change was the result of increasing recognition of the importance of strengthening the power of the governing council by making it both the source and the goal of tribal honors, thus enhancing its authority and at the same time emphasizing the desirability of tribal unity. All that the writers have been able to ascertain concerning the change in the composition of the council from hereditary to competitive membership has been that it took place several generations ago, how many could not be learned.

According to Fletcher and La Flesche there were two orders of chiefs, the principal one called the "dark chiefs" and the second order the "brown chiefs." Membership in the order of brown chiefs was unlimited, though dependent upon the consent of the dark chiefs. Advancement to either order could be achieved only through certain acts or gifts for which ostensibly there was no material return or personal gain, made in these cases to "the seven chiefs." Only brown chiefs could become dark chiefs, and then only when a vacancy occurred. Although the number of gifts required to become a lower chief was not prescribed, a graded sequence of seven gifts or acts was required to become a dark chief. When a vacancy occurred, it could be filled by the brown chief who could "count" the most gifts or acts of the appropriate kind. "The order and value of these graded acts were not generally known to the people, nor even to all the chiefs of the Xu´de [lower group of chiefs]. Those who became possessed of this knowledge were apt to keep it for the benefit of their aspiring kinsmen. The lack of this knowledge, it is said, occasionally cost a man the loss of an advantage which he would otherwise have had" (Fletcher and La Flesche 1911, 204).

The seven chiefs of the council were all dark chiefs. Fletcher and

La Flesche say in fact that they represented that order. But they leave unstated how many dark chiefs there were—whether only seven, as seems to be implied, or perhaps more. There were five other persons in the council who had special responsibilities; although they lacked the rights and powers of the seven chiefs, the chiefs were dependent upon them in various ways. These five were the keeper of the sacred pole (Leader clan), the keeper of the sacred buffalo hide (Leader clan), the keeper of the two sacred tribal pipes (Black Shoulder clan), the keeper of the ritual used when filling them (Flashing Eyes clan), and the keeper of the sacred tent of war (Elk clan).

The two men who could count the greatest number of prescribed gifts were the principal chiefs, and according to Fletcher and La Flesche (1911, 208) each represented one of the two halves of the tribe. Whenever one of the two offices became vacant, the place was taken by the person with the greatest "count," either another of the seven chiefs or some new entrant from among the dark chiefs. A principal chief could be replaced only when he died or resigned, so that evidently it was not possible to supplant a sitting principal chief by exceeding his "count."

Fletcher (1884a, 616) comments on the repeated place of the number seven in tribal government. Seven pipes or equivalent articles were distributed by seven old men. The pipes are seven spans in length. There are seven ceremonial movements or positions for the pipes. There are seven parts to the ceremonies connected with the pipes. These ceremonies require seven articles in their performance. Finally, seven has astronomical reference.

Dorsey writes (1884, 217) that "beside the chiefs proper are the seven keepers of the sacred pipes, or pipes of peace." Later (p. 357) he records, "The keepers of the sacred pipes are regarded as chiefs in some sense though they are not allowed to speak in tribal assembly." These claims appear to contradict Fletcher and La Flesche. In giving his version of the legend (Dorsey 1884, 222), Chief (Gahi´ge) says that the clans that had pipes also had chiefs at first. Of course, a pipe-holding subclan could easily have appointed one man as pipe keeper and another as its representative on the council, but no one has suggested that this was actually the Omaha procedure. In fact, most of the historical chiefs of the Omahas came from non-pipe-owning clans or subclans. Neither Blackbird, who belonged to the so-called Sacred (Xu'be) subclan of the Earth Makers, nor for that matter any of the several head chiefs from the Elk clan belonged to a pipe-holding group. The same is true for all the other known chiefs except Chief of the Black Shoulder Pipe subclan, who was both a chief and a keeper of the two tribal sacred pipes, his predecessor Little Chief of the same group, and Lion of the Deer Head Pipe subclan, who was a "paper" or government-appointed chief as well as a pipe keeper.[2] Lion is not actually an exception, since he did not become a chief by traditional procedures. Legend therefore conflicts with tribal reality in historical times in a significant respect. It may be well to bear in mind that the two sources for the legend, Chief and Half-a-Day (Anbahebe of the Deer Head clan) both belonged to pipe-holding subclans.

It is also important to note that, although legend speaks of the distribution of seven pipes, and though the receiving subclans are actually called pipe keepers, the tribe possessed only two real pipes, which represented the two halves of the tribe and were in later years in the safekeeping of Chief. The Eagle subclan of the On the Left Side clan received not a real pipe but a buffalo skull that counted as a pipe, and Dorsey speculates (1884, 222) that the remaining five groups never had pipes but had objects that were regarded as equivalent to them.

Fortune (1932, 156) has observed an apparent contradiction in the method of establishing claim to chieftainship through gift giving and the observation that the exact list of gifts required was kept secret so it could be used to the advantage of kinsmen. Fortune considered Omaha political theory democratic but therefore in conflict with Omaha political reality. It is interesting to contrast Fortune's stance with the interpretation of Fletcher and La Flesche. For them the council may once have been hereditary, before changing to competitive membership. In Fortune's interpretation, competitive membership was in practice hereditary. Fortune (1932, 1) was uncertain that he could prove hereditary succession for the lower five of the seven chiefs, but he felt he had done so for the first two.

However, his proof depends upon accepting that the Elk clan held one of the principal positions by hereditary right. In fact the various legendary accounts of the establishment of the council specifically mention the Elk clan as one of three that had been passed over in the distribution of the pipes and therefore council chieftainships.

These quandaries may perhaps best be addressed by clearly distinguishing the organization of the tribe during the period for which there are records from the state of affairs that may have preceded this time. During the historical period the tribe experienced increasingly significant change as the Omahas lost their autonomy by stages and as representatives of the United States government intervened more and more decisively in the process of selecting leaders. The various petitions, letters, and treaties signed by tribal leaders over the years never attempted to distinguish the several ranks and grades of chiefs and soldiers. They therefore cannot be readily used to determine who the seven chiefs were at any period or indeed if the institution was intact. A passing reference to the seven chiefs made by Francis La Flesche suggests, however, that the group did still exist and act together in 1878 (Dorsey 1884, 224).

There are conflicting reports concerning the pattern of succession at the beginning of the nineteenth century. According to Long, White Buffalo (usually referred to in the literature as White Cow or Tesa^n), mentioned above, succeeded to the position held by Big Rabbit after very few years. In 1851 the Swiss painter Kurz (1937, 65) wrote of a Tamegache (Ton$'$won$gaxe or "Village Maker"), son of Blackbird, who had become lame and surrendered his claim as chief in favor of the young "Elk." Unfortunately Kurz's remarks on this point are inconsistent, and it is uncertain how much he understood. The order of succession given by Dorsey (1884, 357) shows Blackbird and White Buffalo as the first principal chiefs, followed by White Buffalo and White Elk of the Elk clan. Dorsey was unaware of the tradition that White Buffalo had replaced Big Rabbit after the death of Blackbird. Dorsey then indicates that White Elk was replaced by his younger brother Big Elk (ca. 1772–1846) while White Buffalo retained the other office.

At this stage contemporary documents and later reports begin to confirm each other. Long says of White Buffalo that, being governed by an unambitious wife, he remained inactive, leaving it to the next important man Big Elk to take the principal position of leadership. However, on 11 May 1811 the trader Hunt was confronted by Big Elk and White Buffalo, who wanted him to decide on behalf of the United States government which of them was preeminent (Bradbury, 1904–7, 89). Hunt refused, but for reasons not known White Buffalo (who lived into the 1860s) was later replaced as second chief by Yellowish Skin (Waha'xi, commonly known on treaties as "Big Eyes") of the Flashing Eyes clan, Real Flashing Eyes subclan. The same man appears on the treaty of 6 October 1825 as "The Man That Cooks Little in a Small Kettle" (a name sometimes rendered "Small Boiler") (Peters 1848, 282–84). Big Elk and Hard Walker (Small Birds subclan of On the Left Side) head the list of eight Omaha signatories to the treaty of 20 July 1815 (Peters 1848, 128). Big Elk and Big Eyes were the two chiefs acknowledged by Major O'Fallon in 1819 (James 1905, 14:262).

Catlin wrote (p. 28) that the head chief of the Omahas was Gahige-washushe, Brave Chief, a man of the Black Shoulder clan, Hoop subclan, and that Big Elk was placed next to him in standing and reputation. Though Dorsey ignored Brave Chief, his name does appear at the head of an Omaha deputation that visited Washington in 1837, and Big Elk's name appears second on the list.[3] Big Eyes did not sign the treaty of 15 July 1830, though Big Elk was the first of the signers, but Big Elk and then Big Eyes were the first two to do so on 15 October 1836 (Peters 1848, 328–32, 521–26). This series of contradictory reports with their overlapping dates suggests a fluid state of affairs and no doubt factional disagreement during the 1830s. Fletcher and La Flesche say (1911, 496) that Big Eyes had a son whom he wanted to become chief, but the son died prematurely.

James (14:281) writes, "Big Eyes is a large and remarkably muscular man. His nose is that of the European, the opposite to the Roman curve; he is second chief of the Omawhaws." Fletcher and La Flesche (1911, 495–96) tell stories of his generosity. Much was written of Big Elk during his lifetime. On 8 March 1820 he visited Long. James says of him (p. 281), "The Big Elk, principal Omaha chief, is much pitted with small-pox, and is of commanding presence. He speaks with great emphasis, and remarkably distinct." Big Elk emphasized that the Omahas had never killed a white man and said he thought "that he should, at a future date, be a white man himself." His skill in council has been frequently described (James

1905, 14:291–92; McKenney and Hall 1838, 134–39; Bradbury 1904–7, 222–23). McKenney and Hall say he was one of the few Indians who could state his own age accurately. They include a large color print of him. He was also painted by Catlin.

Big Elk retained his office until 1843, three years before his death, though a letter from the agent Miller shows that at times his position was embattled. Big Elk visited Miller to complain that the trader A. L. Papin was giving medals to the younger men and by this means undermining Big Elk's influence. Big Elk even claimed that his life had been threatened by one of the younger men.[4] Records of the La Flesche family[5] indicate that Big Elk died of chills and fever.

One of the signers of the treaty of 15 July 1830 is called "Iron Eye, Chief's son." Presumably this person was the son who replaced Big Elk as principal chief and also bore the name Big Elk. I^n-shta´mo^{n}çe (rendered variously as Iron Eye or Metal Eye) is an Elk clan name, and the second Big Elk conferred it upon Joseph La Flesche when he adopted him into the Elk clan. Since no two Omaha men should bear the same name at the same time, a reasonable inference is that the latter Big Elk adopted his father's name after his father's death and that he had previously been known as Iron Eye. There was, however, another Iron Eye who was the son of the first Big Elk's brother and predecessor White Elk. Not much is known about this man, though he might equally well be the person who appears on the 1830 treaty.[6]

At any rate, according to Dorsey (1884, 357) Big Elk's son of the same name had already taken Big Elk's place in 1843, while Standing Hawk (ca. 1812–86) took the place of Big Eyes. Standing Hawk was the son of White Buffalo; so in this case the chieftainship returned to the Small Birds subclan of the On the Left Side clan. Big Elk the younger died in 1853 and was replaced by the half-French trader and interpreter Joseph La Flesche, Jr. In fact, there was a brief contest for the chieftainship between La Flesche and another half-French interpreter, Logan Fontenelle, which came to an end with Fontenelle's death at the hands of the Sioux in 1855. This interesting episode in Omaha history throws some light on traditional patterns of succession. The second Big Elk had adopted La Flesche and cleared the path for him to assume the chieftainship on the promise that La

Flesche would care for Big Elk's younger son "Cross Elk" and later help him become chief.[7]

In 1854 the commissioner of Indian affairs, George W. Manypenny, wrote to the Omaha agent, George Hepner, to say he had information that Logan Fontenelle had never been appointed by the Omahas as principal chief and requesting Hepner to investigate the matter.[8] Hepner called a council of the tribe and reported[9] that

a boy of the name of Cross Elk, about 8 years old, under care and protection of Joseph La Flesche, is the head chief by hereditary descent, that at present they have no head or principal chief, that they have many ways by which an Indian becomes chief, such as by transfer, acts of charity, bravery &c &c, besides they have a way of making chiefs by smoking the pipe, taking into consideration the curl and ascent of the smoke &c, though this mode is becoming obsolete. I find that the delegates who were at Washington last winter were all chiefs on par and that they are so yet. I then took the names of the principal men and who they wished me to recognize as chiefs, to wit, Standing Hawk, Mixed Fire, Little Chief, Village Maker, The Noise, Big Eye, Joseph La Flesche and Logan Fontenelle, these names were read over to the council, no objection being made. . . . This question of chiefship is a delicate one to handle and when it was mentioned old White Cow [i.e., White Buffalo] took the floor, his first expression was, "Now you shall hear it." You could hear a buz[z] throughout the room, all hands seemed to be somewhat electrified, but in the end all passed harmoniously. Logan Fontenelle was no doubt recognized as chief from the fact of his liberality in making feasts for the head men, braves &c together with some other influence which the Department well understands. . . . Joseph La Flesche spoke in Council and seemed to be well pleased with the results.

Fontenelle had been dismissed as interpreter in 1851 for selling liquor in the village and for "constant drunken and notorious conduct," but he was reinstated the following year.[10] Despite Hepner's statements given above, he later spoke of Fontenelle as their main chief when reporting his death in 1855.[11] The other influence working for Fontenelle, "which the Department well understands," was Major Gatewood, who brought an Omaha party to Washington in 1853 and whom Manypenny accused of conspiring to pass Fontenelle off in Washington as a chief instead of merely the interpreter, his official capacity for the government. Seven men signed the treaty of 16 March 1854 in Washington—the first two were Logan Fontenelle and then Joseph La Flesche (Minot 1855, 1043–47). The charged atmosphere that resulted when White Buffalo rose to speak about the chieftainship is readily understood when we recall that he was at one time a head chief himself and rival to the elder Big Elk and that his son Standing Hawk had claims to one of the chieftainships at the time White Buffalo was speaking. Some Omahas might well have felt that the rightful chiefs were the boy Cross Elk, for whom La Flesche was merely the regent, and Standing Hawk, whereas Fontenelle clearly had no proper claims on office other than the bestowal of gifts. Hepner's mention of the pipe is explained by the employment of the two sacred tribal pipes in the ceremony for electing a man to one of the lesser chieftainships (Fletcher and La Flesche 1911, 203–4).

La Flesche's ward eventually died, and La Flesche maintained the chieftainship while acting as official trader to the tribe until 1866, when the agent Furnas deposed him to gain control of the Omaha trade. Thereafter, according to Dorsey, there was "confusion about the head chieftainship, as well as about the chieftainship in general, ending in the election of seven chiefs of equal rank in 1880." Nevertheless, in some respects La Flesche's powers devolved upon No Knife, a captain of the Omaha police, who followed La Flesche when he left the reservation after losing his office and forced him to surrender the tribal archives.[12] No Knife (b. ca. 1820) was also in the Elk clan and appears in the genealogies as son of the first Big Elk's older brother White Elk.

When the tribe elected seven equal chiefs in open council by a show of hands in March 1880, No Knife was not reappointed. None of those who gained office, except Chief, belonged to a pipe group. The same was true of those who were deposed or who stepped down then and also of the additional three who were elected a few months later, bringing the number of chiefs to ten (Dorsey 1884, 358). By 1880 the seven chieftainships had become concentrated in only four clans, three of which were in the Earth moiety. In the election of that year, each of the three clans electing two chiefs chose one from the "Chiefs' party" and another from the "Young Men's" or "Citizens'" party. These were the principal political groupings of the latter half of the century, representing respectively

conservatives and modernizers. The seventh chief, White Horse, belonged to a third minor faction whose other members were Lion
and I´bahoⁿbi (He Is Known). Each belonged to a Sky moiety clan
and had been a government-appointed "paper" chief. Earth moiety
dominated in 1880 with six of the seven chiefs, but the three chiefs
added later increased the Sky moiety representation to four.

Table 1 brings together all the scattered references to the head
chieftainships, excluding only Little Bow, who according to Long
was merely an inferior chief. The complete list in this table may or
may not constitute an accurate record of the order of succession,
but it seems to establish two main points. First, during the 103
years (1777–1880) for which we have evidence, the Elk clan was
associated almost without interruption with one of the two offices,
while the other passed about among no less than five different clans.
Second, whereas during Blackbird's lifetime, and again in 1819
when Big Eyes held office, there was a chief from each moiety, for
most of the period both chieftainships were held by persons of the
Earth moiety.

That White Buffalo remained alive and continued to take part in
tribal affairs for decades after he had ceased to be one of the head
chiefs seems to call into question the statement that a principal chief
could be replaced only when he died or resigned, unless in fact
White Buffalo did resign out of chagrin or for some other reason.
From the days of Blackbird, there was always confusion caused by
whites (traders, soldiers, or agents) who presented medals to
Omaha men whom they then called chiefs. These men used their
ties with the whites to legitimize their places within the tribe. Each
of the prominent chiefs, including Blackbird and Big Elk, received
medals and followed this pattern. At the same time, there were always complaints within the tribe that whites were creating chiefs
who had no right to hold the office. It is clear too that rivalries
within the tribe sometimes lay behind such charges. White interven-
tion intensified, culminating in the government's reorganization of
tribal leadership in 1880. After 1819 official recognition by the
agent was essential; and in 1853 the position passed into the hands
of men partially of French extraction.

Closely related Siouan tribes conferred leadership by hereditary
right; so there would be nothing ethnologically unusual about the

Table 1. Reconstructed Order of Succession to Principal Chieftainships

Chief	Chief	Date
Blackbird (Earthmaker clan)	Forked Horn[a] (Elk clan)	Before 1777?
Blackbird	Big Rabbit[b] (Leader clan?)	Ca. 1795
White Elk? (Elk clan)	Big Rabbit[c]	Ca. 1801
White Elk	White Buffalo (On the Left Side clan)	
Big Elk the elder (Elk clan)	White Buffalo	By 1811
Big Elk	Big Eyes (Flashing Eyes clan)	Ca. 1819, 1836
Big Elk	Brave Chief[d] (Black Shoulder clan)	Ca. 1832, 1837
Big Elk the younger (Elk clan)	Standing Hawk (On the Left Side clan)	1843–53
Logan Fontenelle[e]	Joseph La Flesche (adopted, Elk clan)	1853–55
Joseph La Flesche	Standing Hawk	1855–66
No Knife (Elk clan)	Standing Hawk[f]	1866–80

a. According to Henry Fontenelle (1885, 78).
b. According to James (1905, 14:320).
c. By inference from James.
d. According to Catlin (1841, 28).

e. Fontenelle's position was disputed by La Flesche and others but, according to the agent Hepner, was effective.
f. According to Green (1969, 34).

Omahas' doing so. Howard (1965, 92–93) writes of the Poncas that the head chieftainship, the council of seven, and lesser chieftainships were hereditary positions, though an outsider could hope to acquire by various means any position except the principal one. Chieftainship among the Osages passed through the male line (La Flesche 1921, 68).

At the beginning of his book on Omaha secret societies, Reo Fortune announces he has proved that the two leading chiefs succeeded to office by hereditary right. This "proof" (1932, 156–58) derives from the list given originally by Dorsey (see table 2). This information supports Fortune's interpretation in the following way. Three men of the Elk clan replaced each other (White Elk, Big Elk the elder, and Big Elk the younger), while White Buffalo gave way first to his son-in-law Big Eyes and then to his own son Standing Hawk. Fortune says that the succession is from father to son in each

Table 2. Order of Succession to Principal
Chieftainships According to Dorsey

Chief	Chief	Date
Blackbird (Earthmaker clan, "Sacred" subclan)	White Buffalo (On the Left Side clan, Small Birds subclan)	Before 1800
White Elk (Elk clan)	White Buffalo	Ca. 1801
Big Elk the elder (Elk clan)	White Buffalo	By 1811
Big Elk	Big Eyes (Flashing Eyes clan, Real Flashing Eyes subclan)	Ca. 1819
Big Elk the younger (Elk clan)	Standing Hawk (On the Left Side clan, Small Birds subclan)	1843–53
Joseph La Flesche (adopted, Elk clan)	Standing Hawk	1853–66

case, but in fact White Elk was older brother to the first Big Elk. Two names in the list, however, pose difficulties for Fortune's theories—Blackbird and Big Eyes. Fortune did not bother to consult published or unpublished historical records and therefore ignores the issues they raise. About Blackbird he writes only, "we have to set aside Wazingasabe as having no continuation of his line whatever." Dorsey's genealogies and treaty records show that Blackbird did have sons and grandsons who might have become eligible for leadership. As for Big Eyes, Fortune merely states that "a man sometimes gave his son-in-law his inheritance, above his son, in Omaha."

Fortune sums up his interpretation by claiming that while Omaha social theory is "aggressively democratic," the social practice is aristocratic. Since there is a discrepancy between social theory and practice, aristocratic privilege is kept secret. The evidence, however, is not as Fortune claims "definite and unmistakable," and Fortune's investigation is far from adequate. Certainly he has not proved, as he avers, that we must discount the reports that claims to chieftainship were validated by giving gifts.

For the historical period the ethnographers seem to agree that among the Omahas there was no (active) ideological sanction for hereditary succession, though chiefs were sometimes, but not invariably, successful in passing positions on to close relatives within their clan or clan segment. Dorsey (1884, 357) writes explicitly that "while the chieftainship is not hereditary, each chief tries to have one of his near kinsmen elected as his successor." The evidence available, Fortune notwithstanding, bears out this picture. At the same time, validation of chieftainship by giftgiving was a good deal more than a shallow deception, requiring as it did great expenditure. This transfer of goods, similar to redistribution patterns of exchange familiar to anthropologists elsewhere, did strengthen the hand of an incumbent trying to advance a son, brother, or nephew. No doubt it is an indication of the importance of the system that Fontenelle and La Flesche both made elaborate gifts to the chiefs when they were attempting to gain overall leadership in the tribe. Both at the time were acting as traders to the tribe, handling large sums that made it possible to finance their campaigns for control of the council, and both figured to secure and enhance their business ventures through political advancement. Even in this respect their methods and intentions were not so completely different from those of full-blooded Omaha predecessors like Big Elk and Blackbird. The long, continuous ascendency of the Elk clan may well have had a bearing on the inability of any single descent group to monopolize the second head chieftainship.

Fortune (1932, 1) asserts also that Omaha society was stratified into four classes: priests, chiefs, doctors and doctoring society members, and nonprivileged persons. Membership in a class was passed on in a male line. Certainly there were discrepancies of various kinds in the standing of different Omaha families (see, for example, Green 1969, 165), but there is a possibility that Fortune has confused class with office. He also refrains from stating clearly what he means by social class, so that in his usage it stands for little more than recognition of inequality.

Dorsey had written (1884, 217) that, though there were no slaves, there were several kinds of servants, *wae'gaxtho^n*. Among such servants were numbered the two keepers of the sacred tents of the Leader clan, who were reciprocally servants to each other. Not Afraid of Pawnee told Dorsey that these two old men were "the real governors of the tribe, and are counted as gods." Francis La Flesche flatly denied this characterization and said that they were merely servants of the Leader clan chief. Among their tasks (Dorsey 1884, 284) was tending the fires and kettles for the feast before departures on the annual tribal buffalo hunt. Though they attended the tribal assembly, they could not speak but were expected to prepare food (p. 363). Not Afraid of Pawnee was himself one of the handful of servants of the Elk clan who assisted them in rites connected with thunder and war (pp. 227, 237–38). He was also a distinguished warrior and leader of raiding parties. Servants also included criers (pp. 231, 284, 290) and policemen (p. 363). Under the heading "state classes" Dorsey distinguishes (pp. 216–17) chiefs, who had legislative, executive, and judicial functions; policemen or braves, who were messengers and deputies of chiefs and held extraordinary powers for disciplining the tribe, especially on the buffalo hunt; and finally young men who had not yet distinguished themselves. Men could and did move up from one rank to another, and Dorsey writes that the state classes "have not been clearly differentiated" and that (p. 218) "Social classes are undifferentiated." Bravery in war, bestowal of gifts, or frequent feast giving permitted a man to move up in rank.

Chiefs, who were "civil and religious" leaders, could not serve as war captains and were permitted to join only large war parties. According to Dorsey (1884, 361–62), chiefs might not be deposed. Common people had no voice in the tribal assembly, which was composed only of chiefs. Principal chiefs did not act without consulting the other chiefs. Principal chiefs had the right to order policemen to strike the disobedient, to order the crier to proclaim the decisions of the tribal assembly, to name two braves to ladle food for a feast, to assume the principal seats, and to assign a new chief his seat in the assembly or to promote an older one.

When one of the head chiefs resigns all of the subordinate chiefs change their places in the council, moving nearer to the seats of the principal chiefs. But should the principal chiefs so desire it some of the new chiefs may occupy the seats near them, being promoted over some of the subordinates. A new chief did not always succeed a retiring chief of the same gens.

Subordinate chiefs were empowered to join in deliberations of the assembly, to regulate the buffalo hunt, to approve or withhold permission for a small war party, to form friendly visiting or peace parties to another tribe; they had the right to stop quarrels and fights and to regulate the sending of scouts in case of alarm. Dorsey's choice of the phrase "right" might not be entirely apt. His distinction between principal and subordinate chiefs appears to overlap Fletcher and La Flesche's categories of brown and dark chiefs, and assemblies called by agents were often attended by many more than seven chiefs.

McKenney and Hall give the following picture (1838, 136) of Omaha statecraft.

A sagacious head man, however, is careful to preserve his popularity by respecting the opinion of the tribe at large, or, as we should term it, *the people;* and, for that purpose, ascertains beforehand the wishes of the masses of his followers. Ongpatonga [the elder Big Elk] was a model chief in this respect; he always carefully ascertained the public sentiment before he went into council, and knew the wishes of the majority in advance of a decision; and this is, probably, the most valuable talent for a public speaker, who may not only lead, by echoing the sentiments of those he addresses, but, on important points, insinuate with effect, the dictates of his own more mature judgement.

Though this account is idealized, it seems to reflect accurately the style Big Elk attempted to adopt; and his oratorical powers were a topic favored by writers of his time. Even he must have mixed a degree of intimidation into his political strategy. Without reference to Blackbird, Fletcher and La Flesche (1911, 213) describe the administration of poison as a punishment that might be ordered by the Council of Seven Chiefs. In fact Fortune (1932, 86) says that chiefs, who were barred from the doctoring societies, had sorcery powers by virtue of their membership in the shell society. Though they rarely used these powers, and never used them for collecting gifts (Fortune calls this "graft"), Omahas believed they might use them if their political power were threatened or even for personal political aggrandizement. Possibly stories from the time of Blackbird lie behind these comments.

In addition to public aspects of social organization, Omaha men, and in a much reduced degree women, participated in a variety of secret socities. The early ethnographies present a good deal of understandably fragmentary data about these organizations, and Fortune subsequently published a substantial monograph about them. Fortune has already carried out the task of comparing the earlier information with his own findings. An analysis of their symbolism and ritual (as indeed for the whole culture) remains outstanding, but that job is best left to a scholar who is properly placed to acquire a firsthand knowledge of these matters and who is fluent in the language.

Fortune shows that the workings of these societies are of great importance for understanding the community's sociology, but in the face of the secrecy surrounding them he has not pushed his sociological analysis much beyond his claims about the class basis of tribal relationships. He did learn much about membership in more recent times, but having promised to maintain confidentiality he publishes only the names already made public by Dorsey in the

1880s. Only his comments on class structure will receive attention here.

Fortune argues (1932, 4) that chiefs of the Council of Seven had to belong to one of the sacred societies, while doctors and medicine men belonged to at least one of the others but never the same one as the chiefs. The class division was buttressed by the strong feeling that a person should marry in his or her own class, "chief's daughter to chief's son, doctor's daughter to doctor's son, priest's daughter to priest's son." They also strongly favored marriage between potential members of the same society and thought proper for a man and wife to belong to the same society (pp. 22–23). Claims for membership might be based on having a vision of an appropriate kind. In practice membership was generally acquired by transfer from an established participant. Such transfer was accompanied in some societies by a doctrine of loss of powers and quickly followed death of the initiator. Fortune speaks of an ideology of "patricide," but in fact the elders retained their freedom of choice and initiated other relatives (p. 46).

This freedom strongly qualifies Fortune's claim that, despite the ideal of vision quest, membership was actually through hereditary privilege, an interpretive difficulty that Fortune never satisfactorily resolves. Comparing his information with Dorsey's, Fortune (1932, 170) found that by 1930 in the water monster society in six instances a son replaced his father, in one a daughter did so, in three cases a son-in-law succeeded, once a sister's daughter took a place, once a perhaps unrelated woman replaced another, and two men entered the society without relationship to previous members. This pattern might be due to changing circumstance, but in fact there is no proof that much the same thing was not commonplace in the past. Dorsey occasionally speaks of inheritance of membership, but his evidence likewise shows no sign either that inheritance always took place or that it was the exclusive means of passing on rights of this kind.

Fortune (1932, 171) provides the only list of the seating order of the seven council chiefs. Because the younger Big Elk is first and Standing Hawk second, this list dates to the period 1845–53, for which unfortunately no treaties are available. Overall the sequence does not closely match any previous or subsequent treaty, though there are interesting similarities in the relative positioning of certain pairs of men. Striking in Fortune's version is that all seven chiefs belong to the Earth moiety and that no fewer than four were in the Small Birds subclan of the On the Left Side clan. This proportion exceeds the strength of this group in other records. Internal evidence (p. 180) suggests that Fortune's informant was of the same subclan. On the whole, the list perhaps is not to be taken at face value.

Fortune does not identify persons by descent group membership, but he does attempt (1932, 171–74) to show multiple memberships in the various societies. His own record does not correspond as closely to Dorsey's as might be expected. For the chiefs' society, called by the ethnographers variously *wacicka* dance, shell, and *midewiwin*, Fortune gives his idiosyncratic enumeration of seven chiefs, plus a further number of names more or less the same as those Dorsey supplies (1884, 343). Fortune's main omission is Mon´zhonkide (Watches over the Land), Silas Leaming, Kon´çe Pipe subclan (ca. 1840–89), who receives attention below. For the ghost and grizzly bear societies Fortune provides names, whereas except for two in the latter grouping (1894, 404–5) Dorsey did not. Fortune, however, ignores Dorsey's membership record for the horse and *witciton* dance societies (1884, 348, 350), perhaps because he thought they were of subordinate importance or not secret societies. There were other, more public kinds that Dorsey (1884, 342) calls feasting societies and Fletcher and La Flesche (1911, 459 ff.) call social societies. Many of what Dorsey calls dancing societies, several of them defunct, may not have been secret. There are various other discrepancies between Dorsey and Fortune, most of them probably of little consequence.

Fortune draws a series of conclusions. First, chiefs, who were all in the shell or *midewiwin* society, joined no other except thunderbird (two men) and buffalo (one). Standing Hawk, however, was also in the *witciton* and horse societies, to which Fortune gave no consideration. Second, priests of the tribe did not join societies. By his own showing, however, one of them was in thunderbird and another in *midewiwin*. Third, there was much overlapping among water monster, grizzly bear, and ghost, but the doctors in these groupings stayed out of *midewiwin* and buffalo. Two Crows's father Fear Inspiring Buffalo Bull was, however, in both grizzly bear and buffalo (Dorsey 1894, 405), and Watches over the Land (Mon'zhonkide), whom Fortune omits without comment, belonged to both *midewiwin* and water monster if Dorsey is right (1884, 343, 347). Thunderbird, as Fortune shows, did have fairly widely overlapping membership with all other groups. There are therefore exceptions to most of Fortune's generalizations. His failure to discuss them leaves a rather slapdash impression.[13]

Since there is no way to know for sure the prehistoric constitution of the tribe, it would be futile to speculate on the accuracy of the version given by Fletcher and La Flesche. Naturally the elements that go into it might very well have occasionally served as a dissenter's picture of how the tribe should be governed in contrast to the realities of historical times. Without prejudicing the question of historical accuracy, we can nevertheless consider the formal properties of this legendary tribal constitution.

2: The Tribal Circle

The ten clans of the Omahas were divided into two equal tribal halves, five clans constituting the Leader people (Honˊgashenu), the remaining five belong to the Flashing Eyes moiety (Inshtaˊçunda). Fletcher and La Flesche say these two halves were referred to respectively as the Earth People and the Sky people. They write that the five clans of the southern half of the tribal circle, the Earth moiety, had charge of the physical welfare of the people in the tribe. The five clans of the northern, Sky moiety were "custodians of rites that related to the creation, the stars, the manifestation of the cosmic forces that pertain to life." Except for the last, these rites had been left to fall into neglect. Sky moiety rites pertained to the "creative and directive forces as related to man's social and individual life," but these were necessary to support the Earth moiety rites directed toward warfare, food, and the physical well-being of the tribe. The organization of the tribe symbolized the belief that by union of the sky people and the earth people the human race and all other living forms were created and perpetuated. Both divisions had to be present at any tribal ceremony, negotiation, or consultation, and the council could not act unless attended by one chief from the Sky moiety and two from the Earth moiety. An Omaha elder explained that "The Inshtaˊçunda represented the great power, so that one chief from that side was enough, while two were necessary from the Honˊgashenu" (Fletcher and La Flesche 1911, 194–97).

The two sacred tribal pipes stood for this dual organization. The pipes were placed in the safekeeping of an Earth moiety clan, but the officer responsible for ceremonially filling them belonged to a Sky moiety clan. A council could not commence until the pipes had been presented and smoked, and the authorities interpret them as representing the tribe as a whole as well as the unity and collective authority of the chiefs, rather than that of only a head chief (Fletcher and La Flesche 1911, 207). The two pipes were never separated, even in ceremonial use, but no evidence was forthcoming about which, if either, was specifically associated with Sky people and which with the Earth division (p. 135).

Omaha descent groups were specifically allocated positions in the tribal circle. This prescribed order was called in Omaha *hu'thuga*, a term that "carries the idea of a dwelling" (p. 137). Although lodge sites in permanent villages were selected according to individual choice, when the tribe went out on the annual hunt the women pitched the tents in a circle or horseshoe in which the tents of each group were assigned their proper position (see figs. 1 and 2). Dorsey writes that the road along which the tribe traveled divided the circle into two equal parts corresponding to the moieties, with the tents of the Elk and Flashing Eyes clans opposite each other at the side toward which the tribe was moving. When the tribe was on the return trip, the circle retained the same internal organization, with the Elk and Flashing Eyes tents now on the side closest home (1884, 219–21; 1897, 226–27). Fletcher and La Flesche explain that there was an opening in the circle between these clans that corresponded to the door of a dwelling. This door was always symbolically to the east. While the five Sky moiety clans were in principle to the north, the Earth clans occupied the side that circumstantially passed for the south.[1]

The literal fact is that the opening was actually toward the east only when the tribal ceremonies took place; at all other times it faced the direction toward which the tribe happened to be traveling, but the order of the gentes was always as it would have been had [the] opening faced the east.

An analogy existed between the tribe and the dwelling, and the circle represented the union of male and female principles through the conjunction of Earth and Sky moieties (Fletcher and La Flesche 1911, 122, 137–41).

Mauss (1913) commented that Alice Fletcher's writings on the

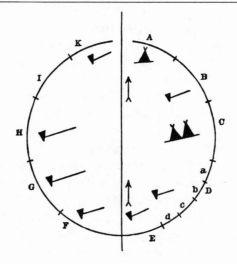

HAÑGACENU GENTES

A. Wejiⁿcte, or Elk.
B. Iñke-sabĕ.
C. Hañga.
D. Çatada:
    a. Wasabe-hit'ajĭ.
    b. Wajiñga-çatajĭ.
    c. ʇe-da-it'ajĭ.
    d. ӿe-'iⁿ.
E. ӿaⁿze.

ICTASANDA GENTES

F. Mañçiñka-gaxe.
G. ʇe-sĭnde.
H. ʇa-da.
I. Iñgçe-jide.
K. Ictasanda.

The sacred tents of the Wejiⁿcte and Hañga gentes are designated by appropriate figures; so also are the seven gentes which keep the sacred pipes. The diameter of the circle represents the road traveled by the tribe, A and K forming the gentes in the van.

Figure 1. The Omaha tribal circle (Dorsey 1884, 220).

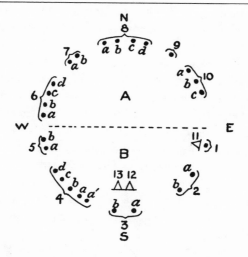

A. IᴺSHTA'ÇUᴺDA DIVISION. B. HOᴺ'GASHENU DIVISION. 1. WE'ZHIᴺSHTE. Subgens: None. 2. IᴺKE'ÇABE. Subgentes: (*a*) Nini'batoⁿ; (*b*) Wathi'gizhe. 3. HOᴺ'GA. Subgentes: (*a*) Waxthe'xetoⁿ; (*b*) Washa'betoⁿ. 4. THA'TADA. Subdivisions: (*a'*) Xu'ka; (*a*) Waça'be itazhi; (*b*) Wazhiⁿ'ga itazhi; (*c*) Ke'iⁿ; (*d*) Te'pa itazhi. 5. KOᴺ'ÇE. Subgentes: (*a*) Tade'tada; (*b*) Nini'batoⁿ. 6. MOᴺ'THI-ᴺKAGAXE. Subdivisions: (*a*) Xu'be; (*b*) Mi'kaçi; (*c*) Mi'xaçoⁿ; (*d*) Nini'batoⁿ. 7. TEÇIᴺ'DE. Subdivisions: (*a*) Teçiⁿ'de; (*b*) Nini'batoⁿ. 8. TAPA'. Subdivisions: (*a*) Tapa'xte; (*b*) Thunder rites; (*c*) Star rites; (*d*) Nini'batoⁿ. 9. IᴺGTHE'ZHIDE. No subdivisions. 10. IᴺSHTA'ÇUᴺDA. Subgens: (*a*) Lost gens; (*b*) Nini'batoⁿ; (*c*) Washe'toⁿ. 11. Sacred Tent of War. 12. Tent of Sacred Pole. 13. Tent of Sacred White Buffalo Hide.

Figure 2. The Omaha tribal circle (Fletcher and La Flesche 1911, 141).

Omahas are marked by occasional vague and seemingly mystical expressions. There are also times when the reader may be uncertain whether he is confronting interpretations or statements of fact. These doubts arise in her description of the symbolic associations of tribal structure, which Mauss subjected to some severe criticisms. In particular Mauss expressed doubt concerning the claim that the moieties are related symbolically as male and female. The authors, however, report that the Omahas regarded the Above as masculine, the Below as feminine, the Sky as the father, the Earth as the mother. In Omaha myths, human beings were born from the union of

Sky and Earth people (Fletcher and La Flesche 1911, 134–35, 601). Perhaps then there was some occasion for the analogy, whether or not it was always present to Omaha minds.

Mauss himself showed a surprising incomprehension of how the two moieties could be considered male and female when by virtue of exogamy each furnished both men and women to the other. The issue of moiety exogamy introduced by Fletcher and La Flesche will be the subject of consideration later. Mauss, however, confused physiological gender with a form of symbolic opposition. That any group of people in a segmentary society necessarily is made up of males and females has nothing to do with the fact that one group may stand as male or female to another. Many examples are known, and an excellent description of an Indonesian case has been made by Onvlee (1949).

A more difficult issue is how the moieties relate to the distinction between right and left. Dorsey (1884, 219) simply states that the Earth moiety was on the right, the Sky moiety on the left. Comparison with his diagram of the tribal circle (see Fig. 1) shows that Dorsey's statement implies that the observer is looking in the direction of travel. Fletcher and La Flesche (1911, 141) say of the Osages that the groups that corresponded to the Omaha Earth moiety camped on the left (i.e., to the south) of the eastern entrance. Describing the configuration of the council meeting, which in its own way conforms to the orientation of the tribal circle, Dorsey (1884, 224) speaks of the chief who could be at the south in the back of the tent as being on the left, with the other chief on the right, implying this time that the observer is looking into the tent through the entrance (see fig. 3). In fact, Dorsey's two diagrams are rotated 180 degrees from each other, and his use of right and left refers merely to the pages upon which they appear. He does not therefore give the true Omaha assignments.

For the closely related Osages, Francis La Flesche (1973; 1925, 115) published a detailed study demonstrating that Osage idiom and practice associated the northern, Sky moiety with the left and the southern, Earth moiety with the right.[2] Moiety divisions among Siouan tribes, as Lévi-Strauss (1966a, 142) observes, are expressed by a variety of oppositions, some of which are given greater or lesser

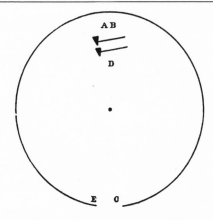

A—The first head chief, on the left. B.—The second head chief, on the right. C.—The two Haṅga wag¢a, one being the old man whom Iñke-sabĕ causes to smoke the pipe. D.—The place where the two pipes are laid. The chiefs sit around in a circle. E.—The giver of the feast.

Figure 3. The position of the chiefs in the tribal circle (Dorsey 1884, 224).

prominence, or are even absent, in different tribes. Certainly the published evidence for the Omahas does not establish the analogy with laterality nearly as explicitly as for the Osages. Nevertheless, there is at least one reasonably clear indication. Fletcher and La Flesche (1911, 208) write that the two principal chiefs sat side by side at the back of the lodge during a council meeting, facing the east and the lodge entrance: "They represented the two halves of the *hu´thuga*, the one who sat on the right (toward the south) representing the Hon´ gashenu, the one who sat on the left (toward the north), the Inshta´çunda."

If we compare this report with Dorsey's diagram (fig. 3), we will see that the top of his drawing lies to the west, the bottom to the east. The symbolic orientation can be better represented in a new figure 4.

So long as the significant orientation is that of the two chiefs sitting at the back of the lodge and facing the east, then the south and the Earth people are on their right, the north and the Sky peo-

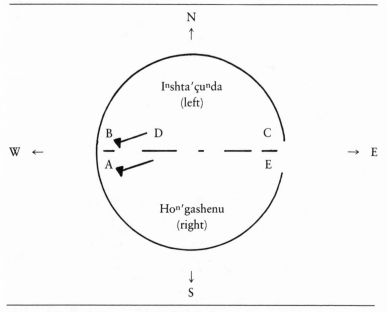

Figure 4. Revised orientation in the tribal council.

ple on their left. This orientation, which parallels that of the Osages, where the relevant relationships are also taken from the
position of a man facing the east (La Flesche 1974, 33), is of course
internal to the lodge. Whether the cardinal points would keep the
same association with right and left in an external frame of reference remains, through lack of evidence, an open question, but there
is no necessity to conclude that they will. The tribal circle, which
corresponds to the positioning of the clan while camping rather
than while on the move, retains this internal orientation.

Fletcher and La Flesche (1911, 337) write that the ground space
of the Omaha earth lodge was as distinctly marked off as if there
were separate rooms. The father occupied the middle of the space to
the left of the fire as one entered, and the mother took her place on
the same side between the father and the door, so that she could
easily slip in and out without disturbing anyone else. Young men of
the family occupied the space near the door on the right. Old people
were also on the right opposite the father, and young girls were
farther back. The interpretation therefore seems justified that for

symbolic purposes the orientation was the reverse of that given by Fletcher and La Flesche; that is, the right side was where the father sat—the right of a person looking out of the lodge. It is also probable that this side was regarded as preeminent.

Additional evidence indicates, as would be expected, that laterality relates to the point of special prominence or honor and therefore depends upon context. The Leader (Hon´ga) clan situates itself in the center of the southern half of the tribe, to the left of the Black Shoulder clan. Leader takes the place that corresponds to the part of the tent reserved for the father of the family. By virtue of their responsibility to call meetings of the council into session, members of Leader clan filled a position within the council "somewhat similar to that of the father toward members of the family under his care." To the left of the Leader clan camped the Tha´tada clan, the name being a contraction of tha´ta tathishon-thonka, "those sitting to the left." Here the point of orientation is clearly that of Leader clan on the south side of the circle. No doubt in principle an explanation is required for this shift, but the ethnographers offer none beyond the meaning of Hon´ga ("leader")[3] and the speculation, based on certain legends and the fact that the name occurs in four closely related patrilineal, Siouan tribes (Omahas, Osages, Kansas, Quapaws), that the name of the common ancestral tribe was in fact Hon´ga (Fletcher and La Flesche 1911, 40–41, 153, 160).

Another example is the orientation of the ceremony associated with the shell society (Fletcher and La Flesche 1911, 516–17, 559). Mauss argues that the tradition concerning the shell society contradicts those associating the Sky moiety with the north and masculinity, the Earth moiety with the south and femininity. The more serious conflict concerns gender; for shell society members explicitly speak of the south side of the lodge as "the masculine side," while the north typifies "the night and feminine forces." The structure here is complex, however. The ceremony is widespread among Algonkian and Siouan tribes and came to the Omahas, according to Fortune (1932, 102), from the Algonkian Sauks and Foxes. Four "children" of the society's myth take specified positions in the lodge in a pattern that Fletcher and La Flesche say is the same in other tribes. The positions stand for cosmic relations and are situated diagonally, not directly, opposite each other. In particular the "eldest son," representing the sun, takes his place at the back on the south side of the lodge, diagonally opposite the "daughter" in the north who represents the moon (see fig. 5). The sun is male and the moon female, and it seems to be this association that on this occasion gives the reversed gender designations for the sides of the lodge. The "second son" (the stars) sits at the back of the lodge on the north diagonally opposite the "youngest son" (the earth) in the south. The stars and the moon therefore are to the north, the sun and the earth to the south. The south is said to be "where the sun travels and causes the earth to bring forth." Plainly the earth, even though represented by the youngest son, is not masculine in this context. The situation of the sun in the south appears to depend as much upon observation of its passage in the northern hemisphere as upon its opposition to the moon.

Among the paraphernalia used by this society that the Peabody Museum at Harvard acquired is a figure made of dressed skin. This figure, formerly in the possession of Big Elk, stood for the master of the society, and its limbs represented the four children of mythology, the left arm being the "eldest son," the right the "second son," the left leg the "daughter," and the right leg the "youngest son." It was explained that the left arm and left leg "went together."

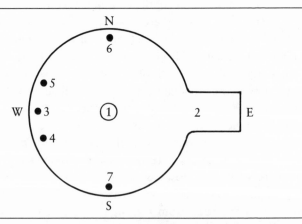

Figure 5. Shell society meeting (Fletcher and La Flesche 1911, 517). 1, fireplace; 2, entrance toward the east; 3, u´zhu; 4, "eldest son" (the sun); 5, "second son" (the stars); 6, "daughter" (the moon); 7, "youngest son" (the earth).

Principles that in the organization of the lodge had been placed diagonally opposite each other were now on the same side—the sun and the moon on the left, the sky and the earth on the right. The figure was a pouch, and in the left arm was kept poison used to punish offenders. In the left leg there were magic shells that permitted the poison to be administered. The right arm and leg contained medicines for healing. The left arm and leg (that is, the poison) were made effectual because, as sun and moon, they were as male and female.

So much for the description as given by the old chief Fire Chief. A permissible inference is that the poison was on the left because it represented death, while the life-restoring medicine was placed on the right side. Because the union of the sun and moon was required to make the poison effective, they became associated with the left. The presence of the poison also indicates that Big Elk was by no means averse to employing a technique more commonly associated with the name of Blackbird. We are by now familiar with the fact that oppositional associations change as contexts vary; indeed they could otherwise hardly be of general use. There is therefore no necessity to regard, as Mauss did, the complex, but nevertheless probably coherent, shell society analogies as conflicting with those of the tribal organization.

We may summarize the description of the tribal circle given by Fletcher and La Flesche as shown in figure 6.

The pattern is the same as that for the Osages, but (especially regarding right and left) not in every respect so clearly manifest.[4] It would be inappropriate to assume for either tribe that the analogies are transitive—that is, to assume, for example, that because the Sky moiety is associated with both masculinity and the left, men necessarily are associated with the left.[5] Then again, we are dealing with analogical features in an ideology that may be at variance with or even quite independent of actual political relations within the tribe.

The analogies serve to express, however, the idea that the unity of the tribe as a whole is prior to the particular ways it is divided up. There are in fact several means of division. The Omahas were first split into halves, made dependent upon each other by the distribution of governmental and ceremonial functions. The tribe was further sectioned into ten clans, five on each side. As will be seen in a

Creative/cosmic forces : Daily affairs

Above : Below

Sky moiety : Earth moiety :: Male : Female

North : South

Left : Right

Figure 6. Analogical associations in the tribal circle.

later chapter, the clans were further subdivided—according to one theory into four segments per clan. Government structure paralleled these splits, since there were two head chiefs, an additional five making up a council of seven superior chiefs, as well as an indefinite number of subordinate chiefs and soldiers. The structure of leadership crossed that of tribal division in two respects. The two principal chiefs "represented" the two moieties, even though for most of the historical period they came only from the Earth moiety. Second, in legend if not in the recent past, the seven council chiefs came from specific clans. Legend and custom compensated for the discrepancy between the seven chiefs and the ten clans by assigning specific functions and qualified council membership to two additional clans, leaving the tenth without privilege or explanation. Fletcher and La Flesche (1911, 207) speculate that there were seven council chiefs because the number seven represented "the whole of man's environment"—north, south, east, west, above, below, and center.

Were we to focus on particular conflicts between these ideal patterns and the record of facts, we might lose sight of the more important point that the ideology resorts to a series of numbers (two, seven, four) to impose the clarity of system upon empirical diversity. The levels of division and subdivision are hierarchically arranged, and the actual groupings correspond best with the higher-order divisions and least well with the lowest.

We may now turn to the formal properties of the idioms whereby Omahas represented human differences as composing an overarching whole. In his famous essay on the comparative method Radcliffe-Brown (1951, 21) placed Australian moiety systems beside those of North America and explained that they represented the principle of the union of opposites. The word "opposition" he thought stressed too much only one side of a relationship—separation and difference—whereas moiety divisions serve to integrate society through opposition. Whether integration of groups is achieved in a society like the Omahas, where history has brought actual relationships so far away from ideal ones, remains a matter for investigation and argument. In any case, integration is not itself a formal property. Radcliffe-Brown implied that social unity had to be achieved through an expression of difference. Empirically this characterization may or may not be correct, but the Omaha ideology presupposes a unity to which articulation is subordinate.

Omaha moieties exemplify in the first place a duality in the organization of authority and governance of a kind familiar in many parts of the world. It has been called dual sovereignty, complementary governance, diarchy, and so on. The literature on the subject is now large, but a recent contribution is a chapter by Needham in *Reconnaissances* (1980). In language not unlike Radcliffe-Brown's, Needham writes (p. 89) that dual sovereignty is characterized by bipartition, opposition, and complementarity. Complementary opposites of course are those where each side fills out or completes what the other side lacks. The Earth moiety ceremonially concerns itself with the daily affairs of the whole tribe, while Sky moiety ceremonies address themselves to securing the position of the tribe within the world. Both kinds of ceremony are ideally necessary, and each presupposes the other. Sky moiety ceremonies, however, are symbolically superior. It is doubtful that complementary opposites ever permit a perfect equality between the sides. A recurrent feature of studies of complementary governance is the superiority of one form of authority, usually the spiritual or mystical.

Lévi-Strauss (1966a, 140–41) states that among Siouan tribes the dualism inherent in moiety systems conceals a principle of tripartition and that the Omahas display tripartition in that one moiety has two chiefs and the other only one. Lévi-Strauss's reading of Omaha ethnography on this point is in fact mistaken, his source being the tradition already mentioned that for a council to be held only one chief of the superior Sky moiety need be present, while at least two from the Earth division must attend. Nevertheless, in his own terms Lévi-Strauss would interpret this passage as evidence of a concealed tripartition comparable to that of the Osages, where one moiety contains seven clans while the other moiety splits into two divisions of seven clans each (La Flesche 1921, 51). Lévi-Strauss's comments here hark back to an earlier paper on dual organization (1956, 1963), in which he argues that alternative tribal models given to Radin by Winnebagos "correspond to two different ways of describing one organization too complex to be formalized by means of a single model." "Even in such an apparently symmetrical type of social structure as dual organization, the relationship between moieties is never static, or as fully reciprocal, as one might tend to imagine" (1963, 134–35). This paper gave rise to a debate concerning the accuracy of his analysis of Winnebago, South American, and Indonesian societies (Maybury-Lewis 1960; Lévi-Strauss 1960), which may be left aside here. With justification, Lévi-Strauss interprets Radin's information as showing alternative theories of society: one based on division into moieties, the other showing a unified tribe set apart from a line of virgin forest on all sides. The first or diametric dual model he describes as static, whereas the second model of concentric dualism is dynamic, containing an implicit triadism (1963, 151). At the very least, the Omaha tribal circle expresses simultaneously the dual division of the tribe and its unity as opposed to the surrounding environment both of nature and of other human groups.

Perhaps what is missing from the preceding characterizations is a precisely formulated idea of hierarchy. Dumont has recently leveled this criticism at modern social anthropology in general (1979, 1980) and more particularly at a study of right and left and other forms of dual symbolic classification. Dumont (1980, 810–11) fears that in speaking of simple polarities or complementarities anthropologists have assumed that both sides of a dyadic pairing are equal. How they might have adopted this position after reading Hertz (1974) on the preeminence of the right hand need not be discussed here. Nevertheless, for Dumont the reference to the whole made by a right and left opposition is hierarchical, and the preeminence of one element necessarily results from differentiation within a whole. Scholars may disagree over how much of the foregoing is novel, but Dumont's analysis of hierarchy is what most distinguishes his views from his predecessors'. Hierarchy in fact is "the encompassing of the contrary," to be distinguished from a chain of command or taxonomic classification. To display his idea of encompassment, Dumont uses two diagrams (1980, 242) that are remarkably similar to the alternative diagrams of Winnebago society published by Radin (see fig. 7). The first is a rectangle cut vertically into equal halves labeled A and B. The second consists of a rectangle labeled X, in the center of which is a second rectangle labeled Y. The first diagram expresses a universe of discourse exhausted by two complementary or contradictory classes. Despite the fact that both A and B are subsumed within the greater whole, Dumont does not speak of their relation to it as hierarchical. The second diagram expresses hierarchy. Like the first figure, there is unity at the superior level and distinction at the inferior stage, and X and Y are related by complementarity and contradiction. Element X, however, both stands in opposition to Y and represents the higher-order unity. Thus right and left exemplify this "hierarchical opposition" on those occasions when the right stands for the whole as well as for part of the internal division.

In speaking both of contrariety and of contradiction while defining hierarchical opposition, Dumont obviously is not applying these ideas in the conventional sense of traditional logic. In the logic of propositions, two statements are contradictions if it is impossible for both to be true and both to be false. Propositions are contraries when both cannot be true though both can be false. Binary opposites are not propositions, but by virtue of their logical form they may figure as predicates. Consequently, as Lyons says (1977, 272), we may speak in a derivative and obvious way of pairs as being contradictories or contraries. Aristotle, from whom we derive the distinction (Lloyd 1966, 161–62), did deal with oppositions between propositions alongside those between terms (contraries, correlative opposites, positive and privative terms). For Aristotle "male" and "female" are contradictories, while "hot" and "cold" are contraries. Not all contraries are opposites ("red" and "blue"); furthermore, contraries are gradable in that the negation of one side does not necessarily imply the confirmation of the other.[6]

The question now arises how the oppositions of Omaha tribal structure are to be classed. To begin with right and left, both Du-

1

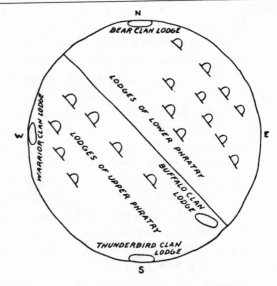

Plan of village according to Thundercloud, of the Thunderbird clan.

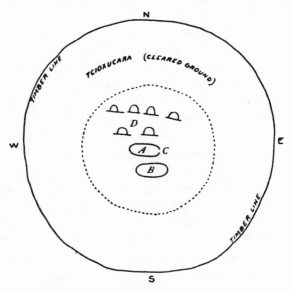

Plan of village according to John Rave, of Bear clan. *A*, Lodge of chief of tribe (Thunderbird clan). *B*, Lodge of chief of Bear clan. *C*, Lodge of Warrior clan. *D*, Lodge of Buffalo clan.

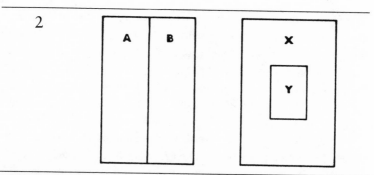

Figure 7. Comparison between Winnebago tribal structure and Dumont's interpretation of hierarchy. 1, Alternative views of Winnebago tribal structure (Radin 1923, 188–89). 2, Dumont's models of opposition versus hierarchy (1980, 242).

mont and Needham treat this opposition as though it permitted no middle term. In fact, insofar as the terms refer to a whole, they very well fit into the tripartite scheme of right, middle, and left (Lloyd 1966, 93). Right and left therefore are natural contraries, in the conventional sense. They have attracted anthropological interest, however, because in analogical classification they are often used in a way implying that they are actually contradictories, permitting no middle term, and it is evidently this commonplace experience that Dumont and Needham have in mind.

The only true contradictories in figure 6 are male and female. Others (above/below, north/south, left/right) allow a middle term—the center or, in fact, the middle. Reference to the middle is by no means excluded in Omaha ceremony. Mediable contraries are just as capable of referring to the whole as are contradictories, though they suggest the potential of tripartite or other plural schemes. The contraries represent Omaha moieties dyadically. This point seems to underlie Lévi-Strauss's hypothesis of an implicit tripartition in any dyadic scheme; for the complementarity of two opposed halves is only a first approximation of tribal relationships.[7]

Aristotle, and others after him (for example, Needham 1980, 51, 58), spoke of the parts of an opposition as species within the genus that is made up by the union of the pair. There is a logical difference between an object belonging to a concept and a concept belonging to a higher-order concept (Frege 1891, 26–27). There are neither right objects nor right concepts, though by analogy both things and concepts are compared to right and left (cf. Needham 1980, 58).

Dumont (1979, 809) describes hierarchical opposition as obtaining "between a set (and more particularly a whole) and an element of this set (or of this whole); the element is not necessarily simple, it can be a sub-set." Furthermore, the element is identical to the set.[8] Hierarchy therefore is a part/whole relationship or synecdoche. Aristotle defined metaphor as a transfer from genus to species, species to genus—therefore really a synecdoche—while applying "metaphor" to all tropes (Brooke-Rose 1958, 4); and rhetorical theory has trod an unending definitional circle ever since. Dumont's theory of hierarchy, however, admits of more precision. For him it is insufficient that a relation of species to genus obtains; hierarchy requires that one species (or half of a pair) be equivalent to the genus, with perhaps a strong interpretation being given to the definition of equivalence. This situation he calls a logical scandal, there being a relation of identity and one of contradiction (that is, difference) in effect at the same time.

Published Omaha data show few explicit signs that one half of the tribe stands for the whole, but the mystical superiority of the Sky moiety places it in association with the cosmos, which of course subsumes daily concerns, the earth, and the tribe. Implicitly, therefore, a relationship of the kind presupposed by Dumont underlies traditional tribal organization. The organization itself is indeed far too complex to be pictured by a single image. The tribe is divided in several ways at different levels, and the levels are organized among themselves in rank order: division into moieties > division into clans > division into subclans > multitude of named individuals.

This rank order may be described in Dumont's terms as encompassed by the highest-order or moiety split. Recall, however, that the pattern is clearest in legendary material, acknowledged by the elders as long being at variance in some ways with the effective relationships within the tribe. Legend stands to the historical past, therefore, rather as *varna* in India does to *jati* (caste). The hierarchical relations are logical—that is, ideal ones—and need not precisely fit actual relations of dominance and subordination among men.

Leach (1954, 278) says that "myth and ritual is a language of signs in terms of which claims to rights and status are expressed, but it is a language of argument, not a chorus of harmony." A question of historical interest therefore is, Who benefited by appeal to this ideology—head chiefs like Big Elk whose position was not entirely legitimized by it, or subordinate rivals for whom it might provide ammunition against the dominant leaders? The multiplicity of images of tribal and government organization, none of which perfectly described the actual position of any group, probably served all of them to some extent. Thus the theory that chieftainship had to be achieved may have been valued by a lineage like those in the Elk clan, who had no claim to chieftainship in the mythical council and who wished to pass the offices they controlled to their descendants. The same version of the constitution equally well supported the ambitions of new claimants to office.

3: Descent Groups

Dorsey (1894, 407, 411) writes that Omaha descent groups are among those things that pertain to Wako^n'da, divinity. There are ten named Omaha clans, five in each moiety. The American authors call these descent groups gens, in keeping with a convention current in their times that labeled patrilineally organized groupings as gens, matrilineal ones as clans. Present usage applies clan to higher-order, named unilineal descent groups, regardless of whether the rule of membership is patrilineal or matrilineal. Since these terms are merely conventions, reference may be made to Omaha clans and subclans, rather than gens and subgens, without implying interpretive disagreements with the ethnographers.

There are of course issues of analysis and characterization that must be addressed. Adopting the classification of his superior at the Bureau of American Ethnology, Major J. W. Powell, Dorsey (1884, 215) describes descent groups as consisting of "a number of consanguinei, claiming descent from a common ancestor, and having a common taboo or taboos." Elsewhere (p. 252) he identifies a variety of *ni'kie* kinship based on descent from the same or a similar mythical ancestor, which may obtain between two clans in different tribes. Dorsey's definition provoked a direct, albeit implicit, disclaimer by Fletcher and La Flesche (1911, 195).

The Omaha gens was not a political organization. It differed from the Latin gens in that the people composing it did not claim to be descended from a common ancestor from whom the group took its name and crest. . . . The

Omaha gens was a group of exogamous kindred who practised a particular rite, the child's birthright to which descended solely through the father; and the symbol characteristic of that rite become the symbol, crest, or "totem," of the gens.

When speaking English the Omahas call their groupings "bands" (Mead 1932, 62, 77). In their own language they refer to clans as *to^n 'wo^{n}gtho^n*, a word that means village. Villages could be distinguished from clans by adding the river name where the village was situated when that sense was required, or *uba'no^n* (implying common kinship) in the case of a clan. Among Omahas or Poncas a person might identify himself by the name of his clan, but in answer to a stranger's question he would name the animal central to the rite of his clan: "I am a buffalo person" or an "elk person." Subclans were *to^n 'wo^{n}gtho^n*, to which a diminutive (*zhi^{n}ga*) or a word meaning "split off" (*uga'çne*) was added. Dorsey's genealogies often specify subclans by use of the word *bate* or "side." In principle each subclan had its name, rite, set of personal names, food avoidances, and assigned place in the camping circle (Fletcher and La Flesche 1911, 136–37).

This description, however, greatly simplifies the situation with which the ethnographers were confronted. To begin with, not all clans were subdivided, while some were segmented in more than one way. Subclans were sometimes designated by a variety of names. The ethnographers were not always successful in establishing a distinctive list of personal names for each of the recognized divisions within a clan. Many of the subclan rites no longer survived by the 1880s. Some subclans were in size and relative independence virtually the equivalent of independent clans, while some clans were relatively insignificant. The ethnographers, and also their informants, disagree on what the subclans are and how many there are in each of the clans.

Dorsey (1884, 216) writes, "There are strong reasons for believing that each gens had four subgentes at the first; several subgentes having become few in number of persons have been united to the remaining and more powerful of their respective gentes." There does appear to have been a view held by some members of the tribe that each clan was divided into four groups. Lion or Wani'tawaxa

(b. ca. 1816) in particular gave Dorsey a list of four subclans for many clans where other Omahas listed fewer or none at all. Two Crows and Joseph La Flesche regularly denied the accuracy of his statements. As a "paper chief" Lion stood apart from the others, and among many Omahas his reputation was low (see Dorsey 1890a, 4). Nevertheless, in some cases his versions were corroborated by others. As a keeper of the pipe in the Deer Head clan, he might well have favored a more traditionalist interpretation of tribal structure. Another factor, however, is that the number four was an archetypical classifier in Omaha culture. The appearance of four in connection with clan segments may in some cases have meant little more than that, in the Omaha view of things, it was appropriate for something to be divided by four or made up of four parts.[1] Another remarkable aspect of Lion's statement on clan division is that he attributed four divisions to each of the subclans of the On the Left Side clan, therefore treating them as though they were on a par with other clans—which in some respects they were.

At this stage, at the risk of submersion in detail, further sociological analysis requires taking up each clan separately.

I. EARTH MOIETY

1. We´zhi^{n}shte (the Elk) clan

Fletcher and La Flesche (1911, 136) write that if an Omaha were asked by another Omaha or a Ponca what clan he belonged to, he would answer by giving its name. A stranger might not know the names of Omaha clans, so he would be answered by naming the animal that was the emblem of the descent group. "I am a buffalo person" or "I am an elk person." "The reply would not be understood to mean that the man thought of himself as a buffalo or an elk, or as descended from one, but as belonging to a group which had charge of rites in which that animal was used as a symbol."

Dorsey says that we´zhi^{n}shte is an archaic word whose meaning has been forgotten. Fletcher and La Flesche attribute to it an etymology that implies it refers to those persons through whom the tribe expressed its anger, turning on their association with war ritual. The clan in any case was commonly designated, by both ethnographers and Omahas, by reference to the associated animal, the elk.

The Elk clan took its place on the south side of the east entrance to the tribal circle. Not assigned one of the original seven pipes, it controlled war rites and the sacred tent of war; but several famous head chiefs in the nineteenth century belonged to this clan by birth or adoption. Whenever another tribe engaged in hostile acts, the keeper of the tent of war was obliged to call a meeting of the seven chiefs and the leading men of this clan, at which he presided. He also presided at the ceremonial bestowal of war honors. At the direction of the seven chiefs, this clan organized scouts to search for danger during the annual buffalo hunt. The clan had charge of rites pertaining to the first thunder heard in the spring. For much of the nineteenth century, the keeper of the tent of war was not one of the head chiefs of the tribe.

Members of the clan might not eat the flesh of a male elk or male deer or wear moccasins of deer or elk skin. At death, however, they were buried wearing such moccasins. Children had their hair shaved to represent the head and tail of the elk (Dorsey 1884, 225; Fletcher and La Flesche 1911, 142–45; see fig. 8). La Flesche (1928, 94–95) relates how Alice Fletcher, who at one time was having difficulty gaining information about descent group hairstyles, made a breakthrough that ended her problems at the home of Badger (b. ca. 1842) of the Herald section of the Black Shoulder clan, when he caught up his young son and subjected him, in spite of his protests, to a demonstration haircut. Thereafter she acquired information of this kind easily.

Although Dorsey supposes there may once have been divisions within the Elk clan, there were none in the 1880s, and tribal legend does not mention them. In 1883 there were fifty-four persons of this clan (see table 3).

Dorsey's genealogical notes show that six persons living in 1883 and reckoned as members of Elk clan were descendants of a pair of brothers whose father had been in the Black Shoulder clan. A laconic marginal note from George Miller says that both were killed by lightning because they had joined the Elk clan.[2] Dorsey was told that the Omahas thought a person killed by lightning should be buried face downward and the soles of his feet slit, so that the spirit

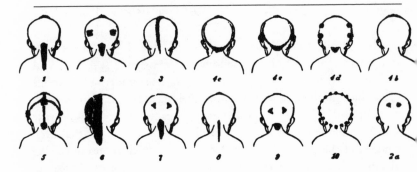

Totemic cut of the Omaha boys' hair. No. 1 is typical of the head and tail of the elk. No. 2 symbolizes the head, tail, and horns of the buffalo. No. 2a—the children of this subgens and those of the Ni-ni'-ba-to^n subgens of other gentes have their hair cut alike; the locks on each side of the bared crown indicate the horns of the buffalo. No. 3 represents the line of the buffalo's back as seen against the sky. No. 4b stands for the head of the bear. No. 4c figures the head, tail, and body of small birds. No. 4d, the bare head, represents the shell of the turtle; and the tufts, the head, feet, and tail of the animal. No. 4e pictures the head, wings, and tail of the eagle. No. 5 symbolizes the four points of the compass connected by cross lines; the central tuft points to the zenith. No. 6 represents the shaggy side of the wolf. No. 7 indicates the horns and tail of the buffalo. No. 8 stands for the head and tail of the deer. No. 9 shows the head, tail, and knobs of the growing horn of the buffalo calf. No. 10 symbolizes reptile teeth. The children of this gens sometimes have the hair shaved off so as to represent the hairless body of snakes.

Figure 8. The hairstyles of Omaha descent groups (La Flesche 1928, 87).

would go at once to the spirit land without bothering the living. According to George Miller and Francis La Flesche, when one of the brothers, Elk Leaps and Flees (Jadegi), was killed by lightning, the Omahas failed to bury him this way and his ghost walked until his brother, Ni'mo^{n}ho^n or Allan Brown, died in the same way and was laid beside him (Dorsey 1894, 420; 1889, 190). Unfortunately, no information is available as to their reason for having switched clan affiliations, but it is interesting to see from the genealogies that the shift had become effective even at such cost. Perhaps the surmise that their deaths resulted from supernatural sanction was reinforced by the responsibility of the Elk clan for thunder rites.

2. Black Shoulder Clan

The Black Shoulder clan was adjacent to the Elk clan in the circle. The name I^nke´çabe is archaic and its meaning uncertain, but it seems to refer to the black shoulder of the buffalo. They received one of the seven pipes, and a member of the clan was keeper of the two tribal pipes. Another person of the clan was vested with leadership in the annual tribal buffalo hunt.

Mythology associates this clan with the buffalo. Dorsey describes young boys of the clan as wearing a two-inch fringe of hair around the crown of the head, with the top shaved except for two tufts representing the horns of buffalo (see fig. 9). Fletcher and La Flesche do not mention this version but ascribe to the Pipe Owning subclan (Nini´bato^n) the same haircut worn in all other pipe-keeping subclans, namely a head completely shaved except for two tufts on the crown at the back. The Hoop subclan left a tuft over the forehead, one on each side of the crown, and a short lock at the nape of the neck, representing the head, horns, and tail of the buffalo.

As for the segments of the clan, Dorsey writes that "There has evidently been a change in the subgentes since the advent of the white man." In 1878 and 1882 Joseph La Flesche gave Dorsey apparently conflicting lists of the divisions, using different names and numbers of divisions (three and four). Fletcher and La Flesche give yet a different account. According to them, there were two subclans, (a) Pipe and (b) Hoop. With the Pipe were associated two further sections, Charcoal (pulverizers of charred box-elder wood) and Heralds. Pipe subclan not only kept the tribal pipes but also held the rites concerned with the cultivation of maize, and they avoided red ears of maize. Charcoal observed an additional prohibition on touching charcoal, deriving as does their name from their responsibility for preparing the paint for the tribal pole and its ceremony. The third small section consisted of a lineage that filled the hereditary office of tribal herald. They also observed the restriction on red ears of maize.

The name of the Hoop subclan refers to a legend (of a class designated as fictitious) in which a hooped rope of a kind used in a cere-

Table 3. Living Members of the Omaha Tribe in 1883

	Male				Female				Grand Total
	Adult	Not Adult	Married	Total	Adult	Not Adult	Married	Total	
I. EARTH MOIETY									
1. Elk	14	15	15	29	10	15	11	25	54
2. Black Shoulder									
a. Pipe									
i. Charcoal	3	3	4	6	4	4	4	8	14
ii. Heralds	2	3	2	5	6	2	4	8	13
iii. Remaining Pipe	16	31	20	47	12	28	18	40	87
Total Pipe	21	37	26	58	22	34	26	56	114
b. Hoop	11	11	10	22	4	16	6	20	42
Unlocated	1	3	1	4	9	2	8	11	15
Total Black Shoulder	33	51	37	84	35	52	40	87	171
3. Leader									
a. Mottled Object									
i. Servers	1	5	1	6		4	1	4	10

ii. Remaining Mottled Object	14	11	15	25	9	13	13	22	47
Total Mottled Object	15	16	16	31	9	17	14	26	57
b. Dark Object	4	2	5	6	2	3	3	5	11
Unlocated					3		3	3	3
Total Leader	19	18	21	37	14	20	20	34	71
4. On the Left Side									
a. Black Bear	13	10	12	23	14	16	19	30	53
b. Small Birds	17	24	17	41	14	29	20	43	84
c. Turtle Bearers	12	10	13	22	7	6	7	13	35
d. Buffalo Head (Eagle)	9	8	9	17	9	21	12	30	47
Unlocated					4	1	5	5	5
Total Left Side	51	52	51	103	48	73	63	121	224
5. Koⁿ'çe	5	7	6	12	9	4	8	13	25
a. Wind	8	3	8	11	4	7	8	11	22
b. Pipe					5		5	5	5
Unlocated									
Total Koⁿ'çe	13	10	14	23	18	11	21	29	52
Total Earth moiety	130	146	138	276	125	171	155	296	572

continued

Table 3 *continued*

	Male				Female				Grand Total
	Adult	Not Adult	Married	Total	Adult	Not Adult	Married	Total	
II. SKY MOIETY									
6. Earth Makers (Wolf)									
a. "Sacred"	12	9	23	21	5	15	6	20	41
b. Pipe	5	3	5	8	4	2	3	6	14
Unlocated					5		5	5	5
Total Earth Makers	17	12	28	29	14	17	14	31	60
7. Buffalo Tail	13	10	14	23	4	23	9	27	50
8. Deer Head									
a. Real Deer Head	8	25	11	33	5	18	9	23	56
b. Thunderbird	8	12	11	20	4	14	6	18	38
c. Star Rites	2	4	3	6	5	2	4	7	13
d. Pipe	8	10	9	18	2	6	3	8	26

Unlocated					10		9	10	10
Total Deer Head	26	51	34	77	26	40	31	66	143
9. Red Dung	10	18	13	28	7	18	9	25	53
10. Flashing Eyes									
a. Pipe	1	2	1	3	5	8	5	5	8
b. Real Flashing Eyes	9	9	11	18	7	16	8	15	33
c. Children Owners	17	30	21	47	13	5	15	29	76
d. Real Thunder	1	1	1	1	9		9	9	10
Unlocated	2		2	3	5		7	10	13
Total Flashing Eyes	30	42	36	72	39	29	44	68	140
Total Sky moiety	96	133	125	229	90	127	107	217	446
Total Omaha[a]	226	279	263	505	215	298	262	513	1,018

a. These figures do not correspond exactly with those given by Fletcher and La Flesche (1911, 33–34) for June 1884, partly because some persons have not been located, partly because Fletcher and La Flesche include several persons tenuously associated with the tribe in various ways.

Figure 9. Dorsey's version of the Black Shoulder clan hairstyle
(Dorsey 1884, 230).

monial game turns into buffalo that provides food for the tribe. The
buffalo hunt leader came from this division. They also had custody
of the songs used in the annual summer He´dewachi ceremony concerned with the cultivation of maize and care of the fields. They
avoided the tongue and head of buffalo. Interestingly, in the tribal
circle the heralds camped not with the other members of the first
subclan but between the Leader clan and the Hoop subclan. Charcoal camped nearest the latter subclan on the other side.

In 1878 La Flesche gave four division names related to prohibitions. Dorsey is clearly correct, however, in concluding that the
names do not refer to four distinct groups. The first two names, Pipe
and Those Who May Not Touch Red Ears of Maize, both designate
the first subclan. The third and fourth names refer to the prohibitions
of the second subclan. In the same year La Flesche said there were
three subclans, the fourth—the Heralds—having become extinct.
These three were Hoop, Those Who May Not Touch Red Ears of
Maize (i.e., Pipe), and They Who Cannot Touch Charcoal. This list
therefore differs from that published by Fletcher and Joseph's son
Francis La Flesche only in according equal status to all four groupings and in the claim that one had died out. In 1882 Joseph La
Flesche and Two Crows told Dorsey that the Heralds were part of
Pipe, which was called by the names referring to the prohibitions on
maize and charcoal. Dorsey's drawing (fig. 10) of the clan assembly
also indicated a configuration of two subclans, with one of them

internally divided as later reported by Fletcher and La Flesche (Dorsey 1884, 228–31; Fletcher and La Flesche 1911, 146–49).

Plainly we are dealing not with incompatible descriptions of the Black Shoulder clan, but with alternative ways of speaking of the same sociological reality. The sources all identify two principal divisions of the Black Shoulder clan, but the standing of the two small sections remains to be explained.

There are two additional sources of information that may help: Dorsey's genealogies and the lists of names by division given by Fletcher and La Flesche (1911, 149–53). The genealogies appear to support the assumption of two principal divisions, but members of the smaller groupings can be identified only with the aid of the later lists of names.

Fletcher and La Flesche accord eighteen names to the Herald division, little indication that they had become extinct. Charcoal receives merely three. The last herald mentioned was an old man named First of Birds (Waxhi^n'ho^{n}ga) or Tsha-hish, Frederick Mitchell (Dorsey 1884, 287). Although this man was alive in 1870, he had

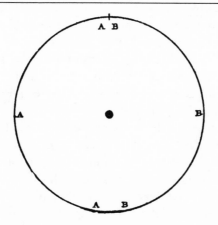

The Iñke-sabĕ Gentile Assembly. A.—The Wa¢igije, or Waqúbe gáxe aká, under Dubama^n¢i^n. B.—The Wata^{n}zi-jide ¢atajĭ; the Ieki¢ĕ, and the Naq¢e-it'abajĭ. These were under Gahige.

Figure 10. Black Shoulder clan assembly (Dorsey 1884, 231).

died by the allotment in 1883 and was survived only by a married daughter, though two nephews, sons of his brother, were living and had large and growing families.

The three Charcoal names are Little Turkey, Samuel Lovejoy (ca. 1823–86), Gashka´wo^{n}gthe (meaning uncertain), Amos Lovejoy (b. ca. 1802 or 1826), and Little Buffalo Horns, Asa Lovejoy (b. ca. 1842). The last man was also named Badger and is the person mentioned above in the anecdote about hair cutting. Amos Lovejoy and his two married daughters were living in 1883, but Dorsey shows him as having no other immediate agnatic relatives. A marginal note identifies this section of the genealogy as belonging to Little Buffalo Horns's or Badger's side.[3] Unfortunately Fletcher and La Flesche list Little Buffalo Horns's other names as belonging to the Herald division. Furthermore, they do the same for Little Turkey's son Fire Eyes and for Little Buffalo Horns's sons Little Hair, Brown Ankles, and Little Knobs on Horns. Given that the authorities agree in assigning the heads of these three families to the same division, and in view of their shared family name of Lovejoy, the conclusion is unavoidable that they were at one time all members of the small Charcoal grouping.

This result throws new light on the discrepancies between Joseph La Flesche's reports of 1878 and 1882. Presumably the last herald died about or just after 1878. Perhaps for reasons unknown the office did not pass to his brother's sons. In any case it seems that both of the small groups charged with special ceremonial duties amalgamated into one that still associated itself with the hereditary office of crier and retained that designation.

The assumption that the Black Shoulder clan was formerly divided into four subclans of equal standing seems to have been made only by Dorsey, based partly on a misunderstanding of Joseph La Flesche's intention (see Dorsey 1897, 227). If so, it is an example of the kind likely to occur when an academically inclined mind confronts the idiom of an unfamiliar culture. Dorsey in particular displayed a weakness for neatly patterned taxonomies. On the other hand, Omaha habits seemed to favor lists of standard numbers like four without regard to whether the components were in all respects comparable. Whatever effect the early epidemics may have had on the demography of the tribe, there is no reason to think the Black

Shoulder group ever had more than two main subclans in the nine-teenth century. It seems even more unlikely that the two smallest segments ever constituted independent groupings. In fact they were nothing more than particular families within the Pipe subclan asso-ciated with particular minor offices or ceremonial duties. That such responsibilities could shift around within the subclan is suggested by the comment (Dorsey 1884, 230) that the ancestors had re-moved the trust of the tribal pipes from the forebears of Na´gu and given it to Chief's paternal grandfather. Dorsey's genealogies indi-cate that the subclan was made of many small family groups whose precise genealogical links with the others were unknown.

In 1883 there were six males and eight females among the fami-lies of the men Fletcher and La Flesche listed as in the Charcoal grouping. The remaining Herald families contained five males and eight females, making an overall total of no more than twenty-seven persons. The rest of the Pipe subclan totaled eighty-seven. The whole subclan comprised more than 114 living members in 1883, if we consider that the clan segment of a small number of people from the clan cannot be identified. The second subclan held forty-two persons. Unlocated members of the clan living in 1883, numbering fifteen in all, bring the total clan size to 171.

3. Leader Clan

The Leader clan occupied the center of the southern half of the tribal circle, its place corresponding to that of the father in the tent. The name has been rendered variously as "foremost," "first," "lead-er," or "ancestral" and occurs as a clan name in several other tribes. They were passed over in distributing the seven pipes but, in Half-a-Day's account, were given a firebrand for lighting them. Joseph La Flesche and Two Crows told Dorsey (1884, 223) that Leader "was the source of the sacred pipes, and has a right to all, as that gens had the first authority." Leader directed a Black Shoulder man to carry the pipes around the circle; and Leader lit the pipes in ceremony. Leader called together the governing council.

There is a single manner of wearing the hair for the children of the whole clan, an erect ridge of hair running from the forehead to the nape of the neck in the image of a buffalo's back as seen against the sky. There were two subclans. "Some said that there were originally four subgentes, but two have become altogether or nearly extinct, and the few survivors have joined the larger subgentes" (Dorsey 1884, 235). There were two sacred tents in the clan, one assigned to each of the subclans, and these were always kept together and erected near each other in front of the clan's tents in the tribal circle. The Mottled Object subclan (referring to the sacred pole) maintained the tent containing the sacred pole, symbolic of the authority of the chiefs, thought to derive from Wakon'da. Fletcher and La Flesche would have it that this tent represented the Sky moiety while the second tent, in the charge of the Dark Object subclan, stood for the Earth moiety. With the second tent (Fletcher and La Flesche 1911, pl. 27) were associated rites pertaining to the quest for food, and it contained the white buffalo hide.

The two subclans had several names, relating either to ceremonial functions or to food prohibitions. The Mottled Object subclan could not eat a special cut of meat from the sides of a buffalo used in the tribal ceremony connected with anointing the sacred pole. They were also forbidden geese, swans, and cranes. A certain set of families in this subclan was distinguished as servers in the sacred pole ceremonies, and they camped adjacent the heralds of the preceding clan, followed by the rest of their subclan.

The Dark Object subclan did not share these restrictions but avoided buffalo tongues. The name indicates that they possessed the "dark object," describing the appearance at a distance of a staff the leader of this grouping held on the annual hunt. Dorsey gives as another name of this subclan "Real Leaders," but Fletcher and La Flesche say this is the name of a division within the subclan responsible for ceremonies connected with maize. These families had an additional prohibition on the outer husk of an ear of maize.

There is some confusion in Dorsey's genealogies concerning the small group of servers that Fletcher and La Flesche assign to the first subclan. The personal names Fletcher and La Flesche give (1911, 157) for the servants all occur in the small extended family of a man named Smell of Buffalo Dung, William Thomas (b. ca. 1840), and in that of Ha'xigi. William Thomas's father, an unidentified Leader man, was the first husband of a woman who took as her second husband Ha'xigi. Dorsey wrote across the portion of the page relevant to William Thomas, "These could *touch* and *arrange* the *tawa-qube* [the prohibited meat from the sides of the buffalo]." Dorsey seems to have been unaware that there was a special family of ceremonial servers, since he nowhere mentions them. Nevertheless, this comment can be taken as confirmation that these were the hereditary servers. However, he also identifies this family by a phrase referring to the white buffalo hide and indicating that they belong to the second subclan, as he does also for the family of Ha´xigi. Most names in both families appear in Fletcher and La Flesche's list of hereditary servers.

The first family, by inference the servers, bear the English family name Thomas, which is exclusive to them. Ha´xigi's family name is Robinson, the same as that of the other members of the second subclan. The obvious explanation appears to be that William Thomas, the last survivor of the servers, had been brought by his mother into the household of her second husband. The two households thus being merged, they came to be associated in people's minds, giving rise to complementary errors by Fletcher and La Flesche and by Dorsey. A conceivable explanation is that William Thomas's ancestors belonged, as reported, to the first subclan and were servers, while Ha´xigi's belonged to the second subclan and were not, at least originally.

Dorsey says that the whole of the second subclan are "Real Leaders," but Fletcher and La Flesche say the Real Leaders are only a subdivision, and they list only two personal names for the subdivision. One of these names is that of Victorious or Richard Robinson (b. ca. 1840), one of the hereditary keepers of the Tent of the White Buffalo Hide. The other personal name is the same as that of the division—Real Leader. Fletcher and La Flesche list this name twice without comment, once here and once among the servers. During the period in question, however, there was only one Real Leader, Thomas Robinson (b. ca. 1842), son of Ha´xigi.

There are some other slight discrepancies in the list of names, but nothing that seems to require comment. Doubts about subclan affiliation of the servers concern only two families. Issues about clan division of the Leader clan are not after all so very different from those concerning the previous clan. By the beginning of the 1880s there were two subclans proper. By further distinguishing families associated with ceremonial functions, the Omahas could arrive at four named groupings of very unequal sociological significance. Demographic decline had blurred even this picture somewhat, leading to some confusion about subclan affiliation for two families, but evidence for four original subclans is very slender (Dorsey 1884, 233–36; Fletcher and La Flesche 1911, 153–59).

In 1883 the first subclan comprised forty-seven living persons. Not counted in this number are ten members of William Thomas's family of servers. Excluding this family, the second subclan consisted of only eleven living persons.

4. On the Left Side Clan

The On the Left Side clan stands out in many respects from all other clans. Its sections had no common rite or symbol. Each subclan had its own separate camping area, though all subclans were adjacent to each other between the Leader and Kon´çe clans. The name of the clan indicates that it camped to the left of Leader. Other than a general association within the tribal circle and a rule of exogamy applying to the whole clan, the four subclans can justifiably be regarded as clans in their own right. Indeed, Dorsey says, "Were it not for the marriage law, we should say Ćatada was a phratry, and its subgentes were gentes." Earlier lists of the clans often err by treating the Tha´tada subclans as though they were self-sufficient. Since there was in fact a real degree of independence between these subclans, different in kind from what was to be found in other clans, it is convenient here to take each subclan separately.

a. Black Bear Subclan.

The first of the subclans in the tribal circle was the Waça´be Itazhi, "Those Who Do Not Touch Black Bear." They were prohibited from touching the skin of this animal or eating its flesh. The subclan once held rites concerned with the black bear, subsequently lost, and at one time they joined in the Elk clan rites connected with the first thunder in the spring. Dorsey describes the hairstyle as consisting of four short locks left on the front and back and two sides of the crown (see fig. 11), but Fletcher and La Flesche mention only a broad lock over the forehead reminiscent of the head of a bear.

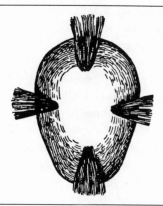

Figure 11. Dorsey's version of the Black Bear subclan hairstyle (Dorsey 1884, 237).

Various Omahas told Dorsey that the subclan contained four divisions: Black Bear, Raccoon, Grizzly Bear, and Porcupine people. Joseph La Flesche and Two Crows mentioned only two divisions. Dorsey concludes characteristically, "It may be that these two are the only ones now in existence, while there were four in ancient times." Not questioned by these two men were the Black Bear proper and the Xu´ka.

Xu´ka refers to instructors in mystic rites, applying to a group of families who acted as hereditary prompters to the Leader clan during rituals of the white buffalo hide and the tribal pole, helping them avoid mistakes. They therefore camped next to the Leader clan, while the rest of the subclan placed their tents farther to the left. Dorsey says the Xu´ka were Raccoon people: "The Black bear and Raccoon people are called brothers. And when a man kills a black bear he says, 'I have killed a raccoon.' The young black bear is said to cry like a raccoon, hence the birth-name Mika-xage" (Dorsey 1884, 237).

Although all Xu´ka are prompters, only one man at any given time acts in this capacity. The Black Bear proper are all servants of the Elk clan and assist them in the thunder ceremonies, but they are accompanied by a few Xu´ka who also act as servants in an unspecified way. Only two men from Black Bear took a prominent part in Elk clan rites, but if they died or were unwilling to act others of their section had to replace them (Dorsey 1884, 236–38; Fletcher and La Flesche 1911, 159–60).

In 1883 this subclan contained fifty-three living persons. Once again, though, there is confusion about the identity of the group with special ceremonial functions. Dorsey (1884, 238) writes that the three brothers—Dangerous, Unkempt or Samuel White (b. ca. 1848), and Digger or Luke White (b. ca. 1841)—were the only ones from whom the Xu´ka could be chosen. None of these men, however, appear in the list of names of the Xu´ka section given by Fletcher and La Flesche (1911, 163). That list contains the names of two small families as well as some other names actually borne by persons in a different subclan. Dorsey's list of names for the Xu´ka division coincides with that of Fletcher and La Flesche to the extent that it includes the same two families just mentioned. However, it also contains names from several other lines throughout the subclan. Several of these names are those of the Elk clan servants, and Dorsey included them only because Not Afraid of Pawnee or Jordan Stabler (b. ca. 1831), a prominent man of the subclan, did so. One of the men named by Joseph La Flesche as an Elk servant is by all other evidence unquestionably a Xu´ka. This man is Rough Clouds or John Jewett (b. ca. 1840). Perhaps he is the Xu´ka who sometimes accompanied the others when they served in Elk clan rites. The last person known to Not Afraid of Pawnee to have acted as a prompter was Dried Buffalo Skull, Lewis Stabler, whose name does not appear in Fletcher and La Flesche's Xu´ka list. It therefore appears that the function had passed more widely through the families of the subclan than suggested by the ethnographers and that, at least by the time of Dorsey's visit, there were no longer two precisely distinguished divisions of the subclan.

b. Small Birds Subclan. This group were the Wazhin´ga Itazhi, "Those Who Do Not Touch Birds." The rites of the subclan concerned protecting the crops from birds but were long in disuse. They described themselves to strangers as Blackbird people. Although they were permitted to eat wild turkeys, geese, ducks, cranes, and when they were ill prairie chickens, they were not allowed to touch any small birds. Their haircut for children consisted of a lock in front and a fringe and broad lock at the base of the skull.

Lion of the Deer Head clan gave Dorsey an elaborate system of division for the subclan, but Joseph La Flesche and Two Crows flatly denied it. "It may be that these minor divisions no longer exist, or that they were not known to the two men." Lion's classification was as follows.

1. Hawk people—under Standing Hawk or Eli S. Parker (ca. 1812–86), a principal chief of the tribe

2. Blackbird people—under Bird Chief, Frank Webster (b. ca. 1834)
a. White Heads
b. Red Heads
c. Yellow Heads
d. Red Wings

3. Gray Blackbird (the common Starling) or Thunder people— under Sound of Tearing with Claws (Wa´thidaxe)
a. Gray Blackbirds
b. Meadowlarks
c. Prairie Chickens
d. Martins

4. Owl and Magpie people
a. Great Owls
b. Small Owls
c. Magpies

Again the division offered is based on the number four, which carries down into further division of two of these sections. Fletcher and La Flesche mention no segments of the subclan and do not discuss the information Lion gave Dorsey. Although Dorsey's genealogy of the subclan does not name separate sections, surprisingly the genealogy does break down conveniently into four groupings around the men Lion named, assuming that the fourth section corresponds to the families who took the English surname Sheridan. There is no way, however, to identify families with the lowest order in the classification, and it is unlikely that these labels applied to permanent lines within lineages where genealogical links were so close (Dorsey 1884, 238–39; Fletcher and La Flesche 1911, 160–61). In 1883 the subclan held eighty-four persons.

c. Turtle Bearers Subclan. Next in the camping sequence came the Ke´i^n or "Turtle Bearers." Dorsey disagrees with Fletcher and La Flesche in this regard, placing the Buffalo Head subclan before them in the circle. They no longer practiced their rites, which they remembered to be intended for bringing rain and dispelling storms or fog. They could not eat turtle flesh. Children wore a short fringe around the head, with a lock at the forehead, two on each side, and one at the back. This configuration depicted the turtle.

Though Two Crows and Joseph La Flesche explicitly denied his report, Lion also named four separate divisions of this subclan. His division follows:

1. Big Turtle—under He Drew Near Hill or Mark Peabody (d. ca. 1878)
2. Turtle That Does Not Flee—under White Claws, Roland Edwards (b. ca. 1811)
3. Red-breasted Turtle—under Buffalo Bull That Is Sleeping (Tenu´ga zho^{n}thi^n´ke) (b. ca. 1808)
4. Spotted Turtle with Red Eyes—under He Alone with Them, George Peabody (b. ca. 1831)

Strangely enough Fletcher and La Flesche, obviously incorrectly, list the names of the heads of the first three divisions as belonging to the Xu´ka division of the preceding subclan. Dorsey's genealogies for this subclan do not neatly fit Lion's scheme, nor do they refute it. The subclan is quite small, consisting of only thirty-five living persons in 1883 (Dorsey 1884, 240–41; Fletcher and La Flesche 1911, 161).

d. Buffalo Head Subclan. Last of the subclans (or, according to Dorsey, third) is the grouping called Te´pa Itazhi, "Who Do Not Touch a Buffalo Head." They may once have had rites pertaining to the buffalo head. They received one of the seven pipes and originally a place in the council, and they are thus the equivalent of the Pipe sections of the other clans. They were forbidden to touch the head of a buffalo and a spoon made of buffalo horn, but they described themselves to strangers as Eagle People, referring to their pipe. Children wore a square tuft over the forehead, another at the nape, and a broad lock over each ear, representing the head, tail, and wings of the eagle. The head of the clan was one of the bearers of the tribal pipes.

Consistent with his other reports, Lion gave four divisions to the subclan (again denied by La Flesche and Two Crows).

1. Keepers of the Pipe or Workers—under Little Eagle (Xitha´zhiⁿga)
2. Those under Only Leader, John Freemont (b. ca. 1830)
3. Those under Real Eagle (Xitha´xti)
4. Bald Eagle—including Yellow Breast (Moⁿge´çi) and Small Hill (Pahe´zhiⁿga)

Dorsey suggests that the first three groups may belong to the three kinds of eagles recognized by the Omahas, the white eagle, the young white eagle, and the spotted eagle. Omahas did not regard the bald eagle as a real eagle but included it in this classification of the subclan.

Dorsey's genealogies of the Buffalo Head subclan are the least complete of any in the tribe. They are badly damaged by rodents, and it is possible that sheets are missing since several persons are left off them though their names are recorded in the genealogies of other clans into which they married. The poor state of Dorsey's record for this subclan is surprising since one of his principal sources was a man of this subclan called Tribal Herald (Waje´pa) or Samuel Freemont (ca. 1835–1906), who went to Washington in the autumn of 1888 and worked with him on the tribe's genealogies until February 1889 (Dorsey 1894, 362). Lion named the heads of families in the last three sections. The only problem posed for Lion's description by the information available is that he places Moⁿ´çeguhe in the second division and Moⁿ´çeguhe's son Small Hill (Pahe´zhiⁿga) in the fourth (Dorsey 1884, 239–40; Fletcher and La Flesche 1911, 161–62). There were forty-seven members of the subclan alive in 1883. There were an additional five females in the clan unlocated by subclan.

Dorsey (1894, 523) presents the assembly circle for this clan when it came together as a whole for a council (see fig. 12). The Black Bear and Small Birds people were described as "sitting on the same side of the fireplace" and as being full kin, while they were only partly related to the other two subclans. Dorsey further interpreted the sections of the clan circle as corresponding to the four elements earth, air, fire, and water, following a theory of Thomas Foster's about the related Winnebago tribe: "The Black Bear people are associated with the ground or earth, as is shown by their personal names; the Small Bird people are Thunder-beings or Fire people; the Eagle subgens consist of "Wind-maker" people; and the Turtle subgens is composed of Water people."

The order of figure 12 corresponds to Dorsey's description of the placing of the subclans in the tribal circle and necessarily therefore differs from that of Fletcher and La Flesche. On the assumption that the underlying orientation of the clan circle is the same as that of the tribal circle (which Dorsey nowhere states), then the first two subclans would oppose the third and fourth as earth and sky. In fact, however, those subclans that in Dorsey's scheme are symbolically

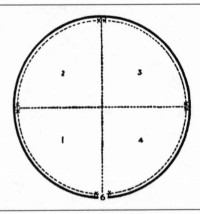

Figure 12. On the Left Side clan circle (Dorsey 1894, 523). 1, Black Bear subclan; 2, Small Birds subclan; 3, Buffalo Head (Eagle) subclan; 4, Turtle Bearers subclan.

lower (earth and water) are numbers 1 and 4, whereas 2 and 3 (Thunder and Wind) might be considered associated with the above. In any event, the evidential basis for Dorsey's symbolic interpretation is scant indeed. The personal names for each of the subclans do not in fact justify Dorsey's assignments to the elements. It is the Black Bear, not the Small Birds people, who take part in Elk clan rites for thunder, and there seem to be no grounds for calling the Eagle subclan wind-maker people.

Of greater importance is that the tradition of a clan circle strengthens the supposition that the clan did have some ideological unity, when the subclans otherwise so often appear self-sufficient in Omaha eyes.

5. Koⁿ´çe Clan

The last clan at the west end of the Earth moiety in the circle was the Koⁿ´çe, whose untranslatable name is the same as that of a related tribe (Kansa) and of the state of Kansas. The entire clan avoided verdigris. The hairstyle for the children represents a design formerly used in rites connected with wind, consisting of tufts on the forehead and nape, over each ear, and at the top of the head, connected by a ridge of hair in a cross pattern. The locks stood for the cardinal points and the center. Men of the clan acted as criers, calling braves to take part in a sham fight after the anointing of the tribal pole before returning home from the annual hunt, and they also initiated the ball game played between the two moieties.

Again, Omahas disagreed about the divisions of the clan. Joseph La Flesche and Two Crows recognized only two subclans: Keepers of the Pipe and Wind people. Lion identified four, each of which he named by giving the headman of the section. Either classification is compatible with Dorsey's genealogies, though they indicate only two subclans. Assuming that the effective split was into Wind and Pipe, then in 1883 in the Wind subclan there were twenty-five persons. The Pipe included twenty-two. There were also five women of the clan alive who could not be assigned to a subclan (Dorsey 1884, 241–42; Fletcher and La Flesche 1911, 169–71), for a total of fifty-two persons.

II. Sky Moiety

6. Earth Maker Clan

Opposite the Kon´çe in the Sky moiety were the Mon´thinkagaxe, the "Earth Makers" or "Earth-Lodge Makers," also known as Wolf or Prairie Wolf people. This was the clan to which the famous chief Blackbird belonged. Rites that are long lost may have had a connection with the gray wolf. Reports differ on the form of the hairstyle for children. Dorsey says that boys wore two locks of hair, one over the forehead and the other at the parting of the hair on the crown. Girls wore a lock in front, one in back, and one over each ear. Fletcher and La Flesche report that for children of three groups of the clan, the hair was shaved clean on the right side and left to grow on the other, but they appear skeptical of the report that this style pictured bare rock and falling rain. The Pipe section cut their hair as did all other Pipe subclans. The clan as a whole observed a prohibition on the swan and upon the clay and soot used to color four stones employed in ceremonies.

The familiar disagreement occurs again concerning clan division. Joseph La Flesche and Two Crows named two subclans, but Lion mentioned four and White Horse, Ellis Blackbird (b. ca. 1835), the head of the clan, listed three. For once Dorsey reflects upon these discrepancies.

This [the division into two subclans] is evidently the classification for marriage purposes . . . ; and the writer is confident that La Flèche and Two Crows always mean this when they speak of the divisions of each gens. This should be borne in mind, as it will be helpful in solving certain seeming contradictions.

Fletcher and La Flesche write bluntly,

There are no subgentes in this gens. Within the last century the groups of families to whom were formerly assigned certain duties connected with the ancient rites have taken names referring to their ancient hereditary office, and as a result these groups have been mistaken for subgentes.

They mention three sections in the first instance: "Sacred" (Xu´be)—charged with the sacred stones; Wolf—charged with rites related to the wolf; Swan—holding duties related to water and the swan. These all cut children's hair as described above. The fourth section are the actual keepers of the pipe. Fletcher and La Flesche nevertheless divide the personal names of the clan into two lists belonging to the divisions mentioned by Joseph La Flesche and Two Crows, namely "Sacred" and Pipe. The sequence in which Fletcher and La Flesche list the sections corresponds to their place in the tribal circle, and it differs on this occasion from that given by Lion only in the order in which the sections are mentioned. White Horse's list differs only in leaving out the Wolf people; for this omission there may be a simple explanation. Dorsey's genealogies fall rather conveniently into the two divisions (although they specify section membership for only one family), and they are at least not incompatible with the classification into four sections (Dorsey 1884, 242–43; Fletcher and La Flesche 1911, 171–75).

By using Fletcher and La Flesche's lists of personal names as a guide to division membership, we find that the sixty living members of the clan in 1883 break down as follows. There were forty-one persons in the "Sacred" subdivision, fourteen in the Pipe subdivision, plus five women from the clan for whom division specification cannot be found.

7. Buffalo Tail Clan

The clan name Teçin'de means Buffalo Tail. Its rites were completely lost, but they pertained to the crow. Members were forbidden to touch the unborn young of any animal, especially of buffalo, and the lower rib where the calf's head touches the mother. They did not eat a calf of either the buffalo or domestic cattle while it was red but might do so when it became black. They were not permitted to touch the buffalo head. The two ethnographies disagree again about the cut of children's hair. Dorsey describes a central ridge long enough to flop over on each side (see fig. 13). Fletcher and La Flesche say that two small tufts on each side of the crown were left on the sides of the head and a lock at the nape, representing the horn stubs and tail of a buffalo calf. Pipe families, however, used the style of the other such subclans.

Fletcher and La Flesche say there are no subclans, but they describe two divisions and give corresponding lists of personal names.

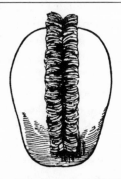

Figure 13. Dorsey's version of the Buffalo Tail clan hairstyle
(Dorsey 1884, 244).

One part camped adjacent to the preceding clan, while the pipe
keepers camped next to the Deer Head clan. Dorsey writes, "For
marriage purposes, the gens is undivided, according to La Flèche
and Two Crows; but they admitted that there were at present two
parts of the gens, one of which was The Keepers of the Pipe." Lion
also knew of only two subclans, the Keepers of the Pipe or Those
Who Do Not Eat the Lowest Buffalo Rib, and Those Who Touch
No Calves or Keepers of the Sweet Medicine. Lion names the head
of each section. Other than a nominal discrepancy concerning the
designation subclan, all authorities for once are in full agreement;
and Dorsey's genealogies bear them out (Dorsey 1884, 244;
Fletcher and La Flesche 1911, 175–77). Fifty Buffalo Tail clan
members were living in 1883.

8. Deer Head Clan

In the center of the northern half of the tribal circle camped the
Tapá or Deer Head clan. This name refers to the Pleiades. Their
rites were lost, but may have been related to stars. Some personal
names of the clan refer to lightning, others to the deer. Members
sometimes painted red lines on their children's arms, indicating
lightning. Persons in the clan were permitted to eat venison, but
they were not allowed to touch the skin of any animal related to
deer, wear deerskin moccasins, or use deer fat as hair oil. They

could not touch charcoal and verdigris, whose colors symbolized the sky. The pipe group used the same haircut as did the equivalent groupings in other clans. For the rest of Deer Head clan, children wore a tuft over the forehead and a thin lock at the nape of the neck.

Once again the various sources disagree as to the nature of Deer Head clan division. Joseph La Flesche recognized three subclans for marriage purposes (which will be explained below). Lion characteristically stated that there were four. Fletcher and La Flesche deny that there were any subclans but acknowledge four divisions based on ceremonial duties formerly possessed. Their list coincides with that given by Lion and with Dorsey's genealogies, which he clearly divided into four subclans. Joseph La Flesche seems to have conflated two of the sections, namely the Pipe and the section under Boy Chief. The authors characterize the groupings variously by name and by the leading man of each group, but no confusion arises from this. The classification below follows the order of the tribal camp (Dorsey 1884, 245–47; Fletcher and La Flesche 1911, 177–83).

a. Real Deer Head—under Glittering Tail, William Hamilton
(b. ca. 1837)
b. Thunder or Thunderbird—under Pawnee Chief, Newlin Smith
(b. ca. 1800)
c. Star Rites—under Boy Chief, Oliver Furnas (b. ca. 1835)
d. Pipe—under Lion, also called Disobedient, Oliver Lyon
(b. ca. 1816)

The sections are as large as the subclans of other clans. The Real Deer Head had fifty-six persons in 1883; the Thunder grouping included thirty-eight. Under Boy Chief there were only thirteen persons, and there were another twenty-six in the Pipe section. There were also ten women of the clan whose section membership is unknown. The entire clan comprised 143 persons.

9. Red Dung Clan

The name of the Red Dung clan refers to the excrement of newborn calves. Members may not eat a buffalo calf, nor may they touch a buffalo fetus. The children's haircut consists of a lock in front, one at the nape, and two on the sides of the head, standing for the head, tail, and horn stubs of a young buffalo. This clan is the only one that in legend was given neither a pipe nor a ceremonial function in the tribal council.

Dorsey says that the clan was undivided for marriage purposes. Fletcher and La Flesche say there were neither subclans nor divisions. Lion, however, mentioned four subclans. Not knowing the names of the sections or their prohibitions, Lion identified them by leading men. Dorsey's genealogies make no distinction by section, but they are not incompatible with Lion's classification (Dorsey 1884, 247–48; Fletcher and La Flesche 1911, 183–85). The clan included fifty-three persons in 1883.

10. Flashing Eyes Clan

The I^{n}shta´çu^{n}da or Flashing Eyes clan camped opposite the Elk clan at the east end of the tribal circle, and it gave its name to the entire northern or Sky moiety. The name relates to lightning. Clan rites pertained to thunder and lightning. Members of the clan were forbidden to touch worms, toads, frogs, snakes or other reptiles, and creeping insects. The children's haircut consisted of a circle of small locks around the crown, representing insect legs. Such vermin, which abound after rain, indicate its fructifying power, and rites of the clan pertain to the sky and its ability to fertilize the earth. Those of a lost subclan may have been connected with the clan prohibition. The clan is sometimes referred to as the Reptile people. The Keeper of the Pipe for the clan also was charged with responsibility for the ceremony of lighting the tribal pipes.

Joseph La Flesche and Two Crows told Dorsey the clan contained three divisions, but Lion of course said there were four. Fletcher and La Flesche explained pessimistically that only one complete subclan and one subdivision survived in 1883, there having once been another subclan that had become extinct. As the result of such changes, they claimed that the distinctive lists of personal names of the various subclans had become confused with one another by the time Fletcher compiled allotment records in

1883. Dorsey's genealogies, however, were organized into four discrete subclans, corresponding exactly with Lion's listing.

a. Pipe—under Lone Buffalo or Arthur Ramsey (b. ca. 1839)
b. Real Flashing Eyes—under Turbulent Day, Alvin Cox
  (b. ca. 1841)
c. Children Owners or Reptile people—under He Is Known,
  Benjamin Hallowell (ca. 1833–4 July 1884)
d. The Real Thunder—under Kidaha´nu

The disagreement between Joseph La Flesche and Lion about this clan is actually slight. The former said that the Keepers of the Pipe and the Real Flashing Eyes constituted the first division. His son Francis told Dorsey that the two were distinct subclans. The Pipe Keepers having been reduced to a single family, they seem to have joined in some way the Real Flashing Eyes. The Children Owners Fletcher and La Flesche identify as the surviving full-fledged subclan. According to Dorsey they were also called Keepers of the Wildcat Claws, which they bind to the left side of a newborn infant's waist. The fourth subclan, Real Thunder, was also called Those Who Do Not Touch the Clam Shell and Keepers of the Clam Shell or Keepers of the Clam Shell and Tooth of a Black Bear. They would bind a clam shell to the waist of a child in their grouping if he was quick to learn to walk. The subclan that Fletcher and La Flesche claim was lost may well be this fourth grouping, for by 1883 Kidaha´nu had died and there was but a single male, himself childless, still living, though there were also nine females. In 1883 there were only eight living persons in the Pipe subclan, the Real Flashing Eyes comprised thirty-three persons, and the Children Owners were seventy-six all together. Thirteen persons were unlocatable by subclan, so the total for the whole clan was 140 (Dorsey 1884, 248–51; Fletcher and La Flesche 1911, 185–94).

The failure of the authorities to reach full agreement on the list of clan segments probably reflects the realities of Omaha life better than would a standard list. Some blurring of patterns did indeed result recently from population decline. No doubt similar processes worked in the past, sometimes swelling one grouping while diminishing another. The ravages of the smallpox epidemics and the depredations of Sioux raiding parties would in any case have ensured that the tribal organization changed during historical times. Nevertheless, misunderstanding can result from giving exclusive attention to such factors. Omaha reasons for distinguishing groupings were various, and not all the means of doing so were simultaneously relevant for a given purpose. Different Omahas obviously carried different pictures in their heads of the internal structure of various clans. Such disagreements evidence not so much incompatible theories as differing interests.

Alice Fletcher seemed to have been most concerned with identifying the effective substantial groupings, so that her list shows the least number of independent divisions (see table 4).

Lion, on the other hand, set about the business of classification in a characteristically Omaha manner. For him division into fours was of more concern than the sociological comparability of the resulting segments. Whereas in some cases his subdivisions correspond to fairly large and tangible groupings, in other cases he is satisfied so long as he can identify single family heads to bear out his quadripartite scheme. On the other hand, Lion insists in dividing up the subclans of the On the Left Side clan as though they were actually clans in their own right, carrying his subdivision down to the point of splitting the segments of the subclans. There is enough corroboration by independent sources to show that Lion's viewpoint is not entirely his personal invention. The outline in table 5

Table 4. Clan Division According to Fletcher and La Flesche

I.	1.			II.	6.	
	2.	a.			7.	
		b.			8.	
	3.	a.			9.	
		b.			10.	a.
	4.	a.				b.
		b.				
		c.				
		d.				
	5.	a.				
		b.				

Table 5. A Supplemented Version of Clan Division According to Lion

I.	1.				II.	6.	a.	
	2.	[a.					b.	
		b.					c.	
		c.					d.	
		d.]				7.	a.	
	3.	[a.					b.	
		b.				8.	a.	
		c.					b.	
		d.]					c.	
	4.	a.	[i.				d.	
			ii.			9.	a.	
			iii.				b.	
			iv.]				c.	
		b.	i.				d.	
			ii.	A.		10.	a.	
				B.			b.	
				C.			c.	
				D.			d.	
			iii.	A.				
				B.				
				C.				
				D.				
		c.	i.					
			ii.					
			iii.					
			iv.					
		d.	i.					
			ii.					
			iii.					
			iv.					
	5.	a.						
		b.						
		c.						
		d.						

presents Lion's representation of the Omaha tribe, supplemented in the earlier clans (indicated by brackets) by similar opinions of other informants where Dorsey does not specifically indicate Lion's interpretation.

Writers may be impelled to look for a coherent system, applying considerations of symmetry and completeness foreign to Omaha culture. Thus, relying largely on Lion, Dorsey presupposes that formerly each clan contained four segments, presumably making forty separate subclans. Lion's actual statements indicate, however, a more complicated structure. Then, too, the various criteria by which groupings are recognized do not always coincide. Judged by descent group name, marriage restrictions, rites, sets of personal names, or avoidance regulations, the list of clan segments would differ slightly in each case.

The effects of such considerations on marriage choices will be taken up below. Another matter requires consideration here. Dorsey and his informants often indicate the heads of various clans or subclans, and Dorsey sometimes calls these men "chiefs" of their descent groups. Even Fletcher and La Flesche (1911, 178) indicate the divisions of the Deer Head clan by naming their headmen, but they qualify this identification by saying these persons "were not chiefs but leading men." Elsewhere (1911, 195, 211) they state categorically that "There was no political or governing chief of an Omaha gens or subgens. . . . No gens had a chief possessing authority over it, nor was there any council of a gens, nor could a gens act by itself."

Dorsey of course speaks in a contrary vein when he identifies the seating pattern of the different clans as they assemble in a clan council. Actually, other than the seating arrangement, no information exists about such meetings or their purpose. Clans did sometimes go out on hunts led by chiefs in the clan. The sociological reality perhaps was that the personal influence of individual chiefs did not strictly coincide with descent group boundaries and that there were changing degrees of prominence among Omaha "leading men."

As Fletcher and La Flesche observe, there were chiefs of one rank or another in every clan, though they deny them individual authority over a descent group. In keeping with their interpretation of the clan as being not a political organization but a group of kin united through a common rite, these two authors number among the leading men in a clan not only chiefs, but also those in charge of rites and those designated to act as soldiers.

Although Fletcher and La Flesche repeatedly emphasized the importance of a common rite, it is well to recall that several clans possessed at best no more than the memory of rites that, if they had ever had them, they had lost at the time their ancestors left the woodlands of the Middle West and moved to the prairie lands of Nebraska and Iowa (therefore probably at the latest by the end of the seventeenth century). Furthermore, as we have seen, ceremonial responsibilities were not always shared in full measure by members of a clan or subclan. Dorsey's evidence suggests that subclans usually consisted of several family groupings that could not trace genealogical connections with each other. For day-to-day concerns such fissures may well have marked limits to mutual dependence, so that the collectivities were further fractured at the lowest level in ways not always reflected in the classifications considered in this chapter.

Lévi-Strauss (1966a, 70) had in mind the numerous deviations in Siouan cultures from the various simple models of order they suggest when he wrote that in societies with unilineal exogamous clans demography pushes the system of clan names toward disorder, which speculative inspiration tends to reorganize. The Omahas exhibit only very imperfectly Lévi-Strauss's model (p. 115) of a "pure totemic structure" in which the differences between species are homologous to the differences between groups.

Omaha descent groups and their associated animals do correspond to this structure in an imperfect way, but, they blur the clarity of the model on the one hand by sharing the same animal among more than one descent group, and on the other by compounding species differences with distinctions not at all on the same plane. While a species (e.g., Elk) may represent one clan, part of an animal of a given species (e.g., Black Shoulder of Buffalo, Buffalo Tail) or the bodily discharges of a species (e.g., Red Dung of a Buffalo Calf) may represent another. Other clans are distinguished not by animals but by human attributes (Ancestral Leader), position in the tribal circle (Left Side), mythical function (Earth Makers) or natural phenomena (Flashing Eyes, implying lightning). Some descent groups may be named by reference to one species, whereas the members describe themselves in conversation by referring to quite a different species. The various subclans of a given clan may be designated by reference to different species. For each procedure an abstract model could be constructed that could in principle be used exclusively and systematically by a culture.

Clan names (as well as personal names) often seize upon a part of a greater whole, suggesting the possibility of, as Lévi-Strauss puts it, retotalization in various ways, for example making names up by reference either to the same part of different animals or to a complete inventory of the parts of a single animal. To the Omaha Black Shoulder and Buffalo Tail clans, there ought to correspond clans named for the head, torso, and legs of the buffalo. The Deer Head clan should be accompanied by Black Bear Head, Buffalo Head, Wolf Head, Eagle Head, and similarly designated clans.

Empirically the systems are jumbled together. Rather than complying with expectation, the Omaha clans turn in other directions, as if to establish their independence as much by the diversity of systems chosen as by distinctions within a given system. They thus seem to deny the very overarching unity that in other ways they appear to be trying to establish. To put the issue another way, the anthropologist might be justified in concluding that Omaha nomenclature is as much concerned with proclaiming the singularity of distinguishable groupings and persons as in subsuming them within tribal structure. Whether this confusion truly results from demographic changes alone—in which theory Lévi-Strauss follows the speculations of the ethnographers—is an open question. Possibly the multiplicity of competing means of classifying groups, imperfectly carried through, is the natural situation where classifications correspond to diverse needs and are propounded by many persons or groups, rather than by a single individual or centralized authority.

Faced with the problem that many societies with unilineal descent groups lack relationship terminologies making corresponding equations, Leslie White (1939, 41) suggested that the relevant terminological features appear once the descent groups have had time to develop. Murdock (1949, 240–41) claims to have found statistical support for the hypothesis. The Omahas are by this theory a society with mature or developed patrilineal descent groups.

Gifford (1940) offers a variety of pertinent criticisms of a comparative kind. The factors he mentions can of course be interpreted in a way that will fit White's generalization, but at the expense of weakening conviction. Buchler (1966, 40) observes that we lack an explicit definition of a strongly developed descent group, necessary for an interpretation of the hypothesis. McKinley (1971a, 238–39) reviews other criticisms and comments that assessing strength by reference to multiplicity of clan functions confuses form and function. More to the point perhaps is that it provides a constantly shifting basis for the comparison in which it is expected to serve as an index. In any event, the grounds are not clear by which we might conclude that Omaha descent groups were stronger than those of such societies as the Ojibwas or Iroquois that lack unilineal terminological equations (cf. Service 1960, 764). Nevertheless, the issue of Omaha clan strength can be assessed only in relation to other tribes and is therefore a comparative question. By some criteria the clans look strong enough, by others rather weak.

4: Personal Names

Dorsey (1886, 396) writes that many Omahas and Poncas could identify the tribe and descent group to which a personal name belonged as soon as they heard it. Fortune (1932, 15) claims to have used in the field an alphabetically arranged dictionary of male personal names that identified the clan of each name, there being no overlapping between clans. Americanists long ago concluded that there were intimate connections between naming clans and naming persons and that such individuating expressions were linked with classifications of natural species.

Because an Indian name implies relationship, it "therefore, shows the affiliation of the individual; grades him so to speak and he is apt to lean upon its implied powers" (Fletcher 1884b, 295). Dorsey (1886, 393) even maintained that "all Indian personal names have meaning, many of which have been preserved to this day." An early witness, Morgan (1959, 87), established a theme that frequently exerted its influence on the imaginations of white observers and provided a basis for often-favored parallels with eastern tribes like the Iroquois, when he noted that the personal names belonging to each clan were kept distinct, no one of another clan being permitted to use them, while the names themselves depicted the animal with which the group associated itself.

Mauss (1913, 108) describes the hierarchy of Omaha classifications as descending from the totem to the subtotems and, by way of personal totems, to the individual. Fletcher and La Flesche for the most part steer the Omahas well clear of the controversies about totemism[1] that were current in their day, confining themselves largely to establishing that clan or personal totems were not objects of worship, but symbols or crests and denying that there was any doctrine of identity with or descent from an animal. Nevertheless, the Omahas belong to the continent and ethnological area for which totemism was classically "discovered," and Lévi-Strauss in part has in mind North American cultures like the Omahas and the Osages when he says (1966a, 149) of their procedures of classification that "the species level can widen its net upwards, that is, in the direction of elements, categories, and numbers, or contract downwards in the direction of personal names."

Like those of the Poncas, Omaha personal names could be said to be on loan for the lifetime of the bearer, reverting to the "name pool" upon his death or earlier for reassignment to a younger member. "The clan [personal] names thus became, in a sense, titles" (Howard 1965, 97). The topic might be thought so well worked out that little remains to be discovered. Yet Dorsey was preparing a major comparative monograph, including his material on Omaha names, that he never completed. The manuscripts reveal two dictionaries of Omaha and Ponca names, alphabetically arranged, in one case by the Omaha language versions and in the other by the English versions. Descent groups and other information about the names are clearly provided.[2] These dictionaries correspond precisely to that described by Fortune. "The average old Omaha has the associations in his head that make quite a large dictionary such as the field worker must use to keep pace with his informant." It would be interesting to know whether Fortune knew of, had access to, and used Dorsey's manuscripts. Such analysis as Dorsey managed to publish (1886, 1890b) was feeble. Like raw ore, the data extracted remain encrusted with unwanted matter, and the vein from which they were drawn is interpenetrated by obscure and contrary-tending interpretations.

Dorsey (1886, 394) writes that the Omahas have four "cardinal birth-names" for each sex (see table 6). Among the Omahas and Poncas such names apply sequentially to the sons or daughters in the family, regardless of whether or not children of the opposite sex have also been born. For example, even if she has elder brothers, the first daughter is still Wi-no$^{n'}$. In this respect the Omahas differ from

Table 6. Omaha Birth-Order Names

Male	Female
1. I^{n}gtho^n	1. Wi-no^n'
2. I^n-ke'	2. Çi-ge'
3. Ka'-ga	3. A-çi'
4. Ka-ge'	4. Wi-he'

Source: Dorsey (1886).

the Dakotas, who take into account a child's place in order of birth of all children.

Implicitly, Fletcher and La Flesche (1911, 314) partially contradict Dorsey's circumstantial report when they write that the firstborn son was called I^{n}gtho^n, the first daughter Wihi. "There were no other special 'baby names' in use among the Omaha." However that may be, these "baby names," as they prefer to call them, which children received on the fourth day after birth, retained currency for the first three or four years of life, after which they were "thrown away" at the Thiku'wi^{n}xe or "turning the child" ceremony. This rite took place after the first thunder heard in springtime, when the grass had grown and the birds were singing. Its purpose was to establish the child as a distinctively human being, a person of the tribe and a member of a descent group. At this time the child received new moccasins and one of the *ni'kie* (ancestral) names of his descent group. Fletcher and La Flesche write that until this stage the child is hardly to be distinguished from all other kinds of living forms. Appropriately, the names for very young children merely indicate the relative sequence of birth, but their new names confer individuality—though to a much greater degree for boys than for girls.

A member of the Black Shoulder Hoop subclan conducted the turning the child ceremony in a tent made ceremonially mysterious or *xube* for this purpose. He placed the child facing the east and introduced it to the four winds, turning it carefully from left to right to the south, west, north, and back to the east. Next the priest gave the child moccasins and its new *ni'kie* name, instructed it in the avoidances of its clan and, if the child was a boy, took it through another ceremony in which he cut its hair. After this ceremony the father finished cutting the child's hair to the pattern of his descent group. He cut his child's hair again every year until the child was seven years old, when he ceased (Fletcher and La Flesche 1911, 117–28, 145, 187). The allotment and genealogical records show that all very young children, even newborn babies, possessed regular names other than the baby names. This circumstance might to some degree be explained by the gradual disuse of the ceremony, but it is conceivable that even in earlier times the Omahas did not always postpone name giving as long as four years.

Dorsey distinguishes the *ni'kie* names of each descent group into several kinds, the principal one being the seven "ordinal" birthnames for each sex. Cardinal and ordinal in Dorsey's usage do not have the sense they have when applied to numbers. Dorsey meant that the cardinal birth names or baby names were used by the whole tribe, whereas each descent group had a distinct set of birth names, at least for males, that they assigned at the turning the child ceremony.

From various sources Dorsey did manage to put together a list of seven birth names for most of the clans, Kon´çe being the only clan for which such names are totally lacking (see table 7). There were a few obvious errors (e.g., Rabbit in the Black Shoulder clan), and Dorsey's informant provided less than a full complement for the Buffalo Tail clan and part of the Tapa clan. Chief gave Dorsey two separate series of birth names for the Black Shoulder clan, one an "Eagle" list, the other "Buffalo." But the names of both series were

Table 7. Descent Group Segmentation Judged by "Birth Names"

I.	1.		II.	6.	
	2.			7.	
	3.			8.	a.
	4.	a.			b.
		b.		9.	
		c.		10.	
		d.			
	[5.]				

available to the whole clan, and in fact in 1883 these names were borne exclusively by males of Chief's Pipe subclan. Joseph La Flesche and Two Crows commented, moreover, that while these names might once have related to order of birth, they were subsequently bestowed without consideration of such matters.

Their observation obviously applies throughout the clans of the tribe, for a check on the "birth names" as they appear in the genealogies shows that they were generally bestowed without regard for actual birth order. No family with several sons employed such names exclusively, nor did they keep rigorously to the sequence; sometimes they began in the middle, skipped several when naming the next son, or resorted to other names. Even the exclusiveness of descent-group ownership was not always inviolable. The Turtle subclan name Big Turtle (Ke'to^{n}ga) was borne by Black Bear men; the Buffalo Tail clan name Little One with Reddish Yellow Hair (Hi^{n}çi'zhi^{n}ga) was also found in the Black Shoulder clan; and Possesses Metal (Mo^n'çedo^n) was popular in both the Red Dung clan and the Turtle subclan of the On the Left Side clan.

Given the uncertainties that arise about these birth names, it is perhaps not surprising that Fletcher and La Flesche have little to say about them. Nevertheless they do write (1911, 147; cf. Dorsey 1884, 229) that in families of the Black Shoulder clan the first son would be called Nigaxude (Muddying the Water). The second son could be either Heba'zhu (Knobby Horns) or Gthadi^n'gthitho^n, "the hungry calf running crosswise in front of its mother and stopping her progress." The third son would be Çiko^n'xega (Brown Ankles), the color of the ankles of the buffalo calf. Besides truncating the sequence (three instead of seven names), the authors also alter the order of the names, substituting the fourth name for the second in the sequence Chief gave Dorsey and then providing an alternative not mentioned by Chief. Obviously, here once again Omaha interpretations of their culture varied from witness to witness. In a study of the Osage child-naming rite, La Flesche (1928, 122ff.) published the Osage personal names that Alice Fletcher had recorded in 1896. Here too for most clans they gave birth-order names for the first three sons and also for the first three daughters.

The names given above and others in the Black Shoulder clan

relate to a legend about a time when buffalo lived underground. A young bull found his way to the surface of the earth, implying the birth of the buffalo species from the earth. The herd followed, crossing a river that looked shallow but was actually deep. Jumping in, the buffalo splashed the water, causing spray and gray froth. After crossing the stream, they found pasture and remained on the earth. The birth-order names therefore derive from the features and actions of the bull calf in the legend.

Fletcher and La Flesche continue by relating that when the same set of sons became adult they could assume new names, the eldest Pe´tho^{n}ba (Seven), the second Mo^n´geto^{n}ga (Big Chest), and the third No^{n}zhi´hto^{n}ga (Big Hair). When they were old men, the eldest could acquire the name He´ubagtho^{n}de (Worn Horns of the Old Buffalo Bull), the second Mo^{n}e´gahi (Arrow Chief), and the youngest Mo^{n}zho^n´wakithe (Land of the Buffalo). Once again the evidence available from the records does little to substantiate this schema. In the 1880s there was only one person—Benjamin Merrick (b. ca. 1841–43)—bearing one of the last group of names, supposedly for old men, and he was in his early forties. Those adults we know to have had one of the three childhood names all later assumed quite different names than we would have supposed from this statement. No doubt there are gaps in the genealogies, and if we had a more complete list of the siblings living and dead in each set, their true dates of birth, and all the names that they bore at various periods, we might find grounds for the theoretical system of naming the first three sons given by Fletcher and her coauthor. As it stands, the passage in question is empirically opaque, and the reader is left uncertain how it is to be understood.

As a criterion of clan segmentation, Dorsey's sets of birth names, if such they are, give yet a different picture from those already considered (see table 7). Only in two clans, On the Left Side and Deer Head, are there distinctive birth names for separate segments. In all other clans such names seem to be available for all men of the clan. Each of the four On the Left Side subclans has its own bundle of names, which is not surprising in view of their relative independence, though even so the subclans did lend and borrow some names back and forth. Dorsey assigns the Deer Head two lists, instead of the expected four. Males of the Pipe section bore Eagle birth names, while boys of the other three sections acquired Deer birth names.

Whereas the tribal birth-order designations applied to each family of the tribe, taking into consideration only the children born into the family, the birth names for descent groups are limited by the regulation that only one person in the clan at a time may bear a given name. If applied rigorously, this rule would by itself ensure an irregular distribution of birth names.

Allotment and census records suggest that for the most part people did avoid giving a child a name in current use. According to Dorsey (1886, 396; 1884, 228), "When the holder of the name changes it for another or dies, another infant can receive the name in question." Dorsey offers the example of Young Black Bear (Waça´bezhi^{n}ga), which was the name of Howard Fox (b. ca. 1840) of the Black Bear subclan before he took Without Gall (Pi´çithi^{n}ge)— the name of a previously prominent Omaha of the same descent group who signed treaties in 1815 and 1836. Edward Stabler (b. ca. 1881) subsequently became Young Black Bear. Although it can be shown that this pattern was often followed, by selecting this example Dorsey ignored several cases in which Omahas apparently broke the regulation.

In fact, in the late 1880s two or more persons concurrently held twenty of the birth names. This figure of course merely reflects what chances to appear on documents and would undoubtedly be reduced if it were possible to double-check with the families in question. To some extent perhaps allotment and census records simply failed to reflect that a person had changed his name. Even so, fourteen of the names were being used by two or more persons born before the allotment of 1883. It therefore may well be that there were long-standing differences in individual practice, with some persons concerned not to duplicate birth names within the clan while others only took care not to do so within the family. Not having the privilege of returning to Dorsey's informants, we cannot guess what special circumstances might explain individual cases of deviation, nor can we estimate with certainty to what extent they may represent disintegration of traditional practices.

Dorsey's assertion that some birth names for females were also tied to descent groups rests upon only two items of evidence (1884, 232, 249). The first of these is Chief's claim that the Black Shoulder clan once possessed them and then lost them. The second and far more substantial basis is He Is Known's actual enumeration of seven birth names for women in the Flashing Eyes clan. Three of those that he lists were popular in other clans too. Dorsey (1886, 396) implies that each of the subclans of the On the Left Side clan had separate lists of "ordinal" birth names for females, but he does not say what they are, and there is no other evidence for them. On the whole, therefore, there is little proof of the widespread use of female birth names by descent groups.

Each group owned a much larger stock of names than those so far under discussion. Dorsey even speculates that the additional names "may have been birth names, resorted to whenever the original seven were already appropriated." Most of the extra names were also *ni´kie* names. Dorsey says (1884, 227; 1886, 394) that *ni´kie* names "refer to a mythical ancestor, to some part of his body, to some of his acts, or to some ancient rite which he may have established." Fletcher and La Flesche say (1911, 607) of *ni´kie* that it is an "example of the expression in a single word of a complex idea derived from social observation and experience."

Fletcher and La Flesche (1911, 136) derive the word from *ni´k*, evidently in their interpretation an abbreviation of *ni´kashiga*, "people," implying those with "words or speech." They also derive *ni´kagahi*, "chief" from *ni´kashiga* and conclude, "Ni´kie signifies a declaration by the people or their chief of consent to a certain proposition." Their attempt at derivation smacks of folk etymology. Those who do not speak the language therefore must merely accept that *ni´kie* is polysemous, used variously in referring to traditional representations and obligations of the tribe and clans. Dorsey also uses *ni´kie* in reference to tents, decorations, and practices characteristic of the clans (1894, 407, 409, 410, etc.). He discusses it (p. 367) in context with *xube*, mysterious in reference to persons or animals ("all animals were persons in ancient times"), and Wakanda, divinity.

The great majority of *ni´kie* names, of which there are many, are owned by only a single group, but Dorsey recognizes a small collection that he found in more than one clan. The only explanation he could muster was that the clans sharing a given name may have had "a common mystical ancestor, or else mystical ancestors of the same genus or species." There were also many names that in one way or other did not conform to the *ni'kie* type. Dorsey mentions names derived from *ni'kie* names in closely related tribes, names borrowed from other tribes, ancient names that had lost their meanings, dream or mysterious names, bravery names, names based on a man's past (often ridicule names), and modern names of various kinds. Fletcher and La Flesche supplement *ni'kie* names with borrowed names, dream names, fanciful names, nicknames, derisive names, names taken from incidents or historical experiences, valor names, and unclassified names. Dorsey found the explanations of some names in the rites and myths of other tribes (1886, 398). These somewhat imprecise characterizations are in general agreement, and individual names can be classed in more than one way.

Dorsey's classification of the names for women, however, is of rather a different kind. Beginning with the four cardinal birth names and the seven ordinal birth names in each clan, Dorsey resorted to the topic of the names in typifying the remaining female denominations: names deriving from clan names (Kansas Female, Ko^{n}çewi^n), vegetation names, wind names, water names, thunder and thunderbird names, animate objects, moon names, mythical names, and unclassified names. Fletcher and La Flesche (1911, 144–45) write that "All female names were of the *ni'kie* class and were never dropped or changed, nor did a woman ever have more than one name." Whereas they claim male (*ni'kie*) personal names always referred to rites and ceremonial paraphernalia, they say female names generally referred to natural phenomena rather than to religious practices (pp. 200, 255).

Like birth names, the other *ni'kie* names were sometimes borne by two living men in spite of the rule against this practice. There are also signs that women may occasionally have changed their names too. Nevertheless, there is a striking contrast between males and females in their access to names and the distinctiveness of the appellations. Women rarely or never had more than one name, and the number of available female names was relatively small, so that there were always many women bearing the same names.

Having stated the law of male *ni'kie* names, that no more than one person in a clan could have any particular name, Dorsey went on to write that the same prohibition applied to some degree also to girls' names (1884, 228; 1886, 396): "If parents know that a girl in the gens has a certain name they cannot give that name to their daughter. But should that name be chosen through ignorance, the two girls must be distinguished by adding to their own names those of their respective fathers."

No other evidence exists for this practice of adding the father's name to that of a daughter. It would be helpful to know whether the passage in question genuinely reflected Omaha statements or whether, as may be suspected, it was elicited by the ethnographer in a search for a nonexistent symmetry. Fortune (1932, 15) spoke only of male names as being strictly linked to descent groups, though even in this respect he overstated the case.

Dorsey's unpublished monograph on Omaha and Ponca names shows just how disproportionate was the relation between male and female names, for he gathered more than six hundred names for boys and men and a mere seventy-seven for women, though in neither respect is his record complete. Omaha men might easily have followed their rule of only one man per name at a given time. For the most part they did, though since they frequently dropped, picked up, and transferred names it was easy for two men to share a name at different times in their lives. Women's names were not generally linked to descent groups, and as many as twenty-two women or girls, scattered among several clans, shared a single name.

Of names available for women, at least thirty-one are moon names, and in 1883 well over two-hundred women bore one or another of these moon names. During the allotment there were no more than twenty-five women or girls who shared their names with no one else. In addition to these twenty-five, of the hundred or so female designations then current another forty-nine appeared to be in use in only a single descent group. However, a very large percentage of women bore appellations found simultaneously in other clans.

With regard to the stated rules and preponderant practice, the names of Omaha males provide men with distinctive individuality while also linking each unmistakably to a recognized collectivity.

The possibility of acquiring multiple names in adulthood enhances individual prominence for men. Such additional names sometimes reflect the activities or characteristics of the bearer. In the case of bravery or valor names, they undoubtedly establish a claim on public esteem. It was the custom on a war party for men who so wished to assume new names after having been under way for four days. On this occasion the name was chosen by its new owner and conferred upon him in a brief ceremony by the leader of the party. Jordan Stabler (b. ca. 1831), for example, chose for himself "Not Afraid of Pawnee." To judge by his account, when changing their names his group made vows as to the deeds of valor they would perform in the anticipated battle (Dorsey 1884, 324–25). Other names commemorated daring acts already accomplished, as in the case of Pawnee Tempter, of Deer Head Pipe subclan, who about 1840 was among a group of Omahas who dressed as white men and succeeded in enticing Pawnees out of the camp and killing three braves. Others, however, received derisive sobriquets, which normally they neither solicited nor wished to retain. One such name, which may be shortened to "Small Boiler," became popular and was passed down and frequently used within the Flashing Eyes clan.

In contrast to the effects of male names, women's names barely rescue their bearers from a general anonymity, neither conferring uniqueness nor indicating group membership. Another factor in this contrast is that names of males were strictly distinguished from those of females, there being no name suitable for persons of both sexes. Admittedly there are many individual exceptions of various kinds already described to the general trend, but the principal contrasts between the situation of men and women may be represented as in table 8.

Omaha names and the procedures for making them up are finite in the trivial sense that at a given period the number of names in currency is small enough to be manageable in human terms. Nevertheless, the conservative Omaha policy of regularly retaining and reusing names should not be confused with rigidity. Omaha names were not immutable, and there evidently was never any prohibition on inventing new names, which were brought into use from time to time, especially for men and less frequently for women. The many

1. Two Crows, Lewis Morris (ca. 1826 to 4 March 1894). From the *Twenty-seventh Annual Report of the Bureau of American Ethnology.*

2. James Owen Dorsey (31 October 1848 to 4 February 1895).
Courtesy of the National Anthropological Archives, Smithsonian
Institution, Washington, D.C.

3. Abandoned, George Miller (b. ca. 1852). National Anthropological
Archives, Smithsonian Institution, Washington, D.C.

4. Wajepa, Samuel Freemont (ca. 1835–1906). From the *Twenty-seventh Annual Report of the Bureau of American Ethnology.*

5. Alice Cunningham Fletcher (15 March 1838 to 6 April 1923). From
the *American Anthropologist* (1923, vol. 25). Courtesy of the Bodleian
Library, Oxford.

6. Francis La Flesche (ca. 1857 to 5 September 1932). From the *Twenty-seventh Annual Report of the Bureau of American Ethnology.*

7. Big Elk (ca. 1772 to ca. 1846). From McKenney and Hall, *History of the Indian Tribes of North America*, vol. 1. Courtesy of the Bodleian Library, Oxford.

8. Betsy Dick (b. ca. 1812?), part-Omaha doctor, mystery woman, and leader of a dancing society. Photograph by W. H. Jackson. Courtesy of the Nebraska State Historical Society.

9. Standing Hawk, Eli S. Parker (ca. 1812–86); Little Chief,
Thomas Wood; and "Noise," or Muttering Thunder. Photograph
1866, Washington, D.C. Nebraska State Historical Society.

10. Louis Sanssouci, part-Omaha interpreter; No Knife, Frederick Tyndall (ca. 1820 to 7 January 1901); and Iron Eye, Joseph La Flesche, Jr. (ca. 1822 to 24 September 1888), Ponca-French, head chief of the Omahas. Photo 1866, Washington, D.C. Nebraska State Historical Society.

11. Chief (Gahíge), Garner Wood (ca. 1820–82). From the *Twenty-seventh Annual Report of the Bureau of American Ethnology.*

12. Fire Chief, Jonathan Parker (b. ca. 1812), and wife. From the *Twenty-seventh Annual Report of the Bureau of American Ethnology.*

13. Standing Hawk, Eli S. Parker, and wife. From the *Twenty-seventh Annual Report of the Bureau of American Ethnology.*

Table 8. Contrasts between Omaha Men and Women in Name Use

Usage	Male	Female
One person at a time per name	+	−
Name exclusive to clan or subclan	+	−
Several names borne by one person	+	−
Names may be changed	+	−

buffalo names, which pertain to the environment the tribe encountered after it moved from the woodlands to the plains, permit us to infer that a gradual replacement of names as well as the adjustment of descent group associations took place in earlier times, just as they did more recently when "modern names" began to be invented. Documents from the eighteenth and nineteenth centuries reveal many individual names that subsequently fell into disuse and were forgotten.

Like the Omahas, the matrilineal Iroquois assign sets of names to descent groups, but the names generally make no reference to the descent group or associated mascot (Goldenweiser 1913a). In this respect they are like Hidatsa names and those numerous Omaha designations that have so often appeared to commentators to lack classification or otherwise to deviate from the established Omaha type. While they do not result from the detotalization of a clan animal, Lévi-Strauss maintains (1966a, 178) that "they do suggest a detotalization of those aspects of social life and the physical world which the system of clan appellations has not already caught in the mesh of its net." Lévi-Strauss concludes that the principal difference between the Iroquois and the Omahas is that the Omahas and similar tribes begin an analysis (i.e., breaking down) of the species in the clan nomenclature that they extend to proper names, whereas in their proper names the Iroquois undertake an analysis on entirely new objects of the same formal type as the Omahas. Of course some Iroquois names refer to species and some do not; so Lévi-Strauss's formulation may or may not tend to obscure the extent to which Iroquois names stray from animal species. As for the Omahas themselves, as we have seen, the contrast Lévi-Strauss identifies between them and the Iroquois occurs in more than one way *within* the collection of Omaha naming practices.

The clan-associated personal names compound the superfluity of redundant principles exhibited in descent group nomenclature. Dorsey's somewhat naive attempt to classify personal names of Siouan tribes (1890*b*, 267–68) at least shows how these multivalent procedures carry across a variety of forms of social organization. The relevant classes are names in which colors are mentioned (often referring to species of animals), iron names, whirlwind names, thunder being names, and composite animal names (e.g., Moon Hawk Female).

Drawing upon an argument of A. H. Gardener's about scientific classification, Lévi-Strauss claims (1966*a*, 201) that proper names have close affinities with species names, and he brings in Omaha names when he writes (p. 216) of "the Omaha priest who defines the social paradigms of a new member of the group by conferring the available name *Old-bison's-used-hoof* on him." The great number of, for example, deer and elk names in the Elk clan brings home the concrete connection between personal names and the animal species. Of course there are other names in the clan, referring, for example, to a mystical being (Waka^{n}dagi), paint used in ceremonies, the moon, bravery, and so on. Even at the concrete level Dorsey was working on, his classification is not the only way of discriminating kinds of names. In other Omaha clans, besides animal names, there are appellations derived from such disparate sources as traditional offices, clouds, tent flaps, ceremonial paraphernalia, knives, dwellings, the sound of drums, personal qualities such as wisdom, activities like cooking, or achievements like victory.

Detotalization in Lévi-Strauss's sense does of course take place, even though it is only one among many procedures and the Omahas never realized its full potential. Whereas Lévi-Strauss finds it convenient to limit his discussion to the possibility of disassembling species, the Omahas apply the same procedure to entities or processes that are not like species at all. Thus they derive names from the passage of lightning, the drumlike sound of thunder, the clear sky after a storm, or the motion or stages of the moon. Other names commemorate moments or events in the life of an individual. The almost myopic attention to the part, the detail, the fragment, rather than the complete being or concept is more general in Omaha life than the concern with species. What is most characteristic of this side of their culture is not the passage from the species to the individual and back, though that unquestionably assumes a prominent place in Omaha attitudes, but the constant exploitation by this or other means of the synecdochic relation of part to whole.

Omaha personal styles are far from being unmeaning marks, which as examples of proper names—according to the tradition of Mill and other philosophers—they should be. In very many cases they are complete predicate expressions, lacking only the subject to turn them into declarative sentences. The prevailing philosophical interpretation of referring expressions would not recognize them as names at all but would regard them, as Howard suggests for the Poncas, as modified titles. Indeed, while translating them into English the ethnographers often distort their syntactic shape to give them an acceptable namelike appearance. For example, Dorsey often parenthetically supplies the implied subject, as in "(Snake) Sheds Its Skin" or "(Thunder That) Walks after Others, at the Close of a Storm"—the Omaha original corresponding only to the words outside the parentheses. Such names therefore contain verbs, adverbs, and adjectives, and the grammatical structure always implies the third person. Dorsey never found a name in the first or second person (Dorsey 1890b, 265).

When such a phrase appears in the subject position in a sentence it creates what seems to speakers of European languages a grammatical scandal, namely a predicate expression acting as though it were a referring one, giving the impression of a predicate within a predicate. However, the elliptical shape of such names does not merely leave a space for a subject; names also imply what that subject is. Almost always Omaha names involve a sharing of reference between the bearer of the name and the animal or thing that could be the subject of an ordinary sentence made up by using the name as a predicate. Omaha names establish a metaphorical relation between the bearer and the nominal subject; and they can be said to be relationship terms in a different sense than terms of "kinship." They lay claim to a symbolic but not real identity between a person and an object, natural process, or animal. Only in the exceptional cases of valor names and derisive names are the actual and the implied subject the same. The question of reference in Omaha names is very complex. Omahas arrive at personal names by means of truncated descriptive sentences, at the expense of the syntactic structure that made the names sentences in the first place—that is, by suppressing their subjects. This end is achieved by a reversal of grammatical value from predicate to subject and the replacement of a hypothetical but grammatically acceptable subject by one that though it actually exists, is only metaphorically appropriate.

There are actually two separate issues disguised, as Frege has shown, in Mill's (1843, 29) assertion that "A proper name is but an unmeaning mark which we connect in our minds with the idea of the object, in order that, whenever the mark meets our eyes, or occurs to our thoughts, we may think of that individual object." On the one hand there is the grammatical point that the name of the subject of a sentence uttered in an actual speech event does not simultaneously act as a predicate—or, as Mill put it, proper names connote nothing. This point is true whether the subject is indicated, to use two of Mill's own examples, by the proper name "John Nokes" or by the definite description "the mayor of the town." A separate issue, recognized by Frege (1892), is whether there is some aspect of meaning in a proper name that accounts for the informational difference between the empirical discovery that $a = b$ and the logical tautology that $a = a$. Frege wished to recognize some not too clearly explained element of meaning in a name that he calls its *Sinn,* sense, as opposed to its *Bedeutung,* reference.

The key to Frege's idea of the sense of a name lies not in searching, as philosophers have sometimes done, for a single invariant explanation, but in recognizing that in empirical rather than hypothetical contexts, people who speak to each other not only share a language but also in some way or other share common experiences. If they can communicate with each other at all, then they can also substitute definite descriptions for proper names. The essential point is that effective substitutes are discoverable, not that each pair of persons would always come up with the same definite descriptions for a given name.

For the Omahas, the analyst's purpose is not to assign personal names immutably to one or the other class, proper names or definite descriptions, but to display the ways they overlap this conventional distinction (cf. Lévi-Strauss 1966a, 188). Sociologically there may be as much to learn by regarding them as modified titles (cf. Strawson 1950) as by resisting this interpretation. In form, most Omaha names are indeed definite descriptions. In actual use, grammatical function tends to draw them toward the model of meaningless signs. History conspires with grammar, for many names are so ancient that their meaning could be recovered only imperfectly or not at all by native speakers of the Omaha language. The specific significance of other names may be comprehended by some but not all members of the tribe. For the great majority of names, however, their meanings are clear enough to everyone.

Lévi-Strauss sums up the intuitions of numerous ethnographers when he writes (1966a, 201–2), "Proper names seemed to us to have close affinities with species names, in particular when their role was clearly that of class indicators, that is, when they belonged to a meaningful system." Frege's quandary about identity of reference would quickly disappear if phrased in Omaha terms. For this reason, theorists in the tradition of Mill would doubtless say they had already moved too far along what Lévi-Strauss calls (1966a, 190) "the imperceptible transition from names to titles." On the other hand, they are what we find when we look for items in Omaha culture that function like our proper names. Lévi-Strauss's assimilation of names to classifications overlooks the fact that American Indian names classify nothing when they appear as subjects of sentences. Furthermore, even when, as in the case of women's names, several persons bear the same one, Omaha names do not have the functions of concept terms. There is no series in Omaha culture made up of things that turn around in bewilderment, things with soft horns, or animals that walk with their head thrown back, even though in Lévi-Strauss's interpretation (1966a, 175–76) precisely this kind of category exists among the Miwoks of California.

There are names in any case that qualify the generalization offered by immediately establishing the connection between name and category. These are those names that contain the species explicitly, like White Buffalo or Big Elk. These are derived from predicates that contain a concept term rather than being concept terms themselves. Very rarely are such predicates trimmed back to leave the species name standing by itself, as in Elk. Even in extreme cases like the last, the personal name Elk does not function like the concept elk.

The relation between Omaha personal names and classification therefore is not a consequence of their grammatical functions in sentences. In fact, the names have not single, but multiple ties to classification. Clan-owned names allow persons to associate the bearer to specific groups because people already know the tie between the name and the group. This connection exists regardless of whether the name is one of those that accept the animal of the appropriate species as the subject, either explicitly or implicitly. Persons in the tribe may be expected to know in advance—and therefore to draw the appropriate conclusions about the bearer— whether a name belongs to the Omaha or the Ponca tribe, whether it is suited for males or for females, whether it is a baby name or an adult name, whether it is an old name or recently invented.

Lévi-Strauss's conception of classification is too imprecise to establish that personal names really classify (cf. Barnes 1980a, 325–28; Tonkin 1980, 658–60). Rather, names—at least Omaha personal names, because they have meaning—often derive from established classifications and therefore permit Omahas to situate persons within those classifications on the basis of the information their names provide and in view of accumulated experiences. By giving a name, an Omaha does convey information about himself or the named or both, but such an act of nomination does not in and of itself constitute an act of classification. Nor does such an act take place on subsequent uses of the name. Omaha names, in other words, do bear significantly on processes of classification, but that bearing is not, as Lévi-Strauss often implies, direct. Furthermore, Omaha names distribute themselves through the different stages that Lévi-Strauss indicates (1966a, 181) exist between identifying marks that indicate a person is a member of a preordained class like a social group and products of free creation.

Lévi-Strauss claims (1966a, 197) that any system that treats individuation as classification (and he asserts that all systems do so) risks rupture of its structure at the birth of every new member. Dorsey's interpretation of *ni'kie* names as substitute birth names, if correct, might provide the best substantiation of this hypothesis. At any event, Omaha practice deviates in a variety of ways from the presumption of a set of terms derived from a specific order of classification, with resulting appellations fixed at a number that might fall short of the population requiring them. Birth-order names certainly face this problem. Otherwise the Omahas have sidestepped it by permitting the invention of names and allowing alternative procedures for coining names—though whether these alternatives are the consequences of indifference or responses to the pressure of the dilemma so defined remains open to argument.

Judged as titles, Omaha names give varying results. Some, such as Chief, derive directly from offices. Valor names figure in the Omaha system of status, wherein successful warriors may hope to advance in public position. The pattern of ascribed status conventionally indicated by personal names could among the Omahas be supplemented by designations signaling positions achieved through initiative and prowess. In this way the preordained structure was able to accommodate the individual ambitions of capable men, though it made no such concessions to women. Valor names, however, were coined for the occasion and in this respect were less like titles than the reusable, standardized names owned by clans, but the latter did not normally indicate occupation of a public trust or a hereditary social position other than descent group membership. There is therefore no uniform respect in which Omaha personal names are analogous to titles except in contrast to an ideal definition of proper names; that is, they all have meaning. Even the analogies relate to their makeup rather than their use. Their function is similar to our use of names rather than our use of titles. In reference they would not require, when rendered into English, the definite article we use with the president, the priest, the mayor. The logicians' ideals of true proper names and of titles are alternative standards that help only by providing analogies to be exploited in analysis.

Like many American peoples, the Omahas did not normally employ a person's name in direct address.

Mention has been made of the custom of never addressing an individual by his personal name; etiquette demanded also that a person's name should not be mentioned in his presence. It may be recalled that a man's name referred to the rites in charge of his gens or to some personal experience—a dream or a valorous deed. The personal name sustained therefore so intimate a relation to the individual as to render it unsuitable for common use. It is doubtful, however, whether this characteristic was the fundamental motive for the custom under discussion; it is more likely that the benefits to be derived from the daily emphasis of kinship as a means to hold the people together in peaceable relations had to do with the establishment of the custom, which was strengthened by the sanctity attached to the personal names . . . while only kinship terms were used in social intercourse, no one, not even children, being called by a personal name. (Fletcher and La Flesche 1911, 334–35).

The situation described above is of course familiar to Americanists and is often encountered in other tribes. Fletcher and La Flesche tell us that an aged Omaha commented unfavorably on white people's custom of addressing one another by name, especially those of the same family. "It sounds as though they do not love one another when they do not use terms of relationship" (1911, 335). At meetings of the Council of Seven personal names were never mentioned, and all present referred to each other by relationship terms (p. 314).

Unfortunately these authors are not entirely consistent on this point. They say (pp. 36–37), for example, that if an Omaha was asked by a stranger who he was, he would answer, "I am [giving his name] the son or the nephew of So-and-so." Elsewhere (p. 335) they assert that "Under no circumstances would politeness permit a person to ask a stranger his name or what business brought him to the tribe," so that emissaries of another tribe might come, complete their negotiations, and leave without anyone's ever learning their personal names.

The prohibition here was evidently a double one, not only preventing the Omahas from calling another man by his name, but also leading them to avoid putting him in the position of having to utter his own name. Like the bobwhite of the southern and eastern United States, the whippoorwill, according to an Omaha saying, sings its own name, translucent skin (ha´kugthi). In the absence of an appropriate relationship term, the Omaha formally addressed a stranger as kage´ha, friend—a usage confined strictly to men. Where respect was required, a man of distinction would be addressed as iⁿsha´ge, aged man. One woman would call another wihe´, younger sister, but she would use kage´, younger brother, for a boy or youth.

Dorsey confirms (1884, 270) in general that "a person is never addressed by name," but he does mention exceptions. When two or more persons present stand in the same relation to the speaker, they must be distinguished by their names. Though the Omahas seldom refer to someone by name when speaking about him, criers call guests by name when inviting them to feasts. The criers recount the deeds of each warrior returning from battle, mentioning him by name. When making presents, a man may mention the name of the recipient.

Except for unusual situations such as these, Omaha personal names commonly lack function in address. Even in reference they compete with relationship terms. The bearer would have little occasion to speak his own name, other than when, exceptionally, he selects one for himself. Furthermore, if Omaha standards of politeness were never breached, he would rarely hear his own name spoken. It was not inappropriate, on the other hand, to refer to deceased kinsmen, except the father (Dorsey 1889, 190), by name. Their deaths did not lead to removing their names from circulation or changing the names for objects or phenomena contained in the names, as occurs elsewhere in the world (Dorsey 1894, 371).

5: Relationship Terminology

The Omaha relationship terminology is without rival the most famous in the world, and many have taken it as the type case of patrilineality. Indeed, Dorsey's record of the Omaha system is the most distinctively original contribution of his monograph and the aspect that assured it classic status. No comparably thorough treatment was available for any other Siouan people until Bowers published his monographs on the Mandans and Hidatsas in 1950 and 1965, and today our knowledge of the systems of many Siouan and other American Indian societies remains far inferior to that for the Omahas.

That all university students of anthropology will at one time or another have heard of the Omaha terminology results not at all from any pronounced taste or enthusiasm among anthropologists or students for topics of this kind. There is of course a world of difference between using relationship terms in daily life and the often wearying enterprise of analyzing dry and unfamiliar lists of foreign words. Both ethnographers and native speakers commonly find it exhausting to check detail by detail the manifold nuances of use. For an Omaha the relationship terms provide the medium through which he expresses his relation with other persons and are therefore intimately bound up with every aspect of his life. Mead (1932, 78–79) found the relationship terms still fully in use despite the many changes Omaha life had undergone in the more than forty years between Dorsey's study and her own. Far from being difficult and technical aridities for an Omaha person, they are so central to his social world that he might well be astonished that anyone should try to acquire competence in his culture while ignoring these basic instruments.

The renown of the Omaha kinship system derives from a combination of factors in the history of anthropology. Dorsey published his account of the Omaha relationship system and organization of descent groups at a moment when scholars of various backgrounds in Europe and America were widely debating issues about the structure of simpler societies. In 1897 the German jurist Josef Kohler contributed a monograph on primitive marriage (Kohler 1975) that gave extensive attention to Dorsey's material, and Emile Durkheim responded in the same year with an important review. What Kohler showed and what Durkheim set forth more plainly was that some features of the Omaha terminology paralleled the patrilineal rule of the descent groups. Indeed, Kohler demonstrated that the same was true in a number of other societies, while a collection of peoples including the Choctaws had terminologies and groups exhibiting matrilineal principles (what Kohler called mother right).

With Kohler the "Crow-Omaha" problem was born, a blanket name for a number of issues related to the question how relationship categories may fit unilineal social institutions. This product of a fledgling anthropology has grown up with the discipline, and many of its ramifications are beyond the scope of this book. Fortunately several writers have reviewed the literature (an accomplished summary may be found in McKinley 1971a; see also Lesser 1958; Tax 1937a; Buchler and Selby 1968; Barnes 1975a, 1976). Once anthropologists had become accustomed to recognizing similarities between the shapes of groups and the shapes of classifications, they began to ask how such resemblances came about. Lacking information on the ancient past of American social organizations, they sensibly set out to employ the method of concomitant variations, which requires criteria for identifying relevant societies. Spier (1925) provided a survey of American cultures of what he called the Omaha and Crow types, based on the distribution of cousin terms taken to be indicative of, respectively, patrilineal and matrilineal descent. At the very minimum, the relevant criteria are the equation under a single term of MB and MBS for the patrilineal or "Omaha" type and a similar identification of FZ and FZD for the matrilineal or "Crow" (called by Kohler the "Choctaw" and by Lowie the "Hidatsa") type, though anthropologists commonly recognize a larger set of similar equations (Lowie 1917a, 151–53; Murdock 1949, 166–67; 1967, 158).

So long as scholars confined themselves to peoples whose ethnological and cultural backgrounds were at least remotely connected, Spier's criteria posed no special problems, even though a good deal of variation occurred from group to group within North America. Investigators tested a series of correlative features, such as the existence of moieties, presence of unilineal groups, strength of groups, practice of exogamy, preference for secondary marriages of certain kinds, and so on. Although some institutions were found in connection with patrilineal terminologies with significant frequency, exceptions abounded. In particular, no necessary and invariable connections were revealed. By 1937 Tax could write in exasperation (1937a, 14), "To say that the Omaha kinship system fits the Omaha clans and the Omaha marriage between a man and his wife's brother's daughter is simply to say that the Omaha kinship system, clans, and marriage customs are all part of a unified Omaha social organization."

Later Needham (1971, 15) quite evidently echoed Tax's sentiment when, after claiming that no useful generalization had been discovered about the "factitious" class of Omaha terminologies, he wrote, "It is surely not surprising that the terminological identification of a man and his son is accompanied by a transmission of status through males." Lesser (1929) pointed out that Spier's indexes could also be found in Africa. In time anthropologists began to apply the terms Crow or Omaha types quite loosely to obviously very different kinds of systems found around the world, without effectively adding to generalized knowledge. In reaction to this practice, Needham protested with conspicuous exaggeration that "there really is no such thing as an Omaha terminology, except that of the Omaha themselves, and it leads only to confusion and wrong conclusions to suppose that there is" (see also Needham 1969, 164).

If taken literally rather than accepted as a rhetorical flourish, this claim would represent an empiricism implying intellectual constraints so stringent that no general understanding would be possible about any aspect of culture. Whatever may be said against accepting as valid the class of Omaha terminologies in worldwide distribution, no one would dispute that, for example, the Ponca terminology results from the same general determinants and circumstances as the Omaha, since both tribes speak virtually the same language and appear to have separated only in a recent era. There are no grounds either for ignoring the almost identical systems of other patrilineal Siouan tribes or even those of the central Algonkian tribes of the same continuous area of North America.

Spier (1925, 73) located terminological systems similar to that of the Omahas in two separate regions of North America: a Great Plains/Midwestern Woodlands area and a Central Californian area. The first region includes, among Siouan tribes, the Winnebagos, the Thegiha group of Omahas, Poncas, Osages, Kansas, and Quapaws, and the Tciwere trio of Iowas, Otos, and Missouris. Also found there were the Shawnees and among central Algonkians the Menominis, Sauks, Foxes, Kickapoos, and Potawatomies, as well as the Miami set of Miamis, Peorias, Kaskaskias, Piankashaws, and Weas. Lesser (1929, 713) added the Yuchis, who potentially constitute a striking contradiction to the proposed correlation of patrilineal groups and terminologies like the Omahas, since they had exogamous matrilineal clans (Lesser 1930, 569). The discrepancy, however, may result from changes in historical times and from a high proportion of marriage with non-Yuchis (Eggan 1937a, 46–49; Speck 1939). Tax showed (1937b) that the principal grouping among the Foxes was the bilateral family, not patrilineal clans. The Foxes therefore offer a very apposite foil to the Omahas; for according to Tax (p. 282) the Fox material indicates the error of succumbing to the temptation, created by the combination of actual clans and moieties with Crow or Omaha categories, to explain one in terms of the other. Eggan (1955, 503–4), on the other hand, has argued again that historical circumstances have led to changes in the formerly exogamous, patrilineal Fox clans.

Some California tribes also lacked the expected exogamous groupings (Lesser 1929, 722)—a factor raised by Gifford (1940) in opposition to Leslie White's hypothesis (1939, 569–70) that unilineal principles receive expression in terminologies after a strong clan system has developed and had time to exert its influence. Lesser (1929, 726) had drawn precisely the opposite conclusion, that the existence of unilineal terminologies offers favorable conditions for developing exogamous lineages. All such historical hypotheses have run into the difficulty that there is no invariable relation between clans and terminologies of the required form. There are also definitional problems of the kind pointed out by Buchler (1966) and McKinley (1971a, 238) in deciding what makes up a strong rather than a weak clan system. Murdock (1949, 241) tried to shore up White's thesis by explaining that portion of his sample that lacked patrilineal groups by the idea that "Omaha societies" were the most mature form and therefore had had longer to lose the original patrilineal groupings. The doctrine is of course plausible, but in the absence of confirmation it looks like special pleading.

These and other hypotheses have been propounded in comparative contexts, where they are also best tested. They may well be borne in mind, however; for even a theory that fails of proof comparatively may nevertheless be valid in the special circumstances of a single society. We are in any case on firmer ground with Lesser's observation (1929, 714–15, 727) that the distribution of Omaha terminologies in the Plains/Woodlands district shows that the system originated there at least once, independent of what may have happened elsewhere, and diffused within a limited region. Mutual transfer of cultural patterns between adjacent Siouan and Algonkian peoples is probable and in many instances is known to have occurred (cf. Lowie 1934, 102).

A complementary factor is that the two language families contain a variety of social practices and forms of classifications. The Siouan family of languages comprises several subgroupings that have been classed in various ways (Wolff 1950; Voegelin 1941; Matthews 1959). Wolff recognized seven separate divisions, whereas Matthews settled for four. Matthews's groupings are:

1. Missouri: Hidatsa, Crow
2. Mandan
3. Mississippi: Dakota, Chiwere, Dhegiha
4. Ohio: Biloxi, Ofo, Tutelo

The languages of the fourth grouping were found in historical times scattered throughout the southeastern United States from Virginia to Mississippi. So little survived of these societies that not much is known about them, though they seem to have had matrilineal institutions. As Aberle points out (1974, 70), cultures in divisions 1 and 2 were adjacent and also matrilineal. Tribes of the Mississippi division were distributed continuously through the Mississippi and Missouri river catchment areas, but the Dakota family of tribes exhibited bilateral or cognatic family organization, while the Chiweres and Dhegihas had patrilineal descent groups and corresponding terminologies. Despite the absence of descent groups, the relationship systems of the Dakota peoples exhibited features compatible with exogamous clans but lacked equations across generations that might be interpreted as evidence of a rule of descent. Lowie (1917a) therefore early wrote of the Dakota (i.e. lineal) principle as the general one, of which the Hidatsa (or Crow, i.e., matrilineal) and Omaha (i.e., patrilineal) systems were specific variations. Eggan (1937b) later proposed an emendation to accommodate the lack of Dakota descent groups.

In the spirit of Lowie's earlier writings, it might be proposed that the original Siouan terminologies were like those of the present-day Dakotas; and this implication lies behind the speculations of some anthropologists, among them White. Matthews (1959, 78) in his reconstruction of the Proto-Siouan kinship terminology concluded, however, that Pre-Siouan had an Omaha, that is, patrilineal, terminology. Aberle (1974) has recently taken the opposite tack, arguing that "matrilineality probably characterized the Proto-Siouan speech community" (p. 71).

Lewis Henry Morgan gathered the first extensive series of Omaha relationship terms in June 1860 with the aid of Muda Martin or Long Wings (ca. 1839–64), an Omaha of the Small Birds subclan, and Henry Fontenelle, the bilingual son of the trader Lucien Fontenelle and an Omaha mother (Morgan 1870, 284; 1959, 89). These he published, with those of many other American peoples, in his famous worldwide comparative monograph on relationship systems. Morgan worked from inflexible standard schedules and generally in ignorance of the language, culture, and social organizations of his subjects, and his results contain mistakes and gaps as well as often being marred by phonetic blunders. Without his efforts, however, for many decades there would have been little basis for comparative studies of this aspect of American Indian cultures. Even today his work has not been in every respect superseded.

Dorsey's description of 1884 (pp. 252–55) is of course more complete and more reliable than Morgan's, though both are broadly compatible. Muda Martin died of a rupture while serving in the United States Army during the Civil War (Dorsey 1891, 119), and Dorsey turned to other informants. Presumably Dorsey began the task when he first started linguistic studies with the Omahas in 1878. He mentions eight Omahas who contributed information of one kind or another, but evidence indicates that he continued his investigations when Joseph La Flesche and Two Crows visited him at Washington, D.C., in 1882 to help him revise his manuscript for publication. In 1883 he was writing to Lucy La Flesche, then at the Hampton Institute in Virginia, to make last-minute inquiries about the terminology.[1] Dorsey seems primarily to be indebted to Joseph and Two Crows. Both Morgan and Dorsey therefore drew their information from a native-speaking Omaha with the further assistance of a bilingual intermediary of Omaha and French ancestry. Morgan did not speak any Omaha, but Dorsey had already acquired a facility in Ponca during his earlier stay and earned his reputation for skill at languages. There are grounds for confidence in the resulting presentation even though it is not the product of a fully modern method of ethnographic research.

Nevertheless, even Dorsey was not entirely thorough. Dorsey published only one form for each relationship term, but Fletcher and La Flesche (1911, 315–17) show that there are significant alterations in pronunciation depending upon whether the referent is addressed, referred to by a relative, or spoken of by an unrelated person. It seems that the last version is regularly encountered in legends when the narrator indicates the relationship between characters (p. 318). Perhaps the authors have misnamed this alternative—the point being not so much that unrelated persons use the terms as that the speaker employs them when he is not himself one of the parties to the relationship mentioned. For sake of convenience, we may press this last version of the relationship terms into service as what linguists call the "citation forms" (cf. Lyons 1977, 1:19), what might pass as the standard dictionary entries for the words.

A thorough account of the Omaha relationship system would show that the application and pronunciation of terms differs according to the sex of ego, that pronunciation and in some cases even the category name varies according to whether the speaker is or is not the same as ego (that is, whether the speaker is party to the relationship), and that pronunciation depends upon whether the speaker addresses or merely refers to the referent (Fletcher and La Flesche 1911, 314). In some societies the range of application changes somewhat between terms of reference and terms of address, but Fletcher and La Flesche give no hint that this is the case among the Omahas.

Dorsey presented the Omaha terminology as a sequence of genealogical charts. Morgan's tables set out the terms for a range of tribes organized in a series of columns, each headed by a genealogical specification. Neither method is suitable for ready access. Until now no publication has reorganized this information in a conventional tabular form (although Lesser 1958 has done so in his thesis and Ackerman, 1976, 559, recently did so for a portion of the terminology). The reader may therefore find it convenient to consult tables 9 and 10, which display the Omaha relationship terms in Fletcher's orthography with genealogical specifications after Dorsey. Where Morgan gave information not obtained by Dorsey, comments in the tables note the additional data. Since terms of address are easily available in Fletcher and La Flesche, they will not be separately listed here. In the absence of counterindications, we may assume that they apply to the same distribution of specifications as the corresponding reference terms.

Because the Omahas have been drawn upon for several advances in the understanding of relationship systems since the very early days of such work, previous scholars have already contributed much of the analysis of their system (see especially Lesser 1958). The first observation to make about the terminology is that, broadly speaking, the terms form a series of reciprocal pairs, corresponding to what Tax called "the rule of uniform reciprocals" (1937a, 19) or "constant reciprocals" (1937b, 254). The Foxes considered relationships to be designated by paired terms, a principle to which they had recourse when in doubt about remote connections—for example, when confronted by an anthropologist collecting a table of terms. Dorsey was not cognizant of this feature when he gathered

Table 9. Omaha Relationship Terms, Male Ego

1. *Iti'go^n*	FF, FFB, FFF, FFFF, FFFBS, FMF, FMB, FMBS, FMBSS, FMZH, MF, MFB, MFF, MMF, MMMF, MMB, MMBS, MMBSS, MMBSSS, WF, WFF, WFB, WMF, WMB, WMBS, WMBSS, WMZH, SWF
	"Though 'My wife's mother's sister's husband' is *witiga^n*, my grandfather, that term, as applied to him, is seemingly without reason"—Joseph La Flesche.
	Morgan adds MMMB and MMMBS and gives *ashe-ah'-ga* (my old man) for WF. He gives *o-keé-yee*, two fathers-in-law to each other.
2. *Iko^n'*	FM, FMZ, FMM, FMBW, FMBD, FMBSD, FFM, FFZ, FFFM, MM, MMZ, MFM, MMM, MMBD, MMBSD, MMBSSD, MMMM, MMMZ, MMMZD, WM, WMM, WMZ, WMBW, WMBD, WMBSD, SWM
	Morgan gives FFFZ, FFZD, WBW. Morgan gives *gah'-ah'*, WM. Morgan gives *o-keé-yee*, two mothers-in-law to each other.
3. *Itha'di*	F, FB, FMZS, FMBDS, FFBS, FFFBSS, MZH
4. *Iho^n'*	M, MZ, MBD, MBSD, MBSSD, MFBD, MFBSD, MFBSSD, MFZ, MMBSDD, MMBDD, MMBDSD, MMZD, MMZSD, MMMZDD, FBW
5. *Iti'mi*	FZ, FMZD, FMBDD, FFBD, MBW
6. *Ine'gi*	MB, MBS, MBSS, MBSSS, MFBS, MFBSS, MFBSSS, MMBSDS, MMBDS, MMBDSS, MMZS, MMZSS
	Morgan gives MB's great-grandson's son, MMBS, MMBSS, MMBSSS, MMBSSSS, MMMBSS, MMMBSSS, MMMBSSSS, MMMBSSSSS, FZH.
7. *Izhi^n'the*	eB, FBSe, FMZSSe, FFBSSe, FFFBSSe, MZSe, MFZSe, MMBDDSe, MMZDSe
	"The husband of my wife's sister is not always my consanguinity, but if he is a kinsman, I call him my elder or younger brother."

continued

Table 9 *continued*

	Morgan gives MBDS, FFBSSe, WZHe. He gives *o-keé-zee* as a general term for brothers.
8. *Içu^n'ga*	yB, FBSy, FMZSSy, FFBSSy, MZSy, MFZSy, MMBDDSy, MMZDSy
	See note for no. 7. Morgan gives WZHy.
9. *Ito^n'ge*	Z, FBD, FMZSD, FFBSD, MZD, MFZD, MMBDDD, MMZDD, MMMZDDD
	Morgan gives MBDD.
10. *Izhi^n'ge*	S, BS, FBSS, MZSS, MFZSS, FFFBSSSS, WBDS, WFZS, WFBDS, WZS, WMBDDS, WMZDS
	Morgan gives FFBSSS.
11. *Izhu^n'ge*	D, BD, FBSD, MZSD, MFZSD, WBDD, WFZD, WFBDD, WZD, WMBDDD, WMZDD
	Morgan gives FFBSSD.
12. *Ito^n'shka*	ZS, FBDS, FFBDS, MZDS, MFZDS, FZS, FMZDS, FFZS
	Morgan gives the same pronunciation for this and no. 13 in the terms used by a woman. He gives FFZDS, MMZDDS.
13. *Iti'zhu^n*	ZD, FBDD, MZDD, MFZDD, MMMZDDDD, FZD, FMZDD, FFBDD, FFZD, ZHBD (p. 257)
	Morgan gives the same pronunciation for this and no. 14 in the terms used by a woman. He gives MB's great-granddaughter, FFZDD, MMBSDDD, MMZDDD, FFFZDDD.
14. *Itu'shpa*	SS, SD, SSS, SSD, SDS, SDD, DS, DD, DDS, DDD, DSD, DSS, BSS, BSD, BDS, BDD, ZSS, ZSD, ZDS, ZDD, MFZSSS, MFZSDD, MFZDSD, MFZDDS, MMMZDDDDD, FZSS, FZSD, FZDS, FZDD, FFZSS, FFZSD, FFZDS, FFZDD, FFFBSSSSS, SWB, SWBS, DHZ, DHFZ, WZSS, WZSD, WZDS, WZDD,

continued

Table 9 *continued*

	WFZSS, WFZSD, WFZDS, WFZDD, ZHZ (p. 257), ZHFBD, ZHFBDD, ZHFBSD

Morgan gives great-grandson's child, B's grandchildren, B's great-grandchild, FB's great-grandchild, FB's great-grandson's child, FZ's great-grandson's son, FZ's great-granddaughter's daughter, MB's great-granddaughter's daughter, MZ's great-grandchild, MZ's great-grandson's son, MZ's great-granddaughter's daughter, FFB's great-great-grandchild, FFZDDC, FFZ's great-great-grandchild, MMZ's great-great-grandchild, FFFBSSSSS, FFFZDDDD, FFFZDDDDD, MMMZDDDDD.

15. *Ita'hoⁿ*   WB, WBS, WBSS, WFBS, WFBSS, WMBDS, WMBDSS, WMZS, WMZSS, ZH, FZH, FMZDH, FFZH

Morgan gives FBDH, MZDH.

16. *Ihoⁿ'ga*   WZ, WMBDSD, WMBDD, WMZSD, WMZD, WBD, WBSD, WFZ, WFBD, WFBSD, BW

Morgan gives FBSW, MZSW.

17. *Iti'ni*   SW, SWZ, SWBD, SSW, WBW, DHM, DSW, ZSW, FZSW, FFZSW

Morgan gives BSW, ZSW.

18. *Itoⁿ'de*   DH, DDH, SDH, FZDH, FFZDH, ZDH, DHB, DHF, DHFF

Morgan gives BDH, MBDH.

19. *Igaxthoⁿ*   W

20. WZH = ego = WFZH

Table 10. Omaha Relationship Terms, Female Ego

1. *Iti'go[n]*	FF, FFB, FFF, FFFF, FFFB, FFFBS, FMF, FMB, FMBS, FMBSS, FMZH, MF, MFF, MFB, MMF, MMMF, MMB, MMBS, MMBSS, MMBSSS, HF, HFF, HFB, HFBDH, HFZH, HMF, HMB, HMBS, HZH, SWF, (for the following, see Dorsey 1884, 257:) BWB, BWF, BSWF, BWBS, FBSWB, FFBSWB

Morgan gives MMMB and MMMBS. He gives *o-keé-yee,* two fathers-in-law to each other.

2. *Iko[n]'*	FM, FMZ, FMM, FMBW, FMBD, FMBSD, FFM, FFZ, FFFM, MM, MMZ, MFM, MMM, MMBD, MMBSD, MMBSSD, MMMM, MMMZ, MMMZD, HFM, HFBW, HFZ, HM, HMM, HMZ, HMBD, SWM

Morgan gives FFFZ, FFZD. He gives *o-keé-yee,* two mothers-in-law to each other.

3. *Itha'di*	F, FB, FMZS, FMBDS, FFBS, FFFBSS, MZH
4. *Iho[n]'*	M, MZ, MBD, MBSD, MBSSD, MFBD, MFBSD, MFBSSD, MFZ, MMBSDD, MMBDD, MMBDSD, MMZD, MMZSD, MMMZDD, FBW

Morgan gives MMBSD, MMBSSD.

5. *Iti'mi*	FZ, FMZD, FMBDD, FFBD, MBW

"The wife of *ici'e* [no. 16] is my sister . . . [no.s 9 or 10], my father's sister . . . [no. 5], or my brother's daughter . . . [no. 14], if related to Ego, a female."

Morgan gives MBSW, FFFZDD.

6. *Ine'gi*	MB, MBS, MBSS, MBSSS, MFBS, MFBSS, MFBSSS, MMBSDS, MMBDS, MMBDSS, MMZS, MMZSS

Morgan gives MB's great-grandson's son, MMBS, MMBSS, MMBSSS, MMBSSSS, MMMBSS, MMMBSSS, MMMBSSSS, MMMBSSSSS, FZH.

7. *Iti'nu*	eB, FBSe, FMZSSe, FFBSSe, FFFBSSSe, MZSe, MFBDSe, MFZSe, MMBDDSe, MMZDSe

continued

Table 10 *continued*

	Morgan gives MBDS. Morgan gives *e-zin-tha* as a general term for B.
8. *Içuⁿ'ga*	yB, FBSy, FMZSSy, FFBSSy, MZSy, MFBDSy, MFZSy, MMMBDDSy, MMZDSy
9. *Izhuⁿ'the*	eZ, FBDe, FMZSDe, FFBSDe, MZDe, MFBDDe, MFZDe, MMBDDDe, MMZDDe, MMMZDDDDe
	Morgan gives MBDD. See note for no. 5.
10. *Itoⁿ'ge*	yZ, FBDy, FMZSDy, FFBSDy, MZDy, MFBDDy, MFZDy, MMBDDDy, MMZDDy, MMMZDDDDy
	See note for no. 5. Morgan gives *ihan* as an alternative term used by a woman.
11. *Izhiⁿ'ge*	S, ZS, BDS, FBDS, FZS, FMZDS, FFBDS, FFZS, MZDS, MFBDDS, MFZDS, HBS, HFBSS, HMZSS, HMBDSS
	Morgan gives MMZDDS.
12. *Izhuⁿ'ge*	D, ZD, BDD, FBDD, FZD, FMZDD, FFBDD, FFZD, MZDD, MFBDDD, MFZDD, HBD, HFBSD, HMZSD, HMBDSD
	Morgan gives MMZDDD, MMMZDDDD.
13. *Itu'shka*	BS, FBSS, FFFBSSSS, MZSS, MFBDSS, MFZSS, HZS, HFBDS, HFZS, HMBDDS, HMZDS
	Morgan gives the same pronunciation for this and for no. 12 in the terms used by a man. He gives FFBSSS.
14. *Itu'zhuⁿge*	BD, FBDS, MZSD, MFBDSD, MFZSD, HZD, HFBDD, HFZD, HMBDDD, HMZDD
	Morgan gives the same pronunciation for this and for no. 13 in the terms used by a man. He gives FFBSSD. See note for no. 5.
15. *Itu'shpa*	SS, SD, SSS, SSD, SDS, SDD, DS, DD, DDS, DDD, DSD, DSS, BSS, BSD, ZSS, ZSD, ZDS, ZDD, MFZSSS, MFZSDD, MFZDSD, MFZDDS,

continued

Table 10 *continued*

MMMZDDDDD, FBDS, FBDD, FZSS, FZSD, FZDS, FZDD, FFZSS, FFZSD, FFZDS, FFZDD, FFFBSSSSS, SWB, SWBS, DHZ, DHFZ, HZSS, HZSD, HZDS, HZDD, HFZSS, HFZSD, HFZDS, HFZDD, HFBSSD, HFBSDS, HFBDSS, HFBDDD, HMZSSS, HMZSDD, HMZDSD, HMZDDS

Morgan gives B's grandchild, B's great-grandchild, Z's grandchild, Z's great-grandchild, FB's great-grandson's son, FZ's great-granddaughter's daughter, MB's great-grandson's daughter, MZ's great-grandchild, MZ's great-grandson's son, MZ's great-granddaughter's daughter, FFB's great-great-grandchild, FFZDDS, FFZ's great-great-grandchild, MMZ's great-great-grandchild, FFFBSSSSS, FFFZDDDDD, MMMZDDDDD.

16. *Ishi'e*   HB, HFBS, HMZS, HMBDS, BDH, ZH, FZH, FMZDH, FFZH

See note for no. 5. Morgan gives the same pronunciation as for no. 17. He gives HZH, FBDH, MZDH.

17. *Ishi'ko^n*   HZ, HFBD, HMZD, BW, HMBDD

Morgan gives the same pronunciation as for no. 16. He gives FBSW, MZSW, HBW.

18. *Iti'ni*   SW, SWZ, SWBD, SSW, BSW, DHM, HFZSW, HZSW, FFZSW

19. *Ito^n'de*   DH, HFZDH, DHB, DHF, DHFF, DDH, HZDH, FFZDH

Morgan gives BDH, ZDH, FZDH, MBDH. (On his chart Dorsey mistakenly assigns DDH to no. 18.)

20. *E'gthu^nge*   H

21. HBW = ego = HFBSW

the Omaha terminology, and he frequently failed to report both sides of a distant genealogical relationship. His report is nevertheless very extensive—if possible, in some respects too extensive—and there are really no grounds for doubt about the terms to which the unreported reciprocals would be assigned. Given a general familiarity with the terminology and the rule of pairing, we might loosely say that their position can with confidence be predicted, a word I use advisedly because it has already entered for similar reasons into a theory about how the Omahas and other systems are to be interpreted. For the moment, the point to be apprehended is that the general redundancy of usage, not to speak of repeated practice in day-to-day application, is such that the speaker of Omaha, and with time the outsider too, can easily infer how to classify a person in any recognized genealogical relationship.[2]

At this point Margaret Mead's description of how an Omaha child learns to use the terminology may usefully be recalled. She writes (1932, 79–80) that children were not commonly taught the principles of the system but were instructed the correct term to use for each relative as he was encountered. "Call this man grandfather." "Don't talk with that man, he is your brother" (for a girl suspected of flirting). In the early days, when people lived close together, elders could easily instruct their grandchildren in the right word to use for each particular relative. Furthermore, connections within the camping circle provided grounds for generalizing applications. The underlying genealogical thinking therefore was sociological in character, modified by demographic happenstance no doubt, but determined by concerns of a social nature. Clearly it was not based on a hypothetical scheme of possible biological connections.

The expression "constant reciprocals" might create the impression that for each term there is only one reciprocal term. Evidently Tax did not intend this interpretation, which in any case is not true for either the Foxes or the Omahas. There are in all twenty-six separately pronounced Omaha terms of reference, and these combine in twenty-two distinctive pairings. Whenever two terms are in a pair, one of them indicates superiority in some respect, the other relative inferiority. The greatest degree of superiority is marked by the terms *iti´goⁿ* and *ikoⁿ´*, applied to men and women, respectively; and the greatest distance is marked by these terms and their reciprocals. Included in these categories are all persons of the level of grandparents and beyond (with the exception of MFZ). The terms, however, also designate a series of relatives at lower genealogical levels, namely the direct agnatic descendants of MMF. This last set of equations is among those that have caused scholars to make comparisons with patrilineal social groups. There is a single reciprocal for the relationships in question here, a word that, unusually in this system, makes no distinction as to the sex of the referent. *Itu´shpa* comprehends all persons of the level of grandchildren and below, except for a few affinally related persons, but it also takes in a number of other relatives, including certain affines standing in inferior positions. The terms in question comprise what we would regard as both consanguineous and affinal relationships. This distinction between consanguinity and affinity receives attention below. For the moment it stands naively for English language attitudes as Morgan and Dorsey employ them.

Iti´gon and *ikon´* also have two other reciprocal pairs marking affinal relationships: *iton´de* (including DH) and *iti´ni* (including SW). These five terms enter into the following six pairings:

1. *iti´gon*/*itu´shpa*   4. *ikon´*/*itu´shpa*
2. *iti´gon*/*iton´de*   5. *ikon´*/*iton´de*
3. *iti´gon*/*iti´ni*   6. *ikon´*/*iti´ni*

Each term takes more than one reciprocal.

Next there is *ita´di*, which an Omaha applies to his or her father, the other men in F's line of his level (including male patrilateral parallel cousins of differing degrees), and persons who might well have been born into F's lineage at his level had Omaha marriage expectations (with WZ, WFZ, WBD) been fulfilled at earlier levels (thus FMZS, FMBDS), as well as to the commonplace and appropriate MZH. The reciprocal terms are *izhin´ge* (including S, BS, etc.) and *izhun´ge* (D, BD, etc.), which also apply to certain relatives of a male ego's wife, who might also be his children or brother's children had the appropriate marriages taken place in the proper places (cf. Kohler 1975, 157–58).

These two terms also reciprocate *ihon´*: M and all other women of her patriline at every genealogical level (including MFZ) and other women who might have been born into M's line had the marriage expectations mentioned above been fulfilled, as well as the expected FBW. Neither Morgan nor Dorsey says so, but we may reasonably infer, as does Kohler (1975, 145), that the wives of men called by the same term as F are *iho^n´*, and the husbands of women called *iho^n´* are in turn also *itha´di*. A woman calls HBD by the same term as D or ZD, which again parallels the marriage conventions.

7. *itha´di/izhi^n´ge* 9. *iho^n´/izhi^n´ge*
8. *itha´di/izhu^n´ge* 10. *iho^n´/izhu^n´ge*

Each term reciprocates two, marking difference of sex.

Iti´mi are FZ, her parallel cousins, and other women of her level who might have been born into the line if the familiar condition concerning marriages had been carried out, plus the MBW. The reciprocals are: *itu´shka* (BS, etc.) and *itu´zhu^{n}ge* (BD, etc.). A woman's brother's children belong to her own patriline while her own children do not, and she accordingly distinguishes them. The last two terms take in the children of men she classes with her brothers, as well as affinally connected relatives requiring particular discussion. They are persons who under stated conditions would fall into the same position as the MBW. The equation FZ = MBW is widely encountered, but it is one of those features that run counter to the general asymmetry of the Omaha system and can best be considered later when the overall pattern of the terminology comes under consideration.

11. *iti´mi/itu´shka* 12. *iti´mi/itu´zhu^{n}ge*

The two terms that pair with *iti´mi* have no other reciprocals.

Ine´gi are all males of M's patriline below the MF—the lineal equations upon which the particular fame of the Omaha system rests. *Ine´gi* also comprehends men who would be in M's line if MF had followed the marriage conventions (i.e., MMZS, MMZSS, MMBDS, MMBDSS, MMBSDS). The reciprocal terms are *ito^n´shka* (ZS, FZS, etc.) and *iti´zhu^n* (ZD, FZD, etc.).

13. *ine´gi/ito^n´shka* 14. *ine´gi/iti´zhu^n*

The pairing terms for *ine´gi* have no other reciprocals.

A man or woman applies the same terms to siblings and parallel cousins, in distinction to cross-cousins and similar relatives. Men and women distinguish within the range of relatives according to the absolute sex of the referent. There is no term applied on a simple principle of relative sex, as occurs sometimes—for example, where a Z and a B apply the same term to each other but not to the sibling of the same sex as ego. Women (or girls) distinguish according to age relative to ego. Men (or boys) do so only for male relatives. The term *ito^n'ge*, which a woman uses for females younger than herself, a man applies to all females. A man uses *izhi^n'the* for males older than himself, but a woman uses *iti'nu*. Both men and women use *içu^n'ga* for younger males.

> 15. *izhi^n'the/içu^n'ga*   17. *içu^n'ga/ito^n'ge*
> 16. *iti'nu/ito^n'ge*   18. *izhu^n'the/ito^n'ge*

Ito^n'ge reciprocates three terms, *içu^n'ga* two. Each of the other three terms pairs with only one other term.

The remaining terms are strictly affinal. *Ita'ho^n* is self-reciprocal and in this respect displays another symmetrical feature of the terminology. The term applies to men in W's line at WB's level or below and reciprocally to men in ZH's line at his level and above or to persons who could be in those positions had appropriate marriages taken place. This term makes a series of patrilineal equations involving WB and descendants and ZH and ascendants. Although the term is symmetrical in making the equations WB = ZH, it corresponds to the general asymmetry of the terminology through the fact that the patrilineal equations in one line involve only junior relatives, while in the other line they take in elder relatives.

For the parallel relation between men and women there are two terms, *iho^n'ga* (WZ, etc.) and *ishi'e* (ZH, etc.). This relationship applies to the corresponding range of relatives as *ita'ho^n*, given that the sex of the referent is different, and implies the same patrilineal equations. *Iho^n'ga* deviates from the preceding term by also taking in WFZ. However, *iho^n'ga* also designates BW, and *ishi'e* designates HB and similar relatives. The equations WZ = BW and ZH = HB that these terms effect are symmetric indications; but the terms also display the same asymmetric bias mentioned above. *Ishi'ko^n* is self-reciprocal and symmetric, applying to HZ, BW, and similar relatives. H and W are $e'gthu^nge$ and $igaxtho^n$, respectively.

19. $ita'ho^n/ita'ho^n$ 21. $ishi'ko^n/ishi'ko^n$
20. $iho^n'ga/ishi'e$ 22. $igaxtho^n/e'gthu^nge$

None of these six terms pairs with more than one other term.

On the charts Dorsey also indicates the following equations unmarked by terms: WZH = ego♂ = WFZH, HBW = ego♀ = HMZSW.

Tax (1937a, 19) defined his "rule of uniform reciprocals" as stating that "if A and B are terms used between a pair of relatives, then the reciprocal of every A must be B." The convenience of such a rule is that the analyst need know the application of only one of each pair of terms to know the application of the other. The rule could therefore be applied in a mechanical fashion and might just as well be handed over to a machine. If, however, A were to be reciprocated by B or C, further knowledge would be required for man or machine to be able to infer correctly the proper reciprocal for applications of A. Complications increase when, for example, B reciprocates both A and another term, let us say A. Tax claimed that there were rare exceptions to his rule, but he identified one among the Merlavs (Banks Island). The Merlav word for "child" reciprocates words for "father" and "mother," but cross-cousins also call each other "child." Tax does not mean that the fact that two words reciprocate the word for child constitutes an exception, but it is indeed at variance with his rule literally interpreted. The Omahas and Foxes actually utilize four terms in the relations between parents and children. What is exceptional, in Tax's interpretation, is that yet another relationship falls under the term that designates "child."

Actually this circumstance is by no means as unusual as supposed, and it is not very different from the Omaha situation where $iti'go^n$ and iko^n' take three different reciprocals each. To the extent that the Omahas deviate from Tax's rule literally interpreted, the resulting complexities still do not exceed the adjustment capacities of men or machines. Given the appropriate additional knowledge, a person can still generally surmise what term to use, even when he has been given only one side of a relationship. The doctrine of uniform reciprocals is therefore more like a rule of thumb than a law of nature; namely, the pattern of reciprocities is as described above and not otherwise.

Another such rule of thumb concerns "uniform descent" (Tax 1937a, 19; 1937b, 254). An example is: "If somebody whom ego calls A has children whom ego calls B, then the children of everybody whom ego calls A are called B." Again Tax does not really seem to intend that every term is followed by only one other term; he means that there is a recognized order of succession in terms. Through (male) ego's line of reference this sequence is as follows: *iti´goⁿ–ikoⁿ´ > itha´di–iti´mi > izhiⁿ´the–içuⁿ´ga–itoⁿ´ge > izhiⁿ´ge–izhuⁿ´ge > itu´shpa*. In addition to knowledge of the relative positions of these terms, the speaker also must know the sex of the referent and, in the medial level, relative age as well. Mother's line looks somewhat different, there being in her patriline only one transition: *iti´goⁿ–ikoⁿ´ > ine´gi–ihoⁿ´*, the last two categories making the classic Omaha patrilineal equations. However, a longer series runs from MM through M and her uterine descendants: *iti´goⁿ–ikoⁿ´ > ine´gi–ihoⁿ´ > izhiⁿ´the–içuⁿ´ga–itoⁿ´ge > itoⁿ´shka–iti´zhuⁿ > itu´shpa*. As Tax acknowledges, this rule simply does not apply for second ascending generation terms, for those terms cap several different sequences.

Table 11 shows the succession pattern for each term. The reader will see at once that, allowing for difference of sex, there is perfect uniformity of succession in just under half of the terms. Tax's rule of uniform descent requires interpretation for each term. Those he gives, he phrases by reference to genealogical position; thus: "the offspring of persons called 'father' or 'mother's sister' are always 'siblings.'" Because he groups several Fox terms under the same heading (e.g., "sibling"), Tax states only seven interpretations, which Coult (1967, 28) dubbed "rules of succession." Table 11 in effect accomplishes the same thing as the rules of succession but expresses them by the terms themselves rather than by genealogical positions. Tax could not have considered the whole terminology, particularly various affinal positions, for he would have had to explain why uniformity of succession is actually exceptional rather than characteristic.

The counterpart of the rule of uniform descent is that of unifrom

Table 11. Succession Patterns of Omaha Relationship Terms

Male ego

1 > 1 & 2,	3 & 5,	6 > 6 & 4	15 > 12 & 13,
3 & 5,	1 & 4,	7 > 10 & 11	15 & 16
1 & 4,	6 & 4,	8 > 10 & 11	16 > 10 & 11
6 & 4,	15 & 16,	9 > 12 & 13	17 > 14 & 14,
1 & 16,	17 & 14	10 > 14 & 14	14 & 18,
15 & 15,	3 > 7, 8 & 9	11 > 14 & 14	16 & 15
17 & 14	4 > 7, 8 & 9	12 > 14 & 14	18 > 14 & 14,
2 > 1 & 2,	5 > 12 & 13,	13 > 14 & 14	14 & 18
12 & 13,	6 & 4	14 > 14 & 14	19 > 10 & 11

Female Ego

1 > 1 & 2,	3 & 5,	6 & 4	14 > 11 & 12,
3 & 5,	1 & 4,	6 > 6 & 4	15 & 15
1 & 4,	6 & 4,	7 > 13 & 14	15 > 15 & 15
6 & 4,	16 & 17,	8 > 13 & 14	16 > 11 & 12
16 & 17,	13 & 14,	9 > 11 & 12	17 > 13 & 14
13 & 14,	15 & 18	10 > 11 & 12	18 > 15 & 15,
15 & 18	3 > 7, 8 & 9	11 > 15 & 15	19 & 15
2 > 1 & 2,	4 > 7, 8 & 9	12 > 15 & 15	19 > 15 & 15,
11 & 12,	5 > 11 & 12,	13 > 15 & 15	19 & 15
			20 > 11 & 12

ascent, which Tax (1937a, 20) acknowledges to be submerged for the Foxes as often as followed. Among the Omahas, at any event, it applies poorly to the terms for the second descending level.

Another of Tax's principles is "uniform siblings." He intends this regulation for siblings of opposite sex and implies that every term for a male has only one term for sisters of the men it applies to and vice versa; that is, for every female term there is only one corresponding term for the male sibling. Naturally, as Tax states it, the rule immediately runs afoul of the relative age distinction in the sibling categories. The Omaha terms, as applied by a male demonstrate the following sibling pairings:

1–2	6–4	12–13	15–16
1–4	7–9	14–14	15–14
1–16	8–9	14–17	18–14
3–5	10–11	15–19	

Only thirteen of nineteen terms strictly exhibit the "uniform sibling" principle, even though Tax said it was rarely broken. We might nevertheless retain it with a loose interpretation, as for the idea of constant reciprocals: Omahas class opposite-sex siblings by these pairings only.

Very similar results and conclusions obtain for the "rule of uniform mates," which presupposes a similar regularity in terms applied to married couples. The relevant Omaha pairings fit the literally read regulation in thirteen out of eighteen terms.

1–2	8–16	15–17	18–13
3–4	10–17	15–2	18–17
6–5	12–17	15–5	18–11
7–16	14–17	15–9	18–14

Tax's final principle of terminology, "the rule of equivalence," states that "two people who call a third person by the same term should be siblings to each other." Again, Tax has misphrased his rule. Properly he should have said that the persons in question refer to each other by the terms that they also apply to siblings. Tax concedes that "this rule is often interfered with, yet fundamentally it is operative." The rule fails to work in regard to second ascending and descending level terms. In a very simple example, a man's SS and SSS would both refer to him as *iti´gon* but would refer to each other as *itha´di* (F, etc.) and *izhiⁿ´ge* (S, etc.). Dorsey does not list the genealogical specifications for sibling terms that would be required for point-by-point confirmation, but generally speaking this rule fits the Omaha system as well as the preceding ones.

Tax's rules tell us nothing that is distinctive of the Omahas. Instead, they merely make explicit some of the consequences of the expectation that a system of classification will be generally coherent. Above all they do not make it possible to say in advance where deviations will occur, for this knowledge is empirical and must be derived from experience. The same may be said regarding the overall distribution of terms that is the particular Omaha pattern. This configuration derives from a series of choices between alternative principles of classification that have become institutionalized and conventional.

Tax refers dismissively to a series of such principles written about by Kroeber (1909), but today anthropologists generally concede them a regular place in analysis. Kroeber's eight principles specify (1) difference or similarity of genealogical level, (2) distinction or equation of (in Morgan's language) lineal and collateral relatives (e.g., F and FB), (3) attention to relative age, (4) sex of referent, (5) sex of speaker, (6) sex of connecting relatives, (7) difference between consanguines and affines, and (8) a catchall for the position of linking relative (married, unmarried, living, dead, etc.). Kroeber showed that when a system takes into consideration relatively many principles of classification governing the distribution of relatively few terms, some if not all receive only partial realization, and that in this regard the principles are in certain respects in competition.

Kroeber's last criterion has no relevance to the Omahas. Terms like *iti´go^n* and *iko^n´* mark different levels in ego's own line while making equations across levels in the line of MF. They could therefore be counted as simultaneously conforming to and violating Kroeber's first principle. In one way or other fifteen of twenty-six terms make patrilineal equations, leaving only eleven that depart in no respect from principle 1. Omahas do not distinguish lineal and collateral relatives (that is, they make the following equations: F = FB, etc.; M = MZ, etc.; B = FBS = MZS, etc.; Z = FBD = MZD, etc.). Omahas bother to acknowledge age relative to ego only in terms for siblings and parallel cousins (ignoring it for female relatives of a male ego). The sex of the relative determines the use of twenty-five of twenty-six terms.

The sex of the speaker has profound effects; for this reason it has been convenient to follow Dorsey in providing separate lists for male and female egos. In a patrilineal society the position of a woman is necessarily different from that of a man from the moment she marries. For one thing, her children belong to her husband's descent group, not her own, giving rise to the use of different terms for her children and her brother's children, and so on. The difference between the positions of men and women becomes very noticeable in the sibling terminology, where there is only one term that both sexes use in common and in the same way. Furthermore, men and women require different terms for immediate affinal relatives. Some terms (thirteen in all) are used exclusively by men or by women. Other terms are used by both sexes but with somewhat different patterns of distribution. Eight terms are of this kind, but in five of these instances the difference may derive entirely from the ethnographer's neglecting to carry his checking of uses far enough. In any event, there are only five terms that we know for certain a man and a woman use in exactly the same way.

Kroeber's sixth principle is the one by which certain anthropologists distinguish between cognatic terminologies and those appropriate to exogamous unilineal groups. It is also the feature Lowie had in mind when he spoke of the Dakota principle, of which the Omaha principle was a particular variation. The Omahas make no reference to it in the second ascending and second descending levels, but they give it full play in the medial three levels.

F, FB, etc. ≠ MB
B, FBS, etc. ≠ MBS
B, FBS, etc. ≠ FZS

FZ, FFBD, ≠ M, MZ
Z, FBD, etc. ≠ MBD
Z, FBD, etc. ≠ FZD

For a male ego:
S, BS, FBSS, MZSS, etc. ≠ ZS
    or MBSS or FZSS, FZDS

For a female ego:
S, ZS, FBDS, MZDS,
    etc. ≠ BS
    or MBSS or FZSS,
    FZDS

D, BD, FBSD, MZSD, etc.
    ≠ ZD or MBSD or FZSD, FZDD

D, ZD, FBDD, MZDD,
    etc. ≠ BD or MBSD
    or FZSD, FZDD

Kroeber's seventh principle is the distinction between blood relatives and those connected by marriage, between consanguinities and affinities. Morgan (1870, 10–11) made this distinction the foundation stone of his theories of the origin of the forms of relationship systems. Morgan began with two premises: (1) "marriage forms the basis of relationship" and (2) the relationships created by these marriages are consanguineous. McLennan (1876), Starcke (1889), Westermarck (1894), and others attacked the idea that relationship systems express specifically biological rather than social relationships. This distinction between biological and social relationship is now accepted as fundamental to the anthropological understanding of kinship. The issue has been transformed; we are now concerned with how cultures themselves regard relationship by virtue of descent or marriage.

A definitional matter has therefore become a question in translation. Dorsey's monograph does not help us greatly here, because he did not recognize a problem requiring attention. All he has to say (1884, 252) is that Joseph La Flesche and Two Crows recognized four classes of kinship:

1. Consanguineous or blood kinship, which includes not only the gens of the father, but also the gentes of the mother and grandmothers.
2. Marriage kinship, including all the affinities of the consort, as well as those of the son's wife or daughter's husband.
3. Weawa^{n} kinship, connected with the calumet dance.
4. Intergentile kinship, existing between contiguous gentes [in the tribal circle].

There is no indication of a precise Omaha equivalent of the phrase "blood kinship," and we might well wish to have the verbatim statements Dorsey drew upon. Elsewhere Dorsey (1890a, 409–15) transcribed an Omaha text in which there is reference to mixed-bloods of various degrees of "blood," but the interlinear translation shows that where "blood" appears in English the Omaha text speaks only of "part." Following Morgan, Kohler supposed that Omaha relationship terms reflect biological ties; but Durkheim (1897) objected that biological ties do not even become social relationships unless they are recognized as such, whereas social ties may be established (as in the case of adoption) where no biological link exists. Noting that all women in the line of MF at whatever level are called by the same term as M, even when they are younger than ego, Durkheim observed that the term therefore designates all women of the family or clan into which F married. *Ihoⁿ´* (*iⁿ´noⁿha* when used by a child) has nothing to do with the idea of descent "in the ordinary sense of the word" (Durkheim means here direct filiation); and the vocabulary expresses something quite different from consanguinity proper.

Durkheim's critique actually has two purposes, one of which is to undermine the biological interpretation of relationship. The other intention is to show that some relationships hitherto interpreted as showing consanguinity might just as well be said to express the fact that the persons in question are affines of someone in ego's line (such as his F). Dorsey left this course open when he stated blandly and without further comment (1884, 253) that "Many affinities are addressed by consanguinity terms." Durkheim's point has come up again from time to time (recently in Köbben, Verrips, and Brunt 1974, 216; Teitelbaum 1980, 35), occasionally evidently in ignorance of Durkheim. In fact, all Omaha terms apply to some persons with whom the connection may be through links that are in the main or exclusively affinal. There is no point, therefore, in saying as Dorsey does that the terms themselves are consanguineous or affinal.

Coult (1967, 39–40) has recently rediscovered Durkheim's point and elaborated it into an argument that "the marriage tie between two groups is prior to the ties created between the groups on the basis of children born to the marriage." The patrilineal equations in M's patrilineage parallel those in W's patrilineage. Coult therefore concludes that what is in question is ego's classification not of his own and M's patriline, but of his own and FW's patriline. The alliance established by marriage does not extend for more than one generation (more properly phrased, alliance does not involve repetition of marriage at subsequent levels) because of the specific Omaha marriage prohibitions. The way Coult presents the issue bears comparison with Dumont's explanation of the Dravidian systems of symmetric marriage alliance (1953). Perhaps we may draw an observation from the discussion Dumont's work has occasioned. Omaha classification capitalizes on the fact that MB and persons of his line are F's affines, but this circumstance does not preclude ego from recognizing his filiation through M with her line.

Lounsbury (1964) has propounded what he calls a formal analysis of the Crow and Omaha types of kinship terminologies. His discussion of the Omaha type actually concerns the Foxes, and Lounsbury takes his starting point from Tax's two articles. Lounsbury refers to his formal approach as transformational analysis, and he states his aim as reducing the many applications of each term to a primary relative. His approach, he says (p. 381), predisposes him to an extensionist theory, whereby classificatory relationship terms are regarded as resulting from a process of extension out from the primary relatives. In fact the extensionist hypothesis is implicit in his article from the point where he first speaks of primary kin. The doctrine of extension assumes that kinship relations are primarily biological rather than social. Reference has already been made to the criticisms that scholars in the previous century advanced against this premise. Actually, Lounsbury's transformational analysis need not be stated in terms of genealogical ties and is logically independent of the extensionist issue.

Coult (1967) has already shown that "Lounsbury's transformation rules are identical with Tax's rules of succession for the Fox terminology" and that "the only difference between Tax's rules and Lounsbury's rules is that Lounsbury's are worded as reduction rules and Tax's are worded as expansion rules." There is no need to repeat here the details of Coult's careful and convincing demonstration. Another objection is that Lounsbury's wording is far less direct and clear than Tax's and therefore tends to obscure the subject at hand. In fact, Tax's own analysis had already been carried out forty years previously by Josef Kohler (1897, 1975; see Barnes 1975a, 66–67). The only thing really novel about Lounsbury's method is the jargon in which he expresses it; the rules themselves are based on anthropological commonplaces. Thus Lounsbury's "half-sibling rule" corresponds to the observation that children of persons classed with parents are themselves classed with siblings. His merging rule is the reciprocal of Tax's generalization that children of same-sex siblings are classed with son and daughter. His skewing rule is nothing other than an inverted reference to the patrilineal equations in M's line.

Lounsbury left out of consideration the terms in the second ascending and second descending levels, and he also ignored all affinal applications. Coult criticized him for this incompleteness. Lounsbury's avoidance of these issues meant he never encountered the

numerous exceptions to his rules that occur in the actual terminology and therefore did not attempt to explain them. In fact, all
the qualifications that must be made to Tax's generalizations are
unexplained in Lounsbury's approach. Since he adds nothing new,
there is no need to give Lounsbury's version of transformational
analysis further consideration.

In his analysis of the Omahas, Choctaws, and related American
Indian terminologies, Josef Kohler (1975, 188) observed that the
Omaha system derives from "father right," or what today would be
called a patrilineal rule. This observation bore both on unilineal
equations and on the nature of the marriage preference, two issues
that are not entirely separable. The next chapter will take up
Kohler's important contribution to the analysis of the Omaha marriage system and related theories of other scholars.

Kohler did not phrase his discovery of the patrilineal rule as
clearly as he might have done. Durkheim (1897, 312, 316) expressed the point more precisely in a review that is justly famous.
Kohler had shown that the systems of the matrilineal Choctaws and
the patrilineal Omahas were similar except for an inversion in the
distribution of terms that, Durkheim argued, was "the logical consequence of the inversion indicated by the system of filiation." Since
the distribution of terms "varies with the kinship organization, it is
clear that it depends on it and that it expresses it."

In the first instance, the patrilineal bias shows up in the way an
Omaha classes persons in M's line. One term comprises all women
at whatever level in her line, and another single term applies to all
males below MF. There are similar equations in several other lines.
The similarity between the formation of groups and the pattern of
the terminology soon became generally recognized. Anthropological debate turned to questions of causality and to the puzzle why
features that so obviously fit together do not always occur together.
Most of these points had been well rehearsed and widely appreciated by the time Radcliffe-Brown (1941, 10) transformed the lineal
principles into his "principle of the unity of the lineage group."

By the principle of the unity of the lineage group I mean that for a person
who does not belong to the lineage but is connected with it through some
important bond of kinship or by marriage, its members constitute a single

Table 12. Patrilineal Equations

Male	Female
1. MB, MBS, MBSS, MBSSS, MFBS, MFBSS, MFBSSS	1. Same
2. MMBDS, MMBDSS, MMZS, MMZSS	2. Same
3. MFZ, M, MZ, MMMZDD, MBD, MBSD, MBSSD, MFBD, MFBSD, MFBSSD	3. Same
4. MMBDD, MMBDSD, MMZD, MMZSD	4. Same
5. FMF, FMB, FMBS, FMBSS	5. Same
6. MMF, MMB, MMBS, MMBSS, MMBSSS	6. Same
7. WMF, WMB, WMBS, WMBSS	
	7. HMF, HMB, HMBS
	8. BWF, BWB, BWBS
8. FM, FMZ, FMBD, FMBSD	9. Same
9. MM, MMZ, MMBD, MMBSD, MMBSSD	10. Same
10. WM, WMZ, WMBD, WMBSD	
	11. HM, HMZ, HMBD
11. WFZS, WZS, WFBDS, WMZDS, S, WBDS	/12. FFZS, FZS, FFBDS, FMZDS, S, ZS, FBDS, MZDS
12. WFZD, WZD, WFBDD, WMZDD, D, WBDD	/13. FFZD, FZD, FFBDD, FMZDD, D, ZD, FBDD, MZDD
13. FFZS, FZS, FFBDS, FMZDS, ZS, FBDS, MZDS	/14. HFZS, HZS, HFBDS, HMZDS
14. FFZD, FZD, FFBDD, FMZDD, ZD, FBDD, MZDD, ZHBD	/15. HFZD, HZD, HFBDD, HMZDD
15. DHFZ, DHZ, DD, DSD	16. Same

continued

Table 12 *continued*

16. WB, WFBS, WMZS, WBS, WFBSS, WMZSS, WBSS, WMBDS, WMBDSS	
17. WFZ, WZ, WFBD, WMZD, WBD, WFBSD, WMZSD, WBSD, WMBD, WMBDSD	
18. SW, SWZ, SWBD	17. Same
19. DHFF, DHF, DH, DHB	18. Same

Note: The comma replaces the equals sign. A slash before a number indicates that men and women use different terms in that position.

category, with a distinction within the category between males and females, and possibly other distinctions also. When this principle is applied in the terminology a person connected with a lineage from outside applies to its members, of one sex, through at least three generations the same term of relationship.

This passage contains many unavowed and misleading assumptions. There are of course many ways Omaha descent groups may appear unified: groups are named; members are identified with the group by personal names; they must observe common restrictions regarding food; political and ritual obligations attach to groups; marriage prohibitions apply to groups; and so on. These factors are true of all Omaha clans. Hence, if an Omaha recognizes the unity of one clan he must do so for all. If he made patrilineal equations regarding persons in groups with which he had ties, Radcliffe-Brown's principle implies that he would do so in every such group. In fact, there are many lines in the terminology where a speaker applies different terms in every level. Radcliffe-Brown's principle does not even explain the distribution of terms in those lines where patrilineal equations are made. Why, for example, are there two terms for males in M's line and only one for females? Finally, the "unity" of which Radcliffe-Brown speaks is not his discovery, but just another way of stating a commonplace that equations are made where they are and in the way they are. Louis Dumont (1961,

93) has dismissed the principle with the remark that it is nothing more "than a kind of tautological blinkers, preventing any view beyond that of the lineage as a thing-in-itself. Together with the 'principle of the unity of the sibling group,' this principle's function is to reduce complementarity to 'unity,' structure to substance."

An Omaha male makes unilineal equations in nine separate terminological lines. Table 12 presents a complete list of the equations, barring possible slips and oversights.

6: Terminology and Marriage

Kohler's original analysis of the Omaha terminology attempted to show that it reflected a specific form of marriage practice. Since Kohler, several persons have advanced hypotheses involving one or another form of marriage arrangement. Some of these have been wide of the mark; others have been useful without being fully correct. Kohler phrased his own theory in terms current in the ethnographies of his day, and his borrowed jargon, with phrases like "group marriage" and "mother right," now seems very outmoded. He made, however, analytic discoveries that are independent of the particular framework of his evolutionary theories and accordingly have survived. Reconsideration of his explanation will repay our efforts.

Kohler attempted to show that the whole Omaha kinship system rested on group marriage with a woman, her sister, her paternal aunt, and her brother's daughter. He contrasted this form of group marriage with the direct exchange of sisters characteristic of Dravidian society and with a Choctaw version in which a woman marries a man, his maternal uncle, and his sister's son. The Choctaw and Omaha systems, according to Kohler, derive respectively from mother right and father right. An Omaha woman cannot marry as a Choctaw woman does because, given patrilineal descent groups, her husband's mother's brother or sister's son would belong to a different descent group than the husband. An Omaha man may marry the father's sister and brother's daughter of his first wife because they belong to her patrilineal clan (Kohler 1975, 188–89,

204). The intervening decades have brought much greater sophistication in understanding systems of marriage alliance than was present in Kohler's pioneering work, but it would be wrong not to accord him his proper place in the history of ideas.

The notion of the concrete practice of mass marriage has always been somewhat fantastic. Durkheim (1897, 318) wrote that "The hypothesis of a collective marriage has never been anything other than an *ultima ratio,* useful as an aid for imagining strange customs; but it is impossible to overlook all the problems it presents." Furthermore, polygyny and polyandry are different from those forms of group marriage presupposed by Morgan and Kohler, in which "a confused and enormous group of men [marry] an equally indeterminate group of women."

A number of eminent anthropologists, among them Kroeber, Radcliffe-Brown, Murdock, and Lévi-Strauss, have disagreed with Kohler's explanation. The principal objection is that marriage with a wife's paternal aunt or niece is necessarily a secondary marriage, indulged in by only a minority of men. Indeed, in 1883, of 228 married men, only thirty-six had more than one wife. At one time or other eighty-one of the men had had more than one wife, and of that number only twenty-one had with certainty married into the same subclan, sixteen of them with closely related women (FZ/BD 6; Zs 8; FBDs 1; FFBSD/FFBD 1).[1] Since secondary marriages of a specific kind are necessarily rather rare, they seem a weak prop for systematic features of a relationship terminology (Murdock 1949, 123–214).

Radcliffe-Brown (1941, 14) no doubt expressed the situation clearly enough when he wrote, "The special form of marriage and the special system of terminology, where they occur together, are directly connected by the fact that they are both applications of one structural principle." The principle involved is patrilineality, and of course Kroeber (1909, 84) and even Kohler had already said as much before Radcliffe-Brown.

The actual causal link Kohler proposed between the form of marriage and the shape of the terminology is probably wrong for the reasons rehearsed. But the Omaha preference for taking additional wives from among the first wife's close agnatic relatives occurs in the same context as the classification. Like the unilineal descent groups and the terminology, the marriage preference presupposes the same patrilineal ideology.

Kohler, however, failed to give explicit acknowledgment to another aspect of Omaha marriage practices—that Omaha marriage prohibitions ensure that agnatically closely related males of succeeding generations do not take women from the same group. While brothers may marry into the same clan, fathers and sons may not. There are in fact a few terminological equations that would be compatible with a system of marriage alliance: MB = FZH, ZH = WB, FZ = MBW. The preponderance of evidence, however, shows that there is no marriage prescription of any kind:

$$FZH \neq WF \qquad MBS \neq WB \qquad WBS \neq ZS$$
$$MB \neq WF \qquad MBD \neq BW \qquad ZS \neq DH$$
$$FZ \neq WM \qquad MBD \neq FZD \qquad SW \neq ZD$$
$$MBS \neq FZS \qquad FZS \neq ZH$$

There is no marriage prescription implying the continued inheritance of marriage ties between lines, and the Omaha terminology accordingly recognizes a great number of distinct affinal lines. In a prescriptive terminology these would be consolidated into a small number, depending in part upon the nature of the prescription. Here, though, the presumption is that marriage ties will not be repeated, and so there are distinct affinal lines at each genealogical level.

Kohler (1975, 175–85) considers a series of terminological equations that he believes reflect the Omaha marriage preference. These equations take on significance when viewed in conjunction with the absence of equations diagnostic of a marriage prescription, for some Omaha equations might also occur in conjunction with asymmetric alliance. All patrilineal equations, of course, are compatible with the Omaha preference, which is why Kohler was tempted to explain them by the marriage rule. The equation of MFZ and MBD with M fits the assumption that F might have married all these women. In addition to patrilineal equations, the Omahas make another extensive series of equations that would be understandable on the assumption that men had been carrying out the preference systematically. The equation FMBDS = F would make sense on the assumption that FF married his WBD, since the Omahas also equate FB with F. The Omahas make equations of this kind throughout the terminology. All of these equations necessarily also imply patrilineality indirectly because the marriage preference is framed in terms of patrilineality. Table 13 presents such equations; the table takes into account all those Kohler found and a great many more.

Possibly Kohler has not been given adequate credit for this dis-

Table 13. Equations That Conform to the
Preference for Repeated Marriage in W's line

Male	Female
1. FMBDS, F, FB, FFBS, FMZS	1. Same
2. FMBDD, FZ, FFBD, FMZD	2. Same
3. MMBDS, MMBSDS, MB, MFBS, MMZS	3. Same
4. MMBDD, MMBSDD, M, MZ, MFBD, MMZD	4. Same
5. MMBDDSe/y, e/yB, etc.	5. Same
6. MMBDDDe/y, e/yZ, etc.	6. Same
7. MFZSe/y, e/yB, etc.	7. Same
8. MFZDe/y, e/yZ, etc.	8. Same
9. MFZSS, S, etc.	9. MFZSS, BS, etc.
10. MFZSD, D, etc.	10. MFZSD, BD, etc.
11. MFZDS, ZS, etc.	11. MFZDS, S, etc.
12. MFZDD, ZD, etc.	12. MFZDD, D, etc.
13. MFZSSS, SS, etc.	13. MFZSSS, BSS, etc.
14. MFZSSD, SD, etc.	14. MFZSSD, BSD, etc.
15. MFZSDS, DS, etc.	15. MFZSDS, BDS, etc.
16. MFZSDD, DD, etc.	16. MFZSDD, BDD, etc.
17. MFZDSS, ZSS, etc.	17. MFZDSS, SS, etc.
18. MFZDSD, ZSD, etc.	18. MFZDSD, DS, etc.
19. MFZDDS, ZDS, etc.	19. MFZDDS, DS, etc.
20. MFZDDD, ZDD, etc.	20. MFZDDD, DD, etc.
21. FFZS, FZS, FFBDS, FMZDS, ZS, FBDS, MZDS	/21. FFZS, FZS, FFBDS, FMZDS, S, ZS, FBDS, MZDS, MFBDDS

continued

Table 13 *continued*

Male	Female
22. FFZD, FZD, FFBDD, FMZDD, ZD, ZHD, FBDD, MZDD, ZHBD	/22. FFZD, FZD, FFBDD, FMZDD, D, ZD, FBDD, MZDD, MFBDDD
23. FFZH, FZH, FMZDH, ZH	/23. FFZH, FZH, FMZDH, ZH, BDH
24. WMBDS, WB, etc.	/24. HMBDS, HB, etc.
25. WFZ, WZ, WFBD, WMZD, WBD, WFBSD, WMZSD, WBSD	
26. WMBDD, WZ, etc.	/25. HMBDD, HZ, etc.
27. S, WFZS, WZS, WFBDS, WMZDS, WBDS	/26. HFZS, HZS, HFBDS, HMZDS
28. D, WFZD, WZD, WFBDD, WMZDD, WBDD	/27. HFZD, HZD, HFBDD, HMZDD
29. WMBDDS, WZS	/28. HMBDDS, HZS
30. WMBDDD, WZD	/29. HMBDDD, HZD
31. WFZSS, WZSS	/30. HFZSS, HZSS, HFBDSS
32. WFZSD, WZSD	/31. HFZSD, HZSD, HMZDSD
33. WFZDS, WZDS	/32. HFZDS, HZDS, HMZDDS
34. WFZDD, WZDD	/33. HFZDD, HZDD, HFBDDD
35. ZHZ, ZHFBSD (?)	
36. SW, SWZ, SWBD	34. SW, SWZ, SWBD
37. FFZSW, FZSW, ZSW	35. (Dorsey does not give the term for FZSW, ZSW)
	36. HFZSW, HZSW
38. DH, DHB, SDH	37. (Dorsey does not give the term for SDH)
39. FFZDH, FZDH, ZDH	38. FFZDH, DH (Dorsey does not give the term for FZDH & ZDH)
	39. HFZDH, HZDH, DH, DHB

Note: The comma replaces the equals sign. To save space, parallel cousin specifications are replaced by "etc." where no confusion will arise. A slash before a number indicates that men and women use different terms in that position.

covery. It has been neglected largely because of the implausible nature of his causal explanation. Nevertheless, these features are there, and they are an important aspect of the distinctive shape of the Omaha system of relationship. The marriage preference therefore stands to these properties of the terminology in exactly the same way as the patrilineal rule of group membership stands to the patrilineal terminological equations. Whatever style of explanation is offered for the latter resemblance must also be advanced for the former.

Dorsey described not only a marriage preference but also an elaborate series of marriage prohibitions, which in recent years—in response to the speculations of Lévi-Strauss—have increasingly come to attention. Obviously the preferences and the prohibitions are two sides of the same coin; so we may now consider the prohibitions.

Dorsey's book is remarkable for the attention he gives this subject. His specifications of marriage restrictions not only are more elaborate than anything of like kind published at that period, but also surpass anything subsequently published on related American Indian groups. No authority on the Omahas has given information that is anywhere near comparable. For other Siouan peoples, such as the Crows, Hidatsas, or Iowas, it is hard to tell exactly what, if any, restrictions are placed on marriage choice. Yet in a few pages of a slender ethnographic report Dorsey set out such a list of constraints that it raised in his own mind the question how an Omaha man could ever find an eligible mate. His explanation was a good one—that since most prohibitions apply only to segments of relevant descent groups, there were always some wife-providing lineages available.

The information he sets out is baldly stated, first by way of concrete examples, then in a general form. Despite his proven talent as an ethnographic reporter, Dorsey's efforts at analysis are inevitably lame and naive. In this as in other cases, Dorsey does not manage to resolve even the conflicts in his own report, nor does he bother to ponder his information long enough to discover in what ways it is incomplete.

The discussion of marriage follows closely upon the description of the relationship system. Dorsey left his account of kinship and marriage largely undigested. It is impossible to read this section oɪ his book through and completely understand the implications of what he says. To comprehend the system, a reader must spend a great deal of time in preliminary and tedious checking and cross-checking of the various prohibited relationships described. So far no one has taken the trouble to do so, and the value of this section is still largely latent.

Other peculiarities of Dorsey's description have to do with the historical conditions under which he collected his information. Although Dorsey actively investigated Omaha language and culture during his years at the reservation, internal evidence suggests that his information on the marriage restrictions derived almost entirely from Two Crows and Joseph La Flesche when they visited Washington in 1882 to help him revise his manuscript for publication. Both were qualified informants, and the information they gave is no doubt authentic. Perhaps, though, the reader of Dorsey's book may be tempted to dismiss too quickly the views they disagreed with. It is reasonable to acknowledge a degree of diversity within Omaha culture and to accept that La Flesche and Two Crows, like other informants, were often unable to convey to Dorsey more than an incomplete and perhaps inaccurate picture on some topics.

Despite the impressive detail, the description of marriage regulations Dorsey got from them is probably incomplete and may be partially inaccurate. Dorsey begins (1884, 255–58) by describing the people whom La Flesche, Two Crows, and some of Two Crows's relatives had married and whom they could not marry. Dorsey seems to have had little genealogical information in 1882 besides what he presents in this section. Clearly he took the examples given him at face value and subjected them to no further checking. Only seven years later, in 1889, did he complete his record of Omaha genealogies, while preparing his intended monograph on personal names. It is inconceivable that he would have published quite the same description of marriage limitations in light of the information available to him at this later date.

For one thing, in 1884 Dorsey described Joseph La Flesche's mother as a Ponca and specified which Ponca descent groups La Flesche was not permitted to marry into. Later Francis La Flesche refused to give Dorsey further data about his family on the grounds that Dorsey had already published too much information about them. At issue was which tribe Joseph's mother came from. In the monograph Francis published with Alice Fletcher, the woman is explicitly described as an Omaha.

The doubtful evidence derived from Joseph La Flesche may be set aside as being of slight relevance in any case. The evidence from Two Crows cannot be so dismissed, but it cannot be accepted without critical interpretation. Two Crows told Dorsey who some of his ancestors were and into which lines he could not marry. He also explained that two of his brothers, Shaa$^{n\prime}$ and Mixa$^\prime$to^n, were subject to the same restrictions and had married, respectively, women of the Deer Head and Ko$^{n\prime}$çe clans. These facts are accurate so far as they go, but Dorsey would surely have been more cautious had he realized that Shaa$^{n\prime}$ had also married another woman from one of the supposedly prohibited groups and that four more of Two Crows's full brothers had also done so.

Two Crows's MM was a Buffalo Head. His FM was a Black Bear. Dorsey therefore says that Two Crows could not marry women of these subclans. The same prohibitions would also obtain for Two Crows's brothers. As a matter of fact, the set of seven brothers married two Buffalo Head women and two Black Bear women. It would have been essential and most interesting for Dorsey to have found out what explanations Two Crows and his living brothers might have given. One of the women involved was actually the divorced wife of Joseph's son Francis La Flesche, and Two Crows may have suppressed mention of her in deference to Joseph's feelings.

Omaha prohibitions pertain to both primary and secondary marriages. Some of the prohibitions do not come into effect until after a man marries for the first time, whereas all prohibitions obtain after his children have married and had children. Because of these and other considerations it is not a simple matter to count up the number of lines a man might be permitted. Rather than plunging immediately into the complexities of these limitations, we had best begin by trying to draw from Dorsey as clear a view as possible of the choices and restrictions facing a young man considering his first marriage partner.

The first and least problematic rule is, "A man must marry outside his gens." All Omaha descent groups were exogamous, and no

Omaha ever violated this regulation. The Omahas were also forbidden to marry persons in their mothers' clans or anyone in the subclans of their FM, FMM, MM, or MMM. The distinction here, as Dorsey himself notes, between the clan and the subclan is of great importance for maintaining a reserve of eligible partners within the tribe. Initially, therefore, a man was forbidden wives from only two clans and four subclans. Out of the ten Omaha clans he might choose a woman from all or part of the divisions of eight other clans, whereas if there had been a blanket ban on marriage into the entire descent groups of the relatives mentioned above, an Omaha might have found only four clans remaining open.

The genealogies allow an imperfect check on compliance; the results may be found in table 14. For only one or two groups are the records complete enough to provide much of a check on anything other than marriage with women in M's clan. For the remote restrictions on the subclans of MMM and FMM, no meaningful test at all is possible. For various trivial reasons, not worth describing, the available evidence tends to exaggerate slightly the percentage of testable cases that conform to the regulations. More complete data would surely increase the number and probably also the percentage of known violations, especially those involving persons in the descent groups of FM, FMM, MM, and MMM. So far as we can draw reliable conclusions, we may infer that there was a regular though small number of deviant alliances.

There were only three marriages into M's own subclan; all other breaches in this category involved marriage into a different subclan. One or two of these may be due to a mistake in identifying the M's

Table 14. Compliance with Marriage Prohibitions

	Prohibitions, Male Ego					Prohibitions, Female ego	
	FM	FMM	M	MM	MMM	FM	M
Testable cases	45	8	255	43	7	71	234
Known violations	2	0	12	3	0	1	11
Percentage	4.4	0	4.7	7	0	1.4	4.7

subclan. The second instance, however, caught the attention of Dorsey, who penned a comment about it in the margin of the genealogies. A man in the Wind subclan of the Koⁿ´çe clan married his MBSD, an unmistakable breach in every way. Both his mother and his wife were from the Hoop segment of the Black Shoulder clan. He was, however, the second husband of his wife, the first husband being from his own group, though the precise genealogical connection cannot be traced. Dorsey notes that this man's wife was his father's *ihoⁿ´ga* (in this case WBSD) and his own *ihoⁿ´* (here MBSD); see figure 14. Her first husband having been from the Wind group, through him the second "obtained a quasi right to marry her, tho even that occasioned *much comment* among the Omahas."[2]

The two men were roughly of the same generation; so through the first marriage the second husband was able to regard the woman as belonging to the category of eligible women, *ihoⁿ´ga*. This case highlights several aspects of Omaha attitudes about kinship. Obviously the maneuver of reclassifying a woman to bring her into a permitted relationship worked in the sense that the marriage was established and persisted. Nevertheless, public opinion was not entirely satisfied by the ploy.

Second, the man legitimated the marriage, at least in his own eyes, by exploiting a tie through a somewhat distant genealogical kinsman within his segment. The sources generally leave unexplained the extent to which classificatory connections affect the application of the marriage prohibitions. In this instance it appears that reference to them is open to choice. After all, though he did not, the first husband might have regarded his marriage choice as

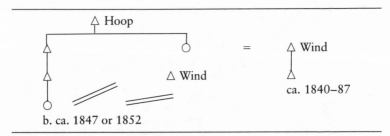

Figure 14. Marriage violation with MBSD.

not permitted on the grounds that an elder classificatory kinsman had already married into the same group. Third, there is no suggestion that the woman gave any consideration to the fact that she married men related to her through her FFZ; and Dorsey fails to mention explicitly a prohibition, though the woman would class such men with her son. These factors bring up the issue of the reciprocity of the regulations, to which further attention will be given below.

Another unusual case involved a woman (a Teton Sioux) who, shortly before George Miller began helping Dorsey with the genealogies (in August 1889), became pregnant by and married the older brother of her daughter's husband (see fig. 15), this being her third marriage. Dorsey's statement of the rules does not mention this possibility, nor does he show how BWM is classed. Only by the inference that a man calls her by the same term as his own WM, $iko^n{}'$, can we conclude that the relation is improper. Although Dorsey expressly marks the connection, he says nothing about how the Omahas reacted to it.

The great unexplored question in Dorsey's ethnography is the extent to which previous marriages of a man's classificatory relatives affect his own range of choice. The question poses itself in several ways. Suppose, for example, that a man was not allowed to marry a woman in the clans of the wives of any of his father's brothers or parallel cousins. This regulation is found among the Samos of Upper Volta, whose elaborate series of prohibitions Héritier (Izard 1968; Héritier 1976, 1981) has compared with that of the Omahas.[3] All it would require to exclude all Omaha women would

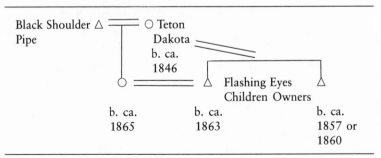

Figure 15. A marriage between BWM and DHB.

be for the men in father's generation to have taken wives from each of the nine other clans. Although the Omahas prefer for a man to take additional wives from among his first wife's relatives, in fact some men managed to marry women from several different groups. Of the eighty-one men who by 1883 had married more than one woman, sixty-one had taken wives from two or more descent groups. Several managed to find wives in up to four separate subclans.

In the larger subclans it would therefore be easy for a generation of men to have acquired women in each of the other clans; but this possibility does not exist for the smallest subclans. The size of one's own group is a factor. Taking men born roughly fifteen years either side of 1850, those in the Children Owners subclan of the Flashing Eyes clan, for example, actually managed to find wives in eight different clans. In fact there is no sign in the genealogies that even the FB's marriages had any effect on a man's choice. A few men and women actually married into the clan or subclan of their FBW.

Less sure is whether a man was concerned about his F's wives other than his M. Six men and three women, at least, show up as having married into FW's clan, where that differed from actual M's clan, but we have no way of knowing whether these should be reckoned additional violations involving M's clan.

The Samos, mentioned above, also prohibit marriage with women from the lineages of the wives of any classificatory B and also repeated marriage into W's lineage and those of certain of her relatives. The aim here is to bar repeated ties of any kind. This aspect of Samo sociology is a point at which there is the widest divergence from the Omahas. In fact, the Omaha preferences presuppose that lineage mates of a given generation will take women from the same groups and that a man may marry two or more women from the same family.

Though some doubt may remain on this score, the interpretation seems justified that the Omahas did not give a broadly classificatory definition to these prohibitions but were concerned only with the direct line of filiation. There is an opposition between group and kin ties to be observed here. A man might marry no woman in his M's clan, regardless of degree of relationship; but he was not, given that the surmise above is correct, concerned with FBW or her female relatives—even though he classed them with his M.

One or two points remain to be considered that bear on the position of a man making his first marriage, but these may be conveniently discussed later. The results so far are that he would probably at most have to avoid one whole clan in addition to his own and four other subclans. No grounds have been found to suggest that Dorsey missed prohibitions through classificatory relatives.

Dorsey sets forth an additional set of prohibitions that in effect would pertain only to remarriages:

1. A woman of the subclan of SW, BSW, or SSW (probably also DSW).
2. A woman of the subclan of DH, BDH, or SDH (DDH). Dorsey then phrases prohibitions by reference, for the first time, to relationship terms:
3. Women classed as *ikon´* who are affines (WM, WMM, WMZ, WMBW, SWM) "because they are the real or potential wives of his fathers-in-law, or of the fathers-in-law of his sons, nephews, or grandchildren."
4. Women classed as "grandchild" (*itu´shpa*).
5. The daughter of any woman classed as *ihon´ga* (WZ, etc.), "as such a daughter he calls his daughter." Furthermore, a man could not marry women of various categories to whom he was related through women of his line:
6. Women whom he calls "sister's daughter," *iti´zhun* (ZD, FZD, FFZD, ZH[B]D, etc.).
7. Women who are ZHZ, ZHFBD, ZHFBDD, or ZHFBSD because they are *itu´shpa* (see no. 4 above.).

Numbers 1 and 2 are the only known instances where consideration is given to persons traced through a collateral relative (B), and they contrast with the negative answer arrived at to the question about FB. The first five have the purpose of keeping separate marriages in different generations, and as such they are the counterparts of those with which we began. An Omaha must strictly avoid his WM, and the possibility of marriage with her is precluded on other grounds. The SW would necessarily also derive from a different line than W for the same reason; it is interesting, though, that here only the subclan is prohibited, a factor relevant to the question about the FW's line.

Rules 6 and 7 have the effect of preventing sister exchange or delayed direct exchange between two lines. The question of direct exchange comes in for detailed treatment below. What is notable is that genealogically close cases of direct exchange are explicitly wrong, while the Omahas said nothing about exchanges between descent groups where the ties are more remote. There are in fact several marriages of the latter kind; at least six men married into the subclan of their FZH, five into that of the ZH, and two into that of BDH. Since there is no genealogical connection or no very close one between the spouses, however, these exceptions are not, so far as is known, incorrect ones. All the more interesting, then, are two marriages that Dorsey went out of his way to label as wrong, one involving the ZHFBD and another the ZHFBSD. Closer examples than these do not turn up. A permissible inference is that the Omahas disliked direct exchange where a close relationship between the partners existed but were indifferent to it otherwise. They again differ somewhat from the Samos, who permit direct exchange in any form.

How the marriage question looks from the point of view of a woman is a matter of some difficulty, requiring careful consideration—the more so since it is often neglected. Dorsey's treatment of the issue is rather summary, consisting of no more than a brief paragraph. She may not marry:

1. S, ZS, FZS, or BDS. All these men might well belong to the same descent group, and she classes them all as *izhiⁿ´ge*.
2. SS, DS, ZSS, FZSS, FZDS, ZDSS, ZDDS. She classes these men as *itu´shpa*.
3. "Any man whom she calls elder or younger brother [i.e., *iti´nu* or *içuⁿ´ga*]." Most such persons are likely to be in her own clan and therefore prohibited by the rule of exogamy.
4. "Any man whom she calls her father's or mother's brother [i.e., *itha´di* or *ine´gi*]." This phrase actually contains two distinguishable prohibitions, one covered in any case by the rule of ex-

ogamy, and the other being the counterpart of the man's avoidance of women in his own M's clan.

5. Her *iti´go^n*, including "her own consanguinities" (i.e., men in her own subclan, such as FF and FFF), her father-in-law, BWB, BWF, BSWF, BWBS, FBSWB, FFBSWB. This way of stating the restriction covers persons in several different lines.

6. Any man who is her *ito^n´de,* namely DH, DHB, DHF, DHFF, FFZDH, HFZDH, HZDH—principally the men in the line into which her D has married.

An important difference between the way Dorsey states this list and his presentation of that for a man is that here he does not mention whole descent groups, whether clans or subclans. A woman expresses her restrictions by relationship category or genealogical connection. This difference constitutes a significant asymmetry in the position of men and women. For example, we have no proof that a woman shares the same restrictions on those groups reported for a man. Héritier (1976, 19) found that Samo prohibitions were framed exclusively from the point of view of a male, so that the situation facing a woman could be arrived at only by inference from that of a man. The Omahas do to an extent describe their system as seen by a woman, but in the main they seem to conceive of it as a pattern imposed upon a man in his search for a partner.

An issue that Héritier (Izard 1968; Héritier 1981, 88 ff.) has shown lies behind the nature of marriage prohibitions is whether they are symmetric for men and women. Her point can be established by beginning with an example taken from prescriptive systems. Anthropologists sometimes say that such systems express or embody a positive marriage rule, or marriage prescription. In fact they are based on a specific configuration of permissions and prohibitions. A symmetric system prescribes marriage with relatives of a certain category, who may be called allies (e.g., bilateral cross-cousins) and at the time prohibits marriage with the remaining kind of relatives. Restricting our view to cousins, for convenience but artificially, an asymmetric system prescribes marriage for a man with a certain kind of cross-relative, including one kind of cross-cousins. Let us say a man marries women in the structural position of MBD, but at the same time he is prohibited women in the structural position of the FZD. The structure is a system of prohibitions as well as a prescription. Using the language of daily speech (rather than mathematical jargon) Héritier describes the FZD as the *inverse* of the MBD. Therefore if we invert the nature of the prescription we invert the nature of the asymmetry.

In what anthropologists oddly call a matrilateral system, women are equally under a prescription that is the *reciprocal* of that for a man—namely, a woman marries a man in the category FZS. An implication of this structure is that a woman is prohibited from marrying men in the structural position of MBS; that is, her prescription is reciprocal, but not *symmetric* with that of a man. These formal relationships of reciprocity, symmetry, and inversion are essential for expressing the difference between symmetric and asymmetric prescriptive structures.

The same formal relationships are also significant for structures that specifically prohibit certain relatives without prescribing an appropriate partner. Héritier has again demonstrated at length how these issues may be addressed. If for the moment we confine our view to the structural positions of cousins, we might say that some structures merely prohibit marriage with one or another parallel cousin or relatives of that position. Others might include in the prohibitions one or other cross-cousin or both. Where there is exogamy, the nature of the structure depends upon the treatment of the cross-cousin position. Paralleling the prescriptive possibilities, a set of prohibitions might or might not be symmetrically applied to both sexes. If a man is prohibited both FZD and MBD, a woman is both reciprocally and, in effect, symmetrically prohibited FZS and MBS. But if a man is prohibited only MBD, the woman reciprocally FZS, it does not follow that a woman (symmetrically) may not marry MBS.

An example where this question becomes important is the Crows. Lowie gave conflicting reports over the years about whether it was permissible to marry into F's clan. His confusion rested in part on his evidence, for he actually collected a handful of cases in which both men and women had done so, and at first he thought that the Crows did not object (Lowie 1912, 201; 1917*b*, 56; 1935, 46–47). But several women felt they should not marry into F's group, at least if the genealogical connection was close. Finally, Lowie concluded that the Crow did not like marriages with F's clan relatives. Later he changed his position again, saying that women could not marry into F's clan, but men could do so when there was no close blood tie. What Lowie failed to consider was whether the prohibition applied to women but not to men. If that were the case, it would have the effect that women would be prohibited, for example, FZS, but permitted MBS; and men would be prohibited MBD and permitted FZD. The structure of prohibitions would be asymmetric.

In fact an answer to the dilemma might be derived from Lowie's statement (1935, 46) that a person ought not to marry anyone who stood to him in the relationship of "parent" or "child." If both parts apply to a female ego (and there is uncertainty about the purport of even this version), then a woman would be prohibited MBS too. It seems reasonable, then, to suppose that the Crows avoided at least close relatives in F's clan, and that the restriction applied symmetrically for men and women. The related Hidatsas, according to Bowers, rarely married into F's clan. It is worth remarking that the Crows and Hidatsas contrast in this respect with the Mandans, who preferred that a woman marry FZS or other relative in F's clan (thus a man could marry MBD). Bowers (1965, 68) says that nearly 25 percent of Mandan marriages were ones in which a woman (presumably) married into F's clan. So the issue of the symmetry or asymmetry of the marriage prohibition is a practical one for the Siouan groups of the plains.

What then of the Omahas? The easiest question to answer concerns reciprocity. If a man is prohibited a woman in a certain relationship, then the woman is necessarily and reciprocally prohibited him too, whether or not in her case the prohibition is given an explicit formulation. The rule of exogamy is both reciprocal and symmetric for men and women, it being impossible for a woman to marry into her descent group if no man does so. There is more of a problem when the other restricted descent groups come up. A man is prohibited even genealogically unrelated women in M's clan. The reciprocal of this rule is that a woman is prohibited any man whose mother comes from her own clan, regardless of genealogical connection or subclan affiliation. There is no evidence that the Omahas have given this consequence a conscious formulation. All that Dorsey gives us is a series of genealogical positions (S, ZS, BDS, FZS) that for a woman reciprocate close genealogical relatives of a man in his M's descent group. Much the same situation obtains for each of the other clan or subclan ties Dorsey mentions, but only when the genealogical connections are rather close; otherwise no test is possible. Dorsey's list of prohibitions for a woman, then, is rather incomplete, presumably because the Omahas give relatively little attention to the topic. He does not mention, for example, any reciprocal of the limitation on FMM's subclan. It is possible—and I have done so—to set up a table showing where Dorsey explicitly mentions the reciprocals, where he leaves them unmentioned, where he gives the relevant relationship term, and where he omits it. The test is useful, but here it is enough to reproduce this summary of the results.

Of rather more significance are the reciprocals for the prohibitions given for a woman. By and large these were already listed by Dorsey, but a handful reveal themselves as new prohibitions for a man. Some are so remote as to be of little practical significance, and in any case they are at present untestable. For example, among the men a woman calls "elder brother" is MMBDDSe, the reciprocal for a man being MMFZDDy. The prohibition on MZD is not surprising, but it is useful to have it confirmed. Of some interest but little systematic importance are WBW, FZSW, ZSW, and DHM.

Héritier (Izard 1968, 11) says that in the absence of any explicit formulation for a woman (which is the situation among the Samos of Upper Volta), looking only at cousins of the fourth degree, it is possible to tell whether the prohibitions on F's, FM's, M's, and MM's lines apply symmetrically for a woman by checking the following relationships (the only ones where the man falls into one of the four lines for a woman, but the woman does not do so for the man): FMBS, MFBS, MBSS, MFBSS, FMBSS, MMBSS. Among relationships forbidden a woman, Dorsey lists men she calls *iti´go^n* (FF, MF, etc.) and those she calls *ine´gi* (MB, MBS, etc.). All seven of the relatives described above fall into one or the other of these two categories. This test, then, gives evidence of the symmetry of the Omaha prohibitions. There is, though, again a discrepancy between application of some prohibitions for a man to whole descent groups and the absence of anything more than genealogically or categorically phrased restrictions for a woman. A woman is prohibited men of F's clan by the rule of exogamy, but we know for sure only that genealogical relatives in M's clan are *ine´gi* or *iti´gon*. With this qualification, these lines are also prohibited. Fletcher and La Flesche (1911, 325) say, "It was obligatory that a man and wife should belong to different gentes and not be of close blood relation through their mothers." Certain men, at least, of MM's line and FM's line are likewise *iti´gon;* so they too are covered by the prohibition.

What then about FMM's and MMM's subclans? Dorsey does not actually give terms for men in these lines. They are so remote that it is hardly likely that either a man or a woman would be much concerned about them. However, it is easy to infer given the treatment of FM's and MM's lines that should there be any occasion to apply terms to them, the men would be *iti´gon* and therefore also unmarriable. Bearing in mind the short Omaha memory for genealogies, about which more below, it is very unlikely that even a man would know what clan his FMM or MMM was in. Nevertheless, in the remote chance that they were of practical effect on marriage choices, they were symmetric for men and women.

The symmetric case for SW's subclan is represented by the woman's restriction on SWF and SWFB, though there is no mention of SWB. The BSW's subclan, SSW's subclan, DSW's subclan symmetries cannot be checked for lack of explicit evidence. DH's subclan is prohibited; BDH's subclan is represented by BDS, SDH's subclan by SDS, and DDH's subclan by DDH and DDHB. The various categorically framed rules are also confirmable as symmetric, at least insofar as the genealogical positions are reasonably close ones. The final check is to look at the symmetricals for the woman's regulations, which turn out to be testable in essential respects and which confirm the overall symmetric pattern.

At this point I must make a summing-up and that requires going back to the circumstances in which Dorsey gathered this information. The Omaha system is perhaps not really based on such elaborate restrictions on marriage choice as we have thought. The appearance of elaborateness is in some ways produced by the circumstances of Dorsey's conversations in 1882 and the way he wrote them up. Two Crows may have been trying to tell him that men of the same local line but of different generations ought not to marry into the same groups so long as (close) kinsmen in these generations are still living or the memory of the tie is fresh. This conclusion is supported by the fact that, having outlined Two Crows's personal restrictions and those of Two Crows's son Ineffectual Striking (Gaiⁿ'bazhi), Dorsey then burdens Two Crows's grandson not only with the corresponding set of restrictions, but also with those specific limitations on clans and subclans that he had just named for the young boy's father and grandfather "if his parents or grandparents were living, and knew the degree of kinship." However, "if they were dead, and he was ignorant of the fact that the women and he were related, he might marry one or more of them." In other words, this crucial section, the locus classicus of "Omaha alliance," is internally incoherent; for according to Dorsey's general statement of the rules, each generation ought to have a separate list of prohibited subclans. His examples indicate, however, that such prohibitions are accumulated throughout the generations so long as there is any memory within the family of a given connection.

Omaha restrictions were not in practice based on absolute limits to ties of a given kind. Instead, their implication and purpose depended upon memory.[4] Where no one living could precisely remember a connection, no restriction existed. Now genealogical memory itself is sociologically determined, and it is a commonplace of anthropology that its character and extent vary greatly from society to society. The Omaha rules therefore might work out very differently in practice in a society like the Emas of Timor, with their long memory for alliance, or the Nuers with their extensive agnatic genealogies. The seminomadic Omahas seem not to have invested much energy in this kind of memory.

The Omaha genealogies are not in general of excessive depth, encompassing three to five generations of adults. When George Miller returned from Washington to the Omahas he took with him a list of questions for further inquiry among Omaha families. In his letters back to Dorsey he apologized for difficulties in completing these questionnaires in some cases, observing, "Some of the people know their grandfather's and grandmother's names and others do not know them at all." "Sometimes they don't know their relatives' names so I can't tell you."[5] Miller had available to him men and women who had been adult in the 1840s and 1850s, and their memories would have included persons whose lives reached back into the 1700s. There is no reason to think that the forgetfulness he encountered would not have been found in earlier generations. This view gains some support from an interesting comment by Alice Fletcher, the first person to collect extensive genealogical information for the Omahas. She reports (in the same year that she was carrying out the allotment; 1883, 395) that if a woman dies when her children are young "it is probable, that, at maturity, they will have forgotten even her name."

Another consideration is that there are only a limited number of names, which are used again and again. Such circumstances militate against detailed memory of ancestors and their marriage connections for a great period into the past. The genealogies contain various marginal notes of interest in this connection. Of one man whose precise family affiliation could not be determined, Dorsey penciled in a query about who his brothers were and later added the answer "Had many, names forgotten." Women and their descent group ties are particularly easy to forget. The marriage prohibitions therefore seem to have worked only within the shorter span of remembered time.

This survey has also shown that, with a few exceptions already mentioned, only the marriages of persons in a direct line of filiation affect marriage choice, the marriages of collateral or classificatory relatives generally being ignored. Except for those instances where a man is forbidden whole descent groups, prohibitions apply to genealogical relatives only, and then usually just to close ones. The structure of the marriage prohibitions is symmetric rather than asymmetric. Direct exchange is permissible except with closely related persons: the Omahas not only explicitly forbid sister exchange, they do not practice it. There is no overt marriage prescription, but, as Kohler showed, marriage preferences encouraging repeated marriage by males within the same generation (with WFZ, WBD, WZ, or where brothers marry sisters) parallel features of the relationship terminology.

7: Marriage, Residence, and Kinship

Marriage is not just a matter of rules and regulations, at least for the persons directly involved. Various authors have written a good deal about Omaha courtship and domestic life, and we can now turn from abstractions to a summary review of these more day-to-day questions. Fletcher and La Flesche (1911, 318–27) provide a description of Omaha courtship that includes several courting songs, and Dorsey covers the same ground (1884, 259–60). Young men and women were not permitted to visit in their homes. Omaha customs favored chastity, and the Omahas were so strict that a young girl or married woman who went walking or riding alone was liable to be regarded as a prostitute. No woman would ride or walk with any man other than her husband; generally women traveled in the company of other women. Young men were not permitted to speak to girls they met on the road unless they were kin (Dorsey 1884, 365). The opportunities for young men and women to become acquainted were limited to tribal gatherings or the confusion attendant on breaking camp. Streams and springs provided opportunities for brief exchanges, and men attempted to attract the attention of girls by means of songs, signals, and intermediaries. It is nevertheless plain from some of Dorsey's remarks that girls did find occasion to steal away and be alone with boys, and in any case cohabitation even of short duration was sufficient to establish a marriage.

In his account of Omaha customs, which was used by James, the Indian agent Dougherty wrote that many Omaha girls were betrothed in infancy (James 1905, 14:322). He seems to have had in mind principally the younger sisters of a woman already married. An Omaha man who marries the oldest daughter "espouses all the sisters successively, and receives them into his house when they arrive at a proper age." Dougherty states that the new bride might be taken into her husband's household at an early age, between nine and twelve. La Flesche and Two Crows expectably denied that such was the Omaha practice, intimating that perhaps the Kansas did so. Dorsey (1884, 259) writes that Omaha women married between fourteen and fifteen but that formerly an Omaha man would wait until he was twenty-five or thirty and women waited until twenty.

Marriage was usually by elopement, though. "The claims on a girl by men holding a potential right to marry her almost necessitated her escaping secretly, if she would exercise her free choice in the matter of a husband" (Fletcher and La Flesche 1911, 324). Elderly men sometimes arranged marriages with the parents of the women, to whom they made large presents. The claims of which Fletcher and La Flesche speak usually derived from ties established by a previous marriage.

If the wife had sisters, these women held a potential relationship to her husband, as they might become his wives either during his wife's lifetime or at her death. According to tribal usage a man had the potential right to marry his wife's sisters and also her nieces [BDs] and her aunts [FZs]. On the other hand, a man was under obligation to marry his brother's widow. Should he fail in this respect, he was liable to suffer in person or property, either by the act of the woman herself or by that of her near of kin, in order to force him to recognize or make good her rights. . . . Approval [is] still expressed when a woman weds the brother of her late husband or a man marries the sister of his dead wife or the widow of his brother; even when there is a marked disparity in the ages of the parties, it is said, "The marriage does not make a break in the family and it shows respect for the dead." (1911, 313)

Whereas Fletcher and La Flesche speak of marriages arranged "with or without" the consent of the girl, Dorsey more sanguinely says, "Parents do not force their daughters to marry against their will." Parents could not compel a daughter to marry a man should she refuse; but they were able to express their disapproval of a suit-

or if approached by returning his presents. In the event of elopement, social pressure usually led to the suppression of signs of anger on the part of the girl's family. Mead (1932, 84–86) writes that wealthier and more privileged families were likely to arrange marriages. Where the girl's relatives initiated negotiations, they were likely to be of higher rank and interested in bringing a young man who was a proven hunter into the household through a matrilocal pattern of residence. In other cases the bridegroom's kin took the first step. "Strong objections on the part of the daughter were usually sufficient to make the father refuse an offer of marriage." Marriages were ratified by the exchange of gifts.

A young husband took his new bride into his father's house. The father and son subsequently prepared a feast and presents for the girl's relatives. Within a few months or a year, the bride's father would return presents of about equal value. The husband then had to work for a year or two in the home of his father-in-law, and for this period the father-in-law sometimes acted as "a tyrant" over his son-in-law's affairs.

There is some doubt concerning where the couple ultimately took up residence. During the period of the hunt families pitched their tents in the tribal circle in the position assigned the husband's descent group. Fortune, however, writes (1932, 24) that during the spring and fall, when the tribe lived in the villages, residence was matrilocal. "Mother and daughter commonly owned an earth lodge, and father-in-law and son-in-law resided together (in place of father and son)." No other authority gives precise information about residence location in the village, and the possibility remains that Fortune may have become confused about the temporary period when the new son-in-law served his wife's father.

Houses in the village were randomly placed, with no consideration of tribal order. Dorsey (1884, 366) says that the chief owners of the earth lodge were jointly the husband and wife who were at the head of the family or household. "Each man caused his lodge to be built wherever he wished to have it, generally near those of his kindred" (p. 219). Coupled with his statement (p. 367) that the eldest son becomes the head of the household or family, Dorsey's report implies that residence is if anything patrilocal, but there is no assurance that he refers here to the earth lodge. He also says that neither husband nor wife could give household property without consent of the other partner. Fletcher and La Flesche, on the other hand (1911, 362), say that "all those things which pertained to the household were the property of the wife." Even the tent they took on the annual hunt was hers, which at least proves that ownership of the dwelling did not necessarily coincide with the rule for locating the residence. Eggan (1955, 505) nevertheless infers from Fortune and other writers that the Omahas and neighboring tribes balanced their patrilineal clans against "permanent earthlodge villages . . . organized in terms of matrilocal residence and an extended matrilocal family."

Mead (1932, 29, 89) confirms that at the late date of her studies (1930) residence during the early years of marriage continued to be predominantly matrilocal. An earlier investigator, she says (p. 77; Alice Fletcher?), had failed in an attempt to establish a census of three historical village sites and had likewise had no success in correlating village residence with clan and subclan membership. No such investigation was any longer possible in 1930. Mead determined that during the winter small groups, mostly from the same clan or subclan, camped in tipis in sheltered ravines. In the permanent earth-lodge villages clan membership was habitually disregarded.

This disregard seems to have been partly due to the tendency of women relatives to build houses close together. Matrilocal residence and house ownership by women both militated against any strict observance of gentile affiliation in an otherwise patrilineal society.

Margaret Mead vividly describes many details of domestic life during the reservation period that have direct or indirect bearing on earlier times, but I shall not summarize that voluminous matter here. Fletcher and La Flesche write (1911, 325) that the father was regarded as the principal authority in the family, but concerning the welfare of the children the mother had nearly equal authority. Dorsey (1884, 268) has it that the parents had no right to put their children to death (there being only one known instance, and that notorious, where a man killed his son), nor, according to Dorsey, could parents force a child to marry against his will. Concerning the welfare of girls, brothers and mother's brothers had even more authority than father and mother, and they had to be consulted before the parents could bestow their daughter in marriage. Two Crows once forbade Susette La Flesche, of whom he was uncle (i.e., classificatory MB) by virtue of an adoption, to take a teaching job in Oklahoma and prevented her trip even though her father and mother approved (Dorsey 1884, 265). Should both parents die, the mother's brother acquired a control of the children that no relative of the father could dispute (Fletcher and La Flesche 1911, 328). Boys often played tricks on their mother's brother and were generally more familiar with him than with their own father, while girls showed more familiarity to mother's brother than to brothers (Dorsey 1884, 270).

Parents- and children-in-law practiced avoidances of various kinds. A man would not speak to his wife's parents or grandparents but had to converse with them by addressing his wife or child and requesting them to repeat the question or statement. A reply would be made through the same channel. A woman would never pass in front of her daughter's husband, and her son-in-law would try not to enter a place when his WM was there alone. Dougherty (James 1905, 15:37–38) says,

If a person enters a dwelling in which his son-in-law is seated, the latter turns his back, covers his head with his robe, and avails himself of the first opportunity to leave the presence. If a person visit his wife, during her residence at the lodge of her father, the latter averts himself, and conceals his head with his robe, and his hospitality is extended circuitously by means of his daughter, by whom the pipe is transferred to her husband to smoke. Communications or queries intended for the son-in-law are addressed aloud to the daughter, who receives the replies of her husband. The same formality is observed by the mother-in-law; if she wishes to present him with food, it is invariably handed to the daughter for him, or if she happens to be absent for the moment, it is placed on the ground, and she retires from the lodge, that he may take it up and eat it.

Mead (1932, 80) says that the avoidance of the parent-in-law of the opposite sex carried a prohibition against sitting next to each other, direct conversation except in emergencies, and contact of any sort. Within the tent the place of the mother-in-law was on the side farthest away from the son-in-law. At small family parties, as well

as feasts, Omaha men sat in rows with
so there would be no danger of placin
each other. Mead relates, however,
even unflattering conversation with
small baby, demonstrated by the foll
ed upon her daughter's husband:
surprised at the way he goes on. I
whole week. He does nothing but
the man retorted in defense, "You
ing, stingy old woman."

A woman would not speak directly to her husband,
she was not similarly constrained regarding her husband's mother.
Omahas would not mention the names of parents or grandparents,
and girls would not speak the name of an *iti´nu* (eB, etc.) (Dorsey
1884, 270). A "joking relationship" obtained between brothers-in-
law and sisters-in-law, as well as between sister's children and
mother's brothers, "classificatory rather than blood." Exchanges
between such relatives, especially where there was at least formal
potential for marriage, were characterized by mocking, ridicule,
and sexual banter (Mead 1932, 82; cf. Lesser 1930, 568).

Parents took charge in training children; a mother particularly
supervised the comportment of a daughter. A grandmother also
acted as instructor and chaperon of granddaughters, while a grandfather taught children myths and trained them in manners and mor-
als (Mead 1932, 82).

Fletcher and La Flesche say (1911, 324) that men and women
were "socially on a moral equality," but they also concede (p. 337)
that women had no official position in the tribe. When a man and
his wife walked together, the man always walked several paces in
front. Most marriages appear to have been stable, but divorce was
easily enough arranged. A woman dissatisfied with her husband
simply took herself back (Dorsey 1884, 262). Fortune (1932, 23)
found it was very common for a man to divorce his wife if his
firstborn son died in infancy. It is impossible to derive reliable statis-
tics on divorce from Dorsey's genealogies, but there are several marriages that he indicates were broken up in this way. In other cases
the inference is plain because both parties were still living in the
1880s and were then married to different partners. The genealogies

to confirm both that divorce was not uncommon
mily was fairly stable (Fletcher and La Flesche 1932,

custom not only permitted a man to hold more than one
multaneously, but it actually gave him a right to marry at
close female relatives of his wife—these being in particular her
sters, her brother's daughter, and even her father's sister. This
preferential claim pertained not only to plural marriages but also to
remarriage after a wife's death. In the genealogies available to
Mead (1932, 87), she found that a high death rate in the middle
years and the tendency to remarry even at an advanced age served
to exaggerate the impression of polygamy. The same may be said of
Dorsey's genealogies. Mead (1932, 86) writes that "it is not possible to obtain any statistical statement of the frequency of plural
marriage, but the genealogies and records suggest that it was infrequent." Nevertheless, by comparing Dorsey's genealogies with the
census and with Fletcher's allotment papers, we come up with reliable approximate figures for plural mating at the time of the
allotment.

In 1883 there were 228 adult males living who were married at
that time or had been married. Of these, 35.5 percent had married
more than once, but only 15.8 percent were currently married to
two or more women (see table 15).

By the time of Mead's study, strong government pressure applied

Table 15. Plural Marriages as of 1883

	Number	Percentage
Men who married more than once	81	35.5
Men who married only once	147	64.5
Total married males	228	100
Men currently married to two or more women (1883)	36	15.8

through the Bureau of Indian Affairs and backed up by financial sanctions (Mead 1932, 28, 64) had led to the tribe's abandoning polygamy. The first move to divide the Omaha lands came toward the end of the 1860s. In 1869 the Omaha agent E. Painter drew up a census (now untraceable) of Omahas entitled to lands, showing age and sex as well as the allotment for each. By this list he found that there were eighteen men with two wives, three with three wives, and one with four wives. Although the 1869 census cannot be recovered, the eventual allotment of 1871 survives, and it names 225 male family heads, including those who were part Omaha. The twenty-two men with more than one wife that Painter counted would be 10 percent of this figure.

Painter proposed that the commissioner of Indian affairs authorize him to withhold indefinitely from men with two or more wives land to which they were entitled beyond 160 acres unless they put away all but one wife. Whatever the response of the commissioner (Painter repeated the request two years later), the 1871 allotment was made null when the Bureau sold that part of the reservation containing the allotted lands to the Winnebago tribe for their reservation. While pressure against plural marriages intensified in the latter half of the century, reinforced by conversions to Christianity and movements to adopt white ways, no effective change in practice seems to have occurred until after the 1883–84 allotment.[1]

Despite the preference for marrying further female relatives of the first wife, most men who did not remain strictly monogamous found women in more than one descent group. Of the eighty-one men who married more than once in table 15, only twenty-one married with certainty into the same subclan, and only sixteen married closely related women (the breakdown has already been given in the preceding chapter).

Only one or two men went through life without marrying, and Dorsey (1884, 269) says there were no single women, since the demand was greater than the supply. People tended to remarry when they lost a spouse. According to Dorsey (1884, 267–68), widows would be expected, especially by the man's kin, to wait four to seven years, though more recently women under forty married two or three years after the death of their first husband and those over forty did not remarry at all. Men too were said formerly to have waited four to seven years, but in Dorsey's time they waited only one or two years. However, these ideal characterizations apparently are to be understood as qualified by the practice of marrying the siblings of a deceased spouse. A man was obliged to marry his brother's widow; while the widow "feels that she honors her husband's memory by remaining in the family, a feeling shared by any unmarried brother of the deceased, who, even if much younger than the widow, promptly becomes her husband" (Dorsey 1884, 258; Fletcher and La Flesche 1911, 313, 641).

Fletcher (1883, 395) writes that when a father died the mother lost all rights in the children. Unless very young, the children went to the family of one of the father's relatives, who would adopt them, permanently separating them from their mother. The widow, who usually married again, was not further burdened with the offspring of her former husband. This report lacks nuance. Obviously much depended on whether the woman married a man unrelated to her former husband and also on the attitude taken by his relatives. Dorsey (1884, 258) makes it clear that marriage of a brother's widow was partly intended to protect the children, and that where such a marriage did not take place a man might adopt his brother's children for fear the widow's new husband might hate them. Concern for the well-being of children expressed itself in the fact that relatives of a deceased spouse, whether man or woman, might punish a widow or widower who remarried too soon (Dorsey 1884, 268).

The census and allotment papers indicate a variety of solutions to the problem of placing orphans. The inference may sometimes be unreliable, but judged by the way such persons are listed, it seems that many were taken into the home of the new husband or wife, even when they belonged to a different family or group from the deceased parent. In many instances, too, some or all of the children were clearly adopted or taken under the protection of someone else—not in every case a close relative. Dorsey says (1884, 262) that when parents separated children sometimes went with their mother, sometimes with their father. A woman could not take her children upon divorce if the husband did not permit her to do so.

Among varieties of kinship, Dorsey lists *weawa^n*, connected with the calumet dance. Dorsey (1884, 276–82) and Fletcher and La Flesche (1911, 376–401) describe the elaborate dance, gifts, and pipes associated with this ceremony, whereby a man adopts a child as his own. The adopted child is thereafter treated as the firstborn, taking precedence over the actual firstborn. The adopter shares his property with the stepchild, "never refusing him anything that he may ask of him." The actual father appears to reciprocate by making gifts to the adopter's actual children. No marriage may take place between members of the two families for four years after the ceremony. Families who wish to maintain this relationship may do so for generations by alternating performances of the dance.

8: The Pattern of Marriage

The place of moieties in determining marriage choices in Siouan tribes has continually given rise to doubt. La Flesche (1921, 51) wrote that the Osages required men of one division to take wives only from the women of the opposite division and that this rule was strictly and religiously observed until the tribe had been reduced by disease and other causes and disturbed by white influences. By the 1950s Nett (1952, 181) could find no evidence of exogamous moieties. Howard (1965, 87) received no confirmation of Dorsey's attribution (1897, 228) of moieties to the Poncas. Radin wrote (1923, 183) that the moieties of the Winnebagos regulated nothing but marriage. If the sample of marriages he adduces (p. 199) is representative, they did at least do that. The Crows lack moieties (Lowie 1912, 207). Hidatsa moieties, by explicit Hidatsa report, had no marriage-regulating function (Lowie 1917b, 2), and half the marriages in Lowie's record were within the same moiety (1917b, 25–26). In Bowers's sample (1965, 69) more than half of Hidatsa marriages were into the same moiety; and though the Mandans claim their moieties were exogamous before the devastating smallpox epidemics, Bowers found that, of fifty Mandan marriages, nineteen were on the same side.

Evidence for the theory of an ancient exogamous dual organization among Siouan peoples (Goldenweiser 1913b, 286–87; Lesser 1929, 717) is therefore thin at best. Fletcher and La Flesche (1911, 135) write that the old men of the Omaha tribe preserved a tradition that their moiety division was for marital purposes. They further claim that a good majority of the marriages in existence "twenty-five years ago [ca. 1880–81]" were between persons on opposite sides of the tribal circle. Dorsey has nothing to say on the matter, and Fortune (1932, 13–14) argues with justification that the theory of Omaha moiety exogamy has no basis in recent practice. Considering only the clans, given clan exogamy, since there are ten clans—five in each moiety—Fortune estimates, admittedly somewhat roughly, that the chances were in any case 5/9 versus 4/9 that a person would marry into the opposite moiety. A majority on these proportions would hence prove nothing. Actually, of 223 marriages in Fletcher's allotment of 1883–84, 128 were on the opposite side, only slightly more than the 124 to be expected from random choice on Fortune's principle. Of 360 marriages in the accumulated record, 59 percent were into the opposite moiety, slightly more than the 56 percent to be expected (see table 16). Fortune ignores the issue of the relative size of each of the clans, however, and the odds for different individuals might vary considerably; but his point is demonstrated adequately, and further refinements are unlikely to change the result significantly. At no time in the nineteenth century were Omaha moieties exogamous.

If we think of the Omaha marriage rules as being intended to prevent family members of different generations from marrying into the same descent groups and to stop brothers and sisters from marrying the siblings of each other's wives or husbands, we may form the impression of the marriages cycling regularly in one direction through the clans and subclans, with very little repetition of ties between any two groups except where brothers or parallel cousins marry closely related women. Lévi-Strauss (1966b) has offered something like this picture with elaborations as the model of "Crow-Omaha" systems of marriage.

In fact, between several subclans there was a significant repetition of marriages, not only at different generations, but also symmetrically where men and women of one descent group married women and men of another. Table 17 shows the number of marriages between each of the Omaha subclans or (where a group had no further divisions for purposes of marriage) clans. The 360 marriages in this table derive from a collation of the genealogies with Fletcher's allotment papers and concern only those unions where

Table 16. Marriages in Same/Opposite Moiety

	Same Moiety		Opposite Moiety		Total	
Subclan	With Male	With Female	With Male	With Female	With Male	With Female
1.	12	9	9	9	21	18
2.a.i.	8	8	17	15	25	23
ii.	1	6	8	1	9	7
iii.	1	0	0	0	1	0
b.	7	6	2	7	9	13
3.a.	12	14	6	6	18	20
b.	3	1	2	4	5	5
4.a.	12	10	16	11	28	21
b.	7	15	19	25	26	40
c.	5	7	6	11	11	18
d.	11	10	15	7	26	17
5.a.	10	4	4	1	14	5
b.	4	3	5	8	9	11
Total	93	93	109	105	202	198
Percentage	46.04	46.97	53.96	53.03		
	46.5		53.5			
6.a.	2	6	5	11	7	17
b.	2	2	3	2	5	4
7.	9	6	14	7	23	13
8.a.	5	9	10	9	15	18
b.	6	1	4	13	10	14
c.	5	3	1	4	6	7
d.	4	1	9	12	13	13
9.	3	6	15	14	18	20
10.a.	2	0	6	1	8	1
b.	4	11	13	13	17	24
c.	8	8	18	19	26	27
d.	3	0	7	4	10	4
Total	53	53	105	109	158	162

continued

Table 16. *continued*

Percentage	33.54	32.72	66.46	67.28
		33.125		66.875
Grand total		146		214
Percentage		40.56		59.44

the precise subclan affiliation of both partners is determinable. Because many of the persons concerned had died before the 1880s, the total is larger than that to be found in the allotment papers alone, and because many men and women married more than once, the number of marriages is not equal to the number of persons involved.

Table 18 abstracts from table 17 only those examples where one subclan was involved in symmetric exchange with another. We can quickly see that size was a factor, the smallest groups being involved in direct exchange rarely if at all. The largest groups correspondingly had more cases of symmetric exchange and, indeed, were likely to have them with each other. Some of these marriages do result from actual violations of rules as they are set out by Dorsey. Many of them, however, give point to the claim that what concerned the Omahas were genealogical relationships—what the ethnographers call "blood" relationships. Although it is not always possible to trace precisely the genealogical ties between persons in the same subclans, Dorsey's genealogies are usually good enough to show when the connection is only distant. Although closely related men and women sometimes married persons in the same subclan, there was no danger of their having violated an Omaha prohibition unless those they married were also closely related to each other. The genealogies tend to break down into family groupings, between whom the ties of common descent are not shown and presumably were often unknown to the Omahas themselves.

Evidently the fact of direct exchange between descent groups per se was of no concern to the Omahas. What caused objections were marriages where genealogical ties of certain kinds already existed. There were twenty-two marriages in Dorsey's record where men

Table 17. Marriage between Omaha Subclans

a \ b	1	2ai	2aii	2aiii	2b	3a	3b	4a	4b	4c	4d	5a	5b	6a	6b	7	8a	8b	8c	8d	9	10a	10b	10c	10d	A	B
1						1 1		1 4	6 2	2 1	3 2					2 2	2 1 1	1 1		1 4	1 1	1	1 2	4	1	21 18	21 18
2ai						2		2	1 2	1	3 3		1 1		1	1 2	1 2	1 1		2 1	1	1 2	2	5 3	1	25 23	25 23
2aii						1		1	1	3	1					1		3	3	1			1			9 7	9 7
2aiii								1			1															1	1
2b	1 1					3		2 2	2			3		1			1			2	2			2 1	2 1	9 13	9 13
3a	1 1	1 2	1		3			1 3	2 2	2 1	1 3	2	1	1 1	1 1	2	2			2	1			2 1		18 20	12 18
3b								1		2 1			1			2	2				2 1					5 5	5 5
4a	4 1	2 1	1		2 1	3 1						5 2	5 2	4 1			3 2	1 1		1 2	1 2	2 3	2 3	3	1	28 21	18 16
4b	2 6	2 1	1		2 2	2 2	1					1	2 2	2 2	2	6 2	2	3			6 1	1 3	6 3	5 3	2	26 40	19 28
4c	1	1 3	3		2 1	1 2	1 2					1		1	1	1	1 1			1	4	1 2	1 2	3 1	3 1	11 18	6 12
4d	2 3	3 1	1	1 1	1 1	1 3	1		1	1		1 1		1	1	1		4	1	4	2 4	1 1	1	1		26 17	16 8
5a					3 2	2		5	1	1				1		2				1 1						14 5	5 4
5b	1 1				1	1		2 2	2					3 1			1 2 1	2	1	1	1			1		9 11	5 8

6a						1		1^{4}	1^{2}	1	^{1}	^{1}	1^{3}				1	^{3}			1	^{1}	^{1}		^{1}	7^{17}	2^{6}
6b		1				^{1}			2		^{1}						^{1}		1	^{1}				1		5^{4}	2^{2}
7	2^{2}	1^{1}	1			2	2		6	^{1}	^{1}	^{2}					1^{1}	^{2}	1	1	1	1	4	1^{2}	^{1}	23^{13}	9^{6}
8a		1^{2}			1	2	1	2^{3}	^{2}	1^{1}			2^{1}	^{1}	1	1^{1}					^{1}		1^{2}	2^{3}	^{1}	15^{18}	3^{7}
8b		1^{1}	^{3}					1^{1}	^{3}		^{4}		2^{1}	3		2					^{1}			1		10^{14}	1^{1}
8c			^{3}						1		^{1}				^{1}	^{1}							3^{1}	2		6^{7}	5^{1}
8d	4^{1}	1^{2}	^{1}		1	^{2}		1		^{1}	^{4}	1^{1}	1		1	^{1}							3			13^{13}	3
9		1^{1}			2	^{1}	1^{2}	1^{2}	1^{6}	4	4^{2}		1	^{1}		^{1}	1	1				^{1}		1^{3}		18^{20}	1^{4}
10a	^{1}	1						2	1	1	1			1							1					8^{1}	
10b	2^{1}	2^{2}	^{1}					2^{3}	6^{3}	^{2}	1^{1}			1		^{4}	2^{1}		1^{3}	^{3}						17^{24}	
10c	^{4}	5^{5}			1^{2}	1^{2}		1^{3}	5^{3}	3	1		1		^{1}	2^{1}	3^{2}	^{1}	^{2}		3^{1}					26^{27}	
10d	1	1^{3}			2				2	1^{1}				1		1	1									10^{4}	

a: Number of marriages with men of subclan x.
b: Number of marriages with women of subclan x.

A: Total marriages per clan.
B: Previously uncounted marriages.

TOTAL 360

Table 18. Symmetric Exchanges

Subclan	With Male	With Female	In Subclan	Subclan	With Male	With Female	In Subclan
1.	1	1	3.a.	4.d.	2	3	1.
	1	4	4.a.		3	3	2.a.
	6	2	4.b.		1	1	2.b.
	3	2	4.d.		3	1	3.a.
	2	2	7.		1	1	5.a.
	1	4	8.d.		2	4	9.
	1	2	10.b.		1	1	10.b.
2.a.	1	2	4.b.	5.a.	1	1	4.d.
	3	3	4.d.		1	1	8.d.
	1	1	5.b.	5.b.	1	1	2.a.
	1	1	7.		3	1	6.a.
	2	1	8.a.		1	2	8.a.
	1	1	8.b.		1	2	8.b.
	2	1	8.d.	6.a.	1	4	4.a.
	1	1	9.		1	2	4.b.
	2	2	10.b.		1	3	5.b.
	5	5	10.c.	7.	2	2	1.
	3	1	10.d.		1	1	2.a.
2.b.	1	2	4.a.		1	1	8.a.
	1	1	4.d.		1	2	10.c.
	2	1	10.c.	8.a.	1	2	2.a.
3.a.	1	1	1.		2	3	4.a.
	1	3	4.a.		1	1	4.c.
	2	2	4.b.		2	1	5.b.
	2	1	4.c.		1	1	7.
	1	3	4.d.		1	2	10.b.
	2	1	10.c.		2	3	10.c.
3.b.	2	1	4.c.	8.b.	1	1	2.a.
	2	1	9.		1	1	4.a.
4.a.	4	1	1.		1	1	5.b.
	2	1	2.b.	8.c.	3	1	10.b.
	3	1	3.a.	8.d.	4	1	1.
	4	1	6.a.		1	2	2.a.
	3	2	8.a.		1	1	5.a.
	1	1	8.b.	9.	1	1	2.a.
	2	1	9.		1	2	3.b.
	3	2	10.b.		1	2	4.a.
	3	1	10.c.		1	6	4.b.
4.b.	2	6	1.		4	2	4.d.
	2	1	2.a.		1	3	10.c.
	2	2	3.a.	10.b.	2	1	1.
	2	1	6.a.		2	2	2.a.
	6	1	9.		2	3	4.a.
	3	6	10.b.		6	3	4.b.
	3	5	10.c.		1	1	4.d.
4.c.	1	2	3.a.		2	1	8.a.
	1	2	3.b.		1	3	8.c.
	1	1	8.a.	10.c.	5	5	2.a.
	1	1	10.d.		1	2	2.b.
					1	2	3.a.
					1	3	4.a.
					5	3	4.b.
					2	1	7.
					3	2	8.a.
					3	1	9.
				10.d.	1	3	2.a.
					1	1	4.c.

married into the same subclan as did one or more of their female relatives. In only three such marriages is there any proven relationship between the spouses. The most interesting example of direct exchange occurred when B and Z married patrilateral parallel first cousins (FBD/FBS). The man therefore married his ZHFBD. Another man and his two sisters married a woman and a man related as FBSD/FFBS. The man therefore married his ZHFBSD. Dorsey mentions both possibilities as being equivalent to a man's marriage with ZHZ (no example of which is to be found); hence these marriages violated Omaha prohibitions. There were five other cases where B and Z married into the same subclan and one instance where second parallel cousins (FFBSS/FFBSD) did so, but the spouses involved were not related to each other.

In another example a man and his BD married persons related as FFBD/FBSS. There were in all four examples of FB and BD marrying into the same group, but the rest did not involve unions of persons who were closely related to each other. According to Dorsey, a man should not marry into his BD's subclan, but by inference from the probable dates of birth of those involved, it was always the FB who married first. The question, then, is whether women were wrong to take husbands where their FB had found his wife. There is no indication that they were restricted in this way. The conclusion has already been reached that even men gave no consideration to the marriages of the FBs. Five men married into the subclans of their FZH, but since they were not genealogically related to their wives, they did not violate the prohibition on women called *iti´zhu^n* (e.g., ZD, FZD).[1]

This survey permits the definite conclusions that Omaha moieties were not exogamous, that their symmetrically structured prohibitions covered only a small field of traceable kin, that direct exchange was otherwise permissible, and that between larger groups marriages tended to go both ways, giving rise in the aggregate to a de facto, but culturally insignificant, pattern of direct exchange. Of 360 marriages there are only nineteen where the husband violated some one of Dorsey's rules. This figure is somewhat low, for there is no way of checking whether the earlier marriages are correct, but the result of about 5 percent that are improper must be near the actual deviation.

9: "Omaha Alliance"

Lévi-Strauss added a new impulse to professional interest in the "Crow-Omaha problem" when he proposed that the way these societies regulate marriage constitutes a distinctive form between those of elementary structures and the random patterns typical in Western industrial societies. At the same time, however, he announced that he had abandoned his own efforts to provide a book on the subject as the second volume of his classic *The Elementary Structure of Kinship* because the difficulties of analyzing such systems "are in the province, not of the social anthropologist, but of the mathematician" (1967, xxiv; 1969, xxvi).

In his Huxley Memorial Lecture of 1965, Lévi-Strauss (1966*b*) does outline a fairly ambitious set of propositions about Crow-Omaha systems. In particular, he holds that we must understand them if we wish to include modern societies in our sphere of investigations and to apply to them the same conceptual framework (namely his own) that he claims has been proved in the investigation of simple communities. He even finds it possible to assert that the very future of anthropology depends upon such a shift in focus.

His speculations have stimulated some interesting work in other parts of the world, notably Alfred Gell's study (1975) of the Umedas in New Guinea, Françoise Héritier's series of papers (1974, 1975, 1976) and recent book (1981) on the Samos of Upper Volta, and a dissertation by Ross Bowden (1977) about the Kwomas of New Guinea. When the aim is to understand the Omahas themselves, the views of this master must be given due attention. In fact the Omahas are less like Lévi-Strauss's model than are some African cultures.

The idea of Crow-Omaha systems does not loom very large in *The Elementary Structures of Kinship*. Lévi-Strauss makes only a few passing references to them, the only one of substance (1969, 465) being the observation that "the combination of the principles of restricted and generalized exchange seems to be at the basis of the so-called Crow-Omaha systems of America (which do not always involve a determination of the prescribed spouse)." Elsewhere (1963, 64) he has repeated the remark, adding that joining the two principles makes it possible "to achieve marriage within remote degrees by using simultaneously two simple formulas, each of which independently applied could lead only to different kinds of cross-cousin marriage." Héritier (1981) has applied these hints in her analysis of Samo society, and I shall consider them below, together with her work.

Lévi-Strauss's published contributions on this topic are largely confined to the Huxley Memorial Lecture, which reappeared in revised form as the preface to the second French edition of the *Elementary Structures* (1967) and the English translation (1969). His definition of Crow-Omaha systems has in the process undergone changes in phrasing. In 1966 (p. 19) he said they were those in which "whenever a descent line is picked up to provide a mate, all individuals belonging to that line are excluded from the range of potential mates for the first lineage, during a period covering several generations."

In the new preface the wording differs insignificantly, except that the English translators mistakenly give the definition a male bias not present in the original English or the French versions by rendering *conjoint* as "wife." "Each time Ego chooses a line from which to obtain a wife [*sic*], all its members are automatically excluded for several generations from among the spouses available to Ego's line" (1969, xxxviii).

This consequence, as he notes, is just the reverse of what occurs in a prescriptive society. In this latter kind, marriage initiates an alliance between lines. Repetition of this alliance is at least allowed. Commonly there is a strongly expressed approval of the repetition of marriage.

There are many obscurities about this definition. Lévi-Strauss derives it from the following description of the marriage rules of the Seniangs of Malekula by Deacon (1934, 132). "Theoretically . . . a man should not marry a woman belonging to a clan into which a man of his own group has married within living memory." Setting aside for the moment the great geographical distance between the Omahas and the Seniangs, the latter are still an extraordinary choice of a culture from which to draw a definition of Crow-Omaha systems. Lévi-Strauss claims that they belong to the Crow (i.e., matrilineal) type. Indeed, they do make the matrilineal equations concerning cross-cousins that have usually been taken as definitive for this type, namely FZ = FZD, F = FZS, BD = MBD, BS = MBS. Terminological features notwithstanding, Deacon's editor tells us that their *clans* are patrilineal. Perhaps Lévi-Strauss might defend his choice of example by commenting that he did not intend to explain the unusual features of Seniang sociology but wanted to take advantage of Deacon's convenient wording. Though we might easily concede so much, the Seniangs still appear strange in this context.

Lévi-Strauss after all is describing the workings of a certain kind of marriage rule in conjunction with a classificatory terminology. He frequently makes allusions to the correspondence between features of terminology and features of descent groups. The implicit assumption seems to be that the same rule of descent will obtain on both levels. Deacon specifies the clans restricted by the Seniangs, including that of the man's mother, "which regulation renders marriage with the mother's brother's daughter impossible." In a patrilineal system of descent groups M and MBD are natal members of the same clan, but not in a matrilineal system. In a matrilineal terminology, such as that of the Seniangs, they belong to different terminological lines. The result is that if the Seniang terminology is indeed ordered by a rule of matrilineal descent, then it cannot govern the marriage prohibitions.

Héritier (1976, 13) criticizes Lévi-Strauss's definition on the grounds that it does not account for lineage exogamy or the prohibition on a man's marrying women of his MM's lineage. She is concerned to compare the definition with the regulations of the Samos, some of which are similar to those of the Omahas. Just as his characterization does not account for all the lines forbidden to a Samo, it has nothing to say about several prohibited an Omaha, not only ego's own line and that of his MM, but also the subclans of his FMM or his MMM. Furthermore, the definition may be faulted (1976, 24; 1981, 78) because it suggests that marriages of lineage members of the opposite sex from ego have the same effect for him or her as marriages of members of his or her own sex. The definition thus permits the inference, for example, that if a man marries a woman from lineage *a*, his Z may not marry a man of lineage *a*.

Samo prohibitions, unlike Omaha ones, are stated only for men, but Héritier has demonstrated that Samo rules are in effect symmetric. As we have seen, in this regard the Omahas display a general, though imperfect, symmetry. Héritier shows (1976, 20; 1981, 89) that the parallel symmetry of Samo regulations does not imply a *symétrie croisée:* "If a man takes a wife in one lineage, nothing indicates that his sister could, or could *not*, take a husband in the same lineage." Among the Samos she can in fact do so; indeed, the Samos actually permit and practice direct exchange of sisters between two men. Samo prohibitions apply, however, only when marriages are contracted by relatives of the same sex as ego. This circumstance represents a serious discrepancy between the definition and Samo ethnography.

The Omahas in this respect are closer to Lévi-Strauss's definition. Omaha men may not marry women they call *itu´shpa*, nor may Omaha women marry *iti´go^n*. In consequence, men are prohibited ZHZ and women correspondingly are forbidden BWB. A man is also prohibited ZD, ZHBD, and ZHFBSD, while a woman is not allowed to marry BWF and BWBS. In each case Dorsey phrases the relevant prohibitions in reference to relationship terms rather than descent groups; so some uncertainty remains whether the entire descent lines of ZH and BW are excluded for men and women respectively. On the other hand, a man may not marry women of DH's, BDH's, or SDH's subclans, nor by terminological prohibition FZD, FFZD, FZSD, or FFZSD. Circumstantial evidence therefore is reasonably strong for the interpretation that Omaha men and women must keep an eye on marriages by opposite-sex lineage mates and that in this respect the definition accurately describes Omaha circumstances. Set against this conclusion is the ambiguity that remains about whether and when whole descent groups are concerned, the rather high frequency of direct exchange displayed in the genealogies, the fact that both men and women marry into FBW's groups, and the number of cases where B and Z married unrelated persons in the same subclan. So far as direct exchange is concerned, therefore, the Omahas not only do not worry about more distant members of their own group, they also care only when there is a close genealogical tie on both sides.

A major respect in which the Omahas contradict Lévi-Strauss's definition is through repetition of marriages, either by one man or by brothers or male parallel cousins. The Omahas give a man preemptive rights over sisters of the wife, and men of the same subclan and generation may marry into the same subclan. This situation, which has entered prominently into theoretical speculations about the Omahas, simply goes unnoticed in Lévi-Strauss's theory. It is in fact the most important single reason for thinking that Lévi-Strauss's speculations about Crow-Omaha systems have nothing at all to do with the Omahas, the Crows, or any other Siouan society.

The Samos, however, who exclude marriage with women of W's lineage as well as those of WM, WFM, and WMM, and who also prohibit marriage into the lineage of any W of any classificatory B, effectively prevent any immediate repetition of an alliance. In this respect they come much closer to Lévi-Strauss's definition of Omaha alliance than do the Omahas. The sociological differences between the Samos and the Omahas in this area are also crucial, and they provide one of several good reasons why the Samo arrangement should be called a Samo, not an Omaha, system of alliance (but see Héritier 1981, 99).

A point about the Omaha rules that has already been made by Héritier (1981, 104–5, 127) but deserves emphasis is that they exhibit not so much interest in unilineal descent as concern with cognatic kinship. Patrilineal descent is involved because the groups themselves are ordered by this principle. Nevertheless, the attachment is through filiation, traced to a comparable extent on either side. We might characterize the Omaha regulations by saying that they prohibit a male from marrying women in a lineage to whom he is tied by a direct line of filiation within living memory. Sometimes only women in families where there is a close genealogical tie are relevant, sometimes all women of a given subclan or clan must be avoided. This description leaves aside ties through what Morgan called collateral relatives, such as FB. It also accounts for most of the prohibitions deriving from marriages of persons younger than ego, with the exception of BSW's and BDH's subclans. The description, which is a modification of Levi-Strauss's definition, fits the Omaha facts better, but still incompletely.

Lévi-Strauss has written (1966, 18) that Radcliffe-Brown and Eggan have taught us that Crow-Omaha systems cannot be represented in a single drawing but require several diagrams, each corresponding to a narrow perspective view of the terminology. In fact, it has been the practice of American anthropologists to exhibit terminologies with more than one chart. Dorsey began the custom when he demonstrated Omaha terms by four genealogical trees, representing consanguineous relationships separately from affinal ones for both sexes. Dorsey did mention that many affines are addressed by consanguinity terms (1884, 253). His distinction in kinds of terms was therefore arbitrary and analytically prejudicial, insofar as he assumed that Omaha ideas of kinship correspond to our distinction between consanguinity and affinity and in his interpretation that certain terms were in their nature essentially words for consanguinity although also applied to affinal relationships.

By splitting the terms up Dorsey did manage a certain visual clarity; but there was no reason in principle why he should have had to do so. The complete Omaha terminology can easily be combined in a single two-dimensional chart (see inside back cover)—Whether the anthropologist does so is purely a question of convenience. Dorsey's diagram can be viewed as representing in two dimensions various lines of relatives distributed in three-dimensional space,[1] and perhaps this factor is the main point of Lévi-Strauss's comments; but by allowing himself a bit more room Dorsey could have managed to get the whole terminology into one figure without sacrificing this advantage.

Lévi-Strauss (1969, xxxvi) says that a satisfactory graphic representation cannot be achieved even within three dimensions, because as one generation follows another new lineages must be brought in through marriage, each requiring its own plane. For each lineage, he says, one man and one woman must be represented at each level;

for otherwise the model would not be in equilibrium. This last comment is perfectly true when speaking of a model of the effects of a given marriage regulation, but a diagram of a terminology requires no more positions than the ethnographers happen to have recorded. In any case there is no practical difficulty in meeting Lévi-Strauss's demands. For every new line required, room may be made simply by expanding the chart laterally, and these accommodations can be made with equal ease in a chart of the terminology or in a model of the marriage regulations. It is not even true that there is any great difficulty in producing such a representation on a single piece of paper. One merely needs a long enough sheet, or the chart may be reduced photographically to fit. If the technology is available, the anthropologist might well find some convenience in reproducing the terminology on several intersecting planes, perhaps made of translucent plastic, but for other purposes he might well prefer the two-dimensional drawing (compare Ruhemann 1967, 91).

Lévi-Strauss speaks of the many spatial dimensions involved, but here his phrasing is metaphorical; there is no reason to think that anything more than the ordinary three dimensions of space and one of time underlie Omaha kinship. Lévi-Strauss says that asymmetric marriage systems are tridimensional, apparently because a good way to represent closure in alliance cycles is to draw them around a cylinder, while he supposes Crow-Omaha systems to require more. He assumes that Crow-Omaha systems exhibit closure, but this assumption remains to be proved. The idea of closed cycles of alliance does not have the same utility in explaining each society with asymmetric alliance, for some explicitly avoid it. Even if we wished to assume closure in the Omaha pattern of marriage, we could still construct a model for it that showed the many intersecting lines in the three dimensions of everyday experience.

Lévi-Strauss further tells us that Crow-Omaha systems unfold through time and therefore require a dimension of time not found in asymmetric alliance. Here again the difference must be made clear between dimensions in the matter being represented and dimensions in the medium of representation. Lévi-Strauss argues that asymmetric systems are timeless whereas Crow-Omaha systems are historical, and that therefore the latter require a time dimension as well in the medium of representation. However, asymmetric systems are not timeless. They simply present a different interpretation of what should happen in time, namely that alliances should be continued and (at least in most such societies) renewed by repeated marriage as generations succeed each other. The claim that a representation of stability through time is the same thing as a denial of time is an entirely arbitrary interpretation. In fact, just this misinterpretation lies behind a common misunderstanding, which assumes that alliances in prescriptive societies work by a kind of inertia. The reality that is present to the people who live in such societies is quite different. Alliances may lapse or dwindle into insignificance through lack of attention, but where groups show an interest in maintaining them the quality of alliance is something they achieve by continuous application. If a man marries into a wife-giving group, raises a substantial bridewealth to give to his mother's lineage, organizes his wife-giver's funeral, or demands a substantial payment when his ZS does not marry his D, he is actually doing something about his alliance, and it seems out of place to accuse him at these moments of ignoring history. What is different between an asymmetric system and the Omaha system is not that one ignores time and the other affirms it. Both recognize the passage of time, but they have decided to organize the social consequences differently. Thus we can with equal justification say of both kinds of society, "for each generation, marriage choices are a function of those that have taken place within previous generations" (Lévi-Strauss 1966, 20).

A moving model of some kind, perhaps produced on a television screen by a computer, could well have advantages in showing how an Omaha descent group has found partners over a period of generations. Such a model, however, is no more necessary to the Omahas than to an asymmetric alliance community, and the advantages it might offer could equally well be exploited for a descent group practicing asymmetric alliance with a number of different wife-giving allies.

At each generation an Omaha family line does face a different pattern of groups into which marriage is permissible; so perhaps Lévi-Strauss is right to speak (1966, 19) of a "state of permanent turbulence." Certainly this state of affairs reverses the regular repetition and cyclical closure of the ideal model of asymmetric alliance.

Rather than its being true that in Omaha life history for the first time comes to the foreground (p. 20), what distinguishes the Omahas is that so far as marriage is concerned the present has a different relation to the past than in a conventional alliance model.

Lévi-Strauss offers another way of distinguishing elementary from Crow-Omaha systems (1969, xxxix; 1966, 19). They seek symmetric and inverse effects. An asymmetric system operates to change kin into affines, while a Crow-Omaha system changes affines into kin. Asymmetric alliance systems, according to Lévi-Strauss, make it either possible or compulsory for matrimonial alliances to be kept within the circle of kin. Crow-Omaha systems make it possible or compulsory for kinship and affinity to become mutually exclusive ties. Lévi-Strauss defines (1969, xxiii) elementary structures as follows:

Elementary structures of kinship are those systems in which the nomenclature permits the immediate determination of the circle of kin and that of affines, that is, those systems which prescribe marriage with a certain type of relative, or, alternatively, those which, while defining all members of the society as relatives, divide them into two categories, viz., possible spouses and prohibited spouses.

Obviously this definition is provisional and imprecise. No prescriptive terminology actually divides relatives into only the two categories of possible and prohibited spouses, since some relatives are of the same sex as ego and do not come into consideration as spouses. The phrase "systems which prescribe marriage with a certain type of relative" seems to mean they prescribe not a specific individual or a specific genealogical relative, but a relative who falls into a specific category in the terminology. Its ambiguity has brought about a large number of sometimes bitter polemic exchanges among those interested in alliance theory, and in his publications of the 1960s Lévi-Strauss used the idea of prescription loosely to cover a variety of not always strictly comparable practices.

Assuming as we always have that an asymmetric system counts as an elementary structure, we encounter a strange discrepancy between this definition and his comparison between asymmetric alliance and Crow-Omaha arrangements. The definition just quoted states that nomenclature in an elementary structure determines the circle of kin and that of affines—that is, sets them apart from each other—exactly what he later said distinguishes Crow-Omaha systems. Furthermore, the text of the preface to the first edition, from which the quotation comes, capitalizes on a linguistic distinction between being kin and being a relative; there both kin and affines are kinds of relatives. The second preface, however, *equates* being kin with being a relative and then sets being a relative off against being an affine. This muddle justifies the criticism made by Köbben, Verrips, and Brunt (1974, 216) that the terms kin and affine are ethnocentric.

The Hidatsas and the Omahas do have distinctive categories for some affinal relatives, but then so do prescriptive societies like the Purums, the Kachins, and the Kédangs. In any case, where there are native ideas that permit translation by the terms "kin" and "affine," a rule of descent-group exogamy is normally enough to secure the distinction in practice. A rule of descent-group endogamy, on the other hand, might be said to convert kin into affines.

In the village of Léuwayang in Kédang, Indonesia, where the formal structure of society corresponds to the model of asymmetric alliance, the patrilineal clans regard themselves as joined by legendary agnatic ties. In this sense agnates, so long as they are not within the clan, may be converted to affines. This way of stating the case amounts to no more than saying that the effective exogamous unit is the clan—a sociological observation of the kind that has long been commonplace. On the other hand, the rule of clan exogamy is strict, and no one may marry another person in his own clan. The Kédang alliance system does not convert members of the clan into affines, and Lévi-Strauss's word "kin" cannot here be translated as "agnates."

A more likely definition of kin is "genealogically related." Using this gloss, we might interpret Lévi-Strauss's generalizations to mean that the Kédangs expect matrimonial alliances to remain within a close circle of genealogical relatives, whereas for the Omahas genealogical relatives may never be married. Contrary to this expectation, among the Kédangs 31 percent of marriages are between genealogically unrelated individuals, while the remainder are often between individuals quite remotely related. The Kédangs might be exceptional in this respect, and their sociological features are very different from those supposed by Lévi-Strauss's original theory. Among the Emas of Timor, Indonesia, where alliance is expressed in terminology and also in strictly observed regulations for affinal alliances among named descent groups, 12 percent of marriages take place between unrelated persons. Furthermore, 79 percent of Ema marriages take place between a man and a woman selected from some wife-giving ally other than the clan of his own mother (Barnes 1978). The import of these figures may be open to debate. In my view they conform to the expectation that some percentage of marriages always establishes new relationships in such communities.

What is to be made in these cases of Lévi-Strauss's assertion that asymmetric alliance systems make it possible or compulsory for alliances to be kept within the circle of kin? If we fix merely on the possibility of doing so, we will discover no structural difference in this respect between prescriptive societies like the Emas, cognatic and endogamous cultures like the Ngadas of Flores, Indonesia, or the British, for that matter. If we place emphasis on the word "compulsory," then Lévi-Strauss's characterization is wrong for asymmetric prescriptive societies like the Kédangs, the Emas, and the Kachins of Burma. The best we can come up with is that there is a tendency in asymmetric societies for marriages to take place between genealogical relatives; but this generalization is also true of most small-scale communities whatever their form of social organization, including even the Samos and to some extent the Hidatsas and the Omahas.

Perhaps Lévi-Strauss was not attempting to isolate the diagnostic features of asymmetric social systems but was merely indicating a significant comparative difference between them and Crow-Omaha societies. Retaining our gloss on "kin" as genealogical relatives, let us examine the assertion that Crow-Omaha systems make it possible or compulsory for kinship and affinity to become mutually exclusive ties.

We will get nowhere by assuming that this proposition merely means that individuals may choose partners to whom they are unrelated because that happens in asymmetric societies too. The best interpretation is that such systems make it possible or compulsory for everyone without exception to marry nonrelatives; and in this version nothing important seems to hang on the difference between "possible" and "compulsory." The difficulty here is that it is a common report of even the Crows, the Hidatsas, the Omahas, and the Osages that members of these societies are typically related by a multiplicity of different kinship links; and some obtain between spouses. In any case, not even the Omahas try to ensure that there is *no* genealogical connection.

Where an alternative was present, the Hidatsas preferred to employ terms indicating (retaining for the moment this conventional distinction) consanguineal ties rather than ones indicating affinity (Bowers 1965, 99); but this does not mean that they did not marry genealogical relatives. Bowers (pp. 92, 103) writes that the Hidatsas considered every member of the tribe a relative (in some sense) and that marriage resulted either in the acquisition of an additional set of relatives or in alteration of the previous classification of relatives. What does happen with the Hidatsas or the Omahas is that relatives within a certain degree of connection may not marry; but restrictions on genealogical degree or kind can occur even within prescriptive societies.

Lévi-Strauss (1966, 19; 1969, xxxix) goes on from the statement just considered to say that, like elementary structures, Crow-Omaha systems frame marriage prohibitions in sociological terms, but like complex structures the nature of the alliance network is aleatory since the only conditions they lay down are negative. Again, his meaning is ambiguous or contradictory. If the Cherokees prefer marriage into FF's or MF's clan, with a relative in the category including GF and GM (Gilbert 1943, 238–45, 280, 310), and the Cherokees are a Crow-Omaha society, then some Crow-Omaha societies do not lay down only negative conditions. In a passage concerning the Seniangs already discussed above, Lévi-Strauss (1969, xxxvii–xxxviii) notes the Cherokee exception and writes, "It would be impossible to conclude from this [his discussion of the Seniangs] that all so-called Crow-Omaha systems necessarily refrain from issuing prescriptions or voicing marriage preferences." If we ignore the remark about negative conditions, then we can acknowledge that Lévi-Strauss is right that the Omaha marriage regulations are sociological institutions, but this generalization is also true of a great variety of societies that are neither elementary nor Crow-Omaha in type, and if we include regulations relating to class or occupation, then it is true of some industrial societies too.

Similar conclusions can be drawn regarding his claim that Crow-Omaha systems are like complex ones in that the actual pattern of marriage is aleatory—that is, probabilistic or resulting from chance. So stated, the characterization fits many kinds of society, including many kinds not considered by Lévi-Strauss; and there is a random aspect for marriages even within elementary structures, as has already been shown and as Lévi-Strauss acknowledged when he wrote (1969, xxiii) that there is no absolute elementary structure "because only exceptionally can a system ultimately determine one sole individual as the prescribed spouse." Elementary structures merely determine the class of relatives to marry, which often is very large, so that there is always some freedom of choice, whereas there is never complete freedom of choice in complex structures. Furthermore (p. xxiv), "elementary and complex structures thus cannot be wholly contrasted, and the line separating them is difficult to define." The foregoing criteria do not therefore clearly establish the difference between elementary and complex structures and consequently cannot specify what is distinctive about some intermediary variety like Crow-Omaha alliance.

Lévi-Strauss's characterizations have a rather rough and ready aspect, like those of a man who is just beginning to settle down to some serious work. In fact, his original writings about elementary structures contain two incompatible definitions, quoted above. One implies that what is essential is the presence of a terminology that prescribes a category of persons who alone may be married. This interpretation was taken up by Needham in *Structure and Sentiment* (1962) and by Korn (1973, 19), who claims that this single, decisive criterion does not permit a third type between elementary and complex. The second definition, however, is the one that Lévi-Strauss has increasingly employed in subsequent decades. It is linked with the notion that an ideal form of prescription would determine absolutely the specific individual, a misunderstanding already exposed in the nineteenth century (for example, by Thompson 1895) for the very reason given by Lévi-Strauss—that the social classification specifies only a class, not individuals. Nevertheless, by use of this alternative criterion we might, as Lévi-Strauss seems to do, presuppose a continuum of societies whose structures are closer to or further from approximating it. What remains uncertain is whether the Omahas occupy any place on this continuum.

Although the presence of sociologically framed marriage rules is not exclusive to elementary structures and to the Omahas, this feature does provide a point of comparison between them, especially if, as Lévi-Strauss prefers to do, we speak about abstracted models for these rules. In such models, but not in any practical interpretation of them, the difference between category and genealogically defined person can be made to disappear. The purpose of positive systems is to predetermine, either by category or by group, the source of the spouse. At these levels the determination of marriage partner is the opposite of a completely random procedure. The Omahas provide certain restrictions on the field, leaving choice otherwise open. So much remains uncontested of Lévi-Strauss's generalizations about elementary, Crow-Omaha, and complex systems.

In 1969 (p. xxxvi) Lévi-Strauss's main characterization of Crow-Omaha systems was as follows. They are

systems which only set up preventions to marriage, but apply them so widely through constraints inherent in their kinship nomenclature that, because of the relatively small populations, consisting of no more than a few thousand persons, it might be possible to obtain the converse, viz., a system of unconscious prescriptions which would reproduce exactly and in full the contours of the mould formed by the system of conscious prohibitions.

Apparently, then, elementary systems are those with overt positive marriage rules, Crow-Omaha systems are those with explicit negative rules, and complex societies are those with no conscious regulations beyond the incest prohibition. In this case there would be two criteria involved, each dividing the three types at a different point: presence of overt regulations, whether positive or negative, and presence of a positive or a negative rule. There are difficulties in trying to reconcile this classification with Lévi-Strauss's own statements. In the passage quoted, Lévi-Strauss attempts to reassimilate Crow-Omaha societies to elementary ones on the grounds that their public prohibitions lead to unconscious prescriptions. On the other hand, prescriptive societies may very well have categorically framed prohibitions, such as those that distinguish asymmetric from symmetric prescriptions. As we have seen, Lévi-Strauss expressly declares that he does not mean Crow-Omaha societies may not have overt positive rules. By 1966 Lévi-Strauss no longer recognizes the distinction between preference and prescription, except as a difference in the degree to which people follow the rule. Therefore the presence of a positive rule, even though publicly recognized, does not in itself distinguish elementary structures from Crow-Omaha structures. The accumulated effect of all of these considerations is that the criteria proposed do not in the long run distinguish elementary from Crow-Omaha systems, as can be seen in table 19. Lévi-Strauss appears to be saying that Crow-Omaha societies tend toward the simplicity of prescriptive societies without ever fully achieving it. So Crow-Omaha systems are imperfect elementary structures that may have no positive rules, covert positive rules, or even overt positive rules.

Whatever may be made of Lévi-Strauss's views on the "Crow-Omaha" type, the Omahas themselves have no overt positive rules. Whether they have unconscious prescriptions remains to be seen. Despite the criticisms his theory has sustained, Lévi-Strauss has left us with an interesting hypothesis—that there may well be structures whose compounded prohibitions amount to an implicit prescription of some kind. Two independent studies have attempted to test this hypothesis: Gell's study of the Umedas and Héritier's of the Samos. Both authors conclude that the societies they are concerned

Table 19. Marriage Rules in Different Types of Society According to Lévi-Strauss

	overt	covert
positive	Elementary, some Crow-Omaha	Crow-Omaha
negative	Crow-Omaha, elementary, complex	

with do not fit the model in various ways, but both claim to have confirmed Lévi-Strauss's hypothesis.

What has so far been lacking from Lévi-Strauss is a thorough description of his model, that is, an explanation of how a society exemplifying his extreme definition would arrive at a covert prescription. To explicate this model the author would have to say for once precisely what he means by prescription—whether he is speaking of a categorical prescription in a relationship terminology, of a genealogical prescription, or merely of constraint to marry a given named individual.

The Umedas of the West Sepik District of New Guinea have patrilineal clans linked by ties of "perpetual alliance," the conditions of which exclude the possibility of further marriage (in subsequent generations) between them (Gell 1975, 50, 53). The ways the Umedas differ from the Omahas are important: their relationship terminology is unlike that of the Omahas, they practice sister exchange, their prohibitions are differently phrased, and of course the political and economic organization is entirely different. Gell argues in fact (p. 67) that the Umedas are a better instance of an intermediary type between elementary and complex systems than are the Crows or Omahas.

The details of his captivating analysis may be left aside here. Gell feels that the Umedas exemplify unconscious prescriptions resulting not from positive injunctions to marry kin but from the operation of negative rules within an extremely restricted marital universe (1975, 75–76). What he refers to is the fact that the Umedas are aware of the possibility of a cyclical return of women by means of reclassifying certain remote relatives so that they cease to be treated as old allies and can therefore again provide wives. The cycles, however, though known as a possibility to the Umedas, are not linked to preferential marriage (with genealogical kin) and do not commit the Umedas to any institutionalized marriage choices. The cycles are "not an institution but an interpretation" (p. 74), and at that an interpretation that the Umedas and their ethnographer must reject as an explanation of their society. Gell says there is no categorical prescription, and he shows that determination of a genealogically defined mate is not a regular result of the Umeda system. The only other interpretation is selection of a named individual, but Gell writes (p. 74) that the Umedas have "no motive for singling out specific partners when reopening exchange relationships with a group of quondam allies."

The Samos of Upper Volta more closely approximate Lévi-Strauss's definition. On the basis of an impressive genealogical record, Héritier has prepared a series of formal studies as well as computer tests. The Samos are probably the most thoroughly known example we will have for some time of how an elaborate system of prohibitions affects actual marriages. They have a non-prescriptive relationship terminology with patrilineal features, agnatic descent, patrivirilocal residence, patrilineal inheritance and succession, and patrilineal lineages, but *no* clans. Their villages are localized and divided into lineages. They have three forms of union, all of which have to obey the marriage rules. Unlike those of the Omahas, these strictly prevent any repetition of marriages between groups but are even more extensive, going back to ego's W's group's own wife-providing groups. Between 60 and 75 percent of marriages were into the village, which may be thought surprising considering the nature of the prohibitions and the frequent practice of polygyny (Héritier 1976, 26–27; 1981, 105–6). Héritier is able to show too that, with insignificant deviations, the Samos obey their rules.

Having established these results, Héritier seeks to prove that they imply there are particular strategies and implicit alliance structures to be discovered, turning upon a preference for marriage between persons whose parents were prohibited from forming an alliance. This criterion implies a preference for marriage among those consanguineously related persons who happen not to be prohibited spouses. Another way of saying it is "there is a preference to marry a blood relative if you can." Some 43 percent at least of marriages were with one or another kind of genealogical relative (1976, 36). Héritier (1976, 37) thinks this figure allows her to say there are preferential unions, which there may well be. Her results satisfy her that Lévi-Strauss was right in supposing that an elaborate system of prohibitions would produce a structure. If she is correct in her interpretation, the Samos may at best be said to practice preferential marriage, but by no definition are they prescriptive, since many dif-

ferent kinds of genealogical connections, and only such connections, are involved. Lévi-Strauss did speculate that the implicit
structure would consist in the plural in "prescriptions"; the best
interpretation of this phrasing would be that he meant not a prescription of some kind, but preferences like those Héritier has in
mind. She has not shown that either the preferences or the practical
frequency with which they are observed result logically and empirically from the prohibitions. There is a marked preference for
village endogamy, which is strongly qualified by the elaborate prohibitions, so that a Samo may marry any of the many kinsmen of
various degrees who are left over. Héritier offers an admirable study
of the effects of the rules, but she gives neither an explanation of
their existence or purpose nor a confirmation of Lévi-Strauss's theory, unless it is given such a mild interpretation as to be entirely
uncontroversial and correspondingly less interesting. Neither Gell
nor Héritier has shown unconscious prescriptions to exist by any of
the alternative definitions of that term. This negative conclusion by
no means constitutes a judgment on the value of their analyses or
on the broader results of their attempts to test Lévi-Strauss's
hypothesis.

Since the Omaha terminology is not a prescriptive one, we must
find some other interpretation of the word "prescription" in order
to see if Lévi-Strauss's hypothesis has any bearing on them. In the
first place, we may consider the possibility that Omaha rules, given
some practical interpretation, combine with the actual number of
marriage groups to leave only one open to an ego. Lévi-Strauss
(1966, 19) writes, "All Crow-Omaha systems have more than four
descent lines: seven among the Cherokee, ten among the Omaha,
thirteen among the Crow." There are ten named major descent
groups among the Omahas, five in each moiety; but for marriage
purposes these are of very unequal standing. Each of course is exogamous, but, as has been seen, beyond that they have quite various kinds of importance for sociological purposes. Empirically, for
those rules specifying subclans, the number of marriage groups was
not ten or forty-four, as in Dorsey's pedantic model, but twenty-
three (eleven in the first moiety and twelve in the second). These
subdivisions were not of equal consequence for all of the rules,

some of which, being linked not to formal groups but to family connections, depended upon the much larger number of effectively independent family lines.

The discussion of Omaha descent groups in an earlier chapter moved from the simple generality of a model—that of Dorsey and of some Omahas—toward the confused particularities of the practical historical and sociological situation. The shift has brought about further movement away from the assumptions of Lévi-Strauss's hypothesis. At the same time the shift has been toward recovering the practical complexities and flexibility of Omaha reality—the context in which individual choices were made. These choices were of course constrained by institutional considerations, but these constraints were not uniform, and they were not likely to be absolute restrictions on freedom.

A man selecting his first wife, or having her selected for him, if his relatives' memories are good, may find that besides the two entire clans of his father and of his mother, the following subclans are also closed: those of FM, FMM, MM, and MMM. Dorsey's illustration of the prohibitions for Two Crows and Two Crows's S and SS raises the possibility that the subclans of FFM and even FFFM and FFMM might be restricted. Since, however, he says these limitations depend on memory, they too may be left aside. The result is that for a first marriage a man is prohibited two clans and a minimum of four other subclans, as well a variety of women specified by category or genealogical connection.

If ego is On the Left Side, clan exogamy removes the four subclans of that clan from his pool of potential suppliers of his wife. If his M were a Deer Head or Flashing Eyes, four more subclans would be removed, so that the total number of restricted subclans would amount to twelve. This figure would still leave him eleven open clans or subclans within the tribe. Three Omaha clans are not subdivided. If ego and his M both belonged to one or the other of these groups, only six marriage groups would be restricted to him, leaving seventeen from which to select a wife. If we computed limits of an extreme example, such as the plight of Two Crows's grandson, to whom Dorsey awarded the accumulated prohibitions of the F and FF, were his parents and grandparents to be living and meddlesome, then the remaining marriage groups would be between eight and fourteen. The conclusion is that in no way would a man find his choice of first spouse limited to a single descent group, even in the reduced circumstances of population during the previous century.

Regarding second and subsequent marriages, a man may not marry women in the subclans of SW, BSW, SSW, DSW, DH, BDH, SDH, and DDH. Here demographic factors come into play, for there is no way to determine without reference to genealogies how many sons, brother's sons, and so on a man has and into how many subclans these persons have married. Let us set as a minimum (quite arbitrarily of course, since for a given person this number could be too high) that each of the genealogical specifications above represents a separate subclan, and that each of these subclans would be separate from those already prohibited in the first marriage. This pair of assumptions would give us eight additional subclans withdrawn from the pool of possible providers of wives. When these eight are added to the figures above they leave between zero and nine lines open.

The object has been to simulate a situation where only one line was left open. If no group is left, or if more than one remains free, then either Lévi-Strauss's hypothesis is wrong for the Omahas or it should not be interpreted to refer to actual descent groups. We can easily add assumptions to increase the number of groups that are forbidden, but we should consider the following points. First, we are already talking only about secondary marriages. Second, some of the assumptions we have already made run counter to the informants' report that the number of groups prohibited depends on memory and on the chance of whether a relative of a certain kind is still living. Third, as we add assumptions we decrease the chances that the results will be uniform for all possible individuals. A certain combination of assumptions could make it impossible for some men to marry while leaving several groups open for others. Fourth, the kinds of additional assumptions necessary to limit choice to one line are no different from the kinds that would guarantee that a man taking a second wife must marry outside the tribe.

This survey provides no useful interpretation of the idea of a hidden prescription or, as yet, of preferences in Héritier's sense. The possibility has not been eliminated that, entirely by chance, an individual looking for a second or subsequent wife might find himself with only a single Omaha woman available to him. This possibility does not justify speaking of a prescription, nor is it a characteristic of a special kind of system. If this consequence was all that was meant in the first place, then there was never any reason not to say quite simply that the happenstances of demography coupled with an unusually rigorous application of the avoidances of connections previously established might leave some men with little or no choice when seeking a second wife.

Another way to check whether specific descent groups emerged as implicitly prescribed, or preferred, would be to check for cases where men married into subclans that had provided women a generation before ego's prohibitions were in effect. The Omaha restriction on the groups of M and FM may be read as limiting marriage into the groups of FW and FFW. Assuming that the restrictions stop at that generation, we would, for example, look for marriages into the subclan of FFFW (FFM). This enticing possibility is untestable empirically because for almost all men there is no way to discover the subclan of their FFM. The Omahas seem usually not to know this connection; so such a preference would hardly constitute a conscious strategy. Ambiguities in Dorsey's example from Two Crows's family suggest that if the tie were known that knowledge would constitute a bar to marriage. The same arguments hold if we look further back.

At Lévi-Strauss's request (1969, xl), Bernard Jaulin computed the permitted varieties of possible marriages in Crow-Omaha societies with only two or three prohibited lineages. Lévi-Strauss does not explain all the assumptions that lay behind this test, but the results ranged between 20,000 and nearly 300,000,000—figures quite out of proportion to the actual size of the populations. On the grounds that these numbers represent a predetermined field within which the small numbers of actual marriages range randomly, Lévi-Strauss writes (p. xli), "a very strict nomenclature and negative rules which operate mechanically combine with two types of chance, one distributive, the other selective, to produce a network of alliances, the properties of which are unknown." These remarks properly belong to problems in applying computer technology to artificially constructed genealogical data and are therefore well away from the anthropological task of interpreting empirical cultural systems. Nevertheless, if these numbers mean what is claimed for them, they tend to confirm that, though the Omaha rules remove a relative large number of persons from the pool of mates, they also leave many in it. Seen in a certain way, no doubt the Omaha system does reveal, as Lévi-Strauss asserts, "a compromise between the periodicity of [models of] elementary structures and their own determinism which relates to probability." There is also no doubt that "individual choices always preserve a certain latitude which is inherent to the system."

Nevertheless, Lévi-Strauss proposes a possible interpretation that, despite its aleatory appearance, a system like that of the Omahas "returns on itself periodically in such a way that, taking any initial state whatsoever, after a few generations a structure of a certain type must necessarily emerge." One way to explore this possibility is to ignore the implications for ego's level in the original definition and to disregard for the moment any empirical test. A system may be proposed in which ego may not marry into the lines from which men of F's and FF's generation have taken women, leaving open lines from which FFF's level have done so. Looking for a prescription, we might experiment with a structure entailing marriage into the same line as the one where FFF took his wife.

Such a structure is theoretically possible, using a rule to marry a woman in the position of the FFMBSSD. Lévi-Strauss attributes closure to Crow-Omaha marriage systems, though there is no empirical evidence of such closure among the Omahas. A diagram of the proposed rule is asymmetric, but if the feature of closure is incorporated the model tends to reveal symmetric traits. When diagrammed for four lines and closure, the rule involves reversals of direction, and, although men at each level may marry FFMBSSD, that position may also include FZD, FFZSD, or FFZSSD. Six lines, on the other hand, involve one generation in direct sister exchange, but this procedure is prohibited for the Omahas. Closure involves conflicts with Omaha prohibitions in one way or another for four, five, or six lines. These may be avoided only with seven lines. Similar incongruities tend to occur in models of FFFMSSSD marriage involving closure. These difficulties disappear if closure does not occur, and since there is no reason to incorporate closure into our models, if desired it may be left out. The result of dispensing with it is that we lose part of the potential of such systems and must specify that closure does not take place or does so only beyond a specified number of lines (perhaps six).

The Omaha terminology can be plotted against a model of some such prescriptive arrangement, for example, a model for FFMBSDD marriage (in this case corresponding also to MFZSD) using seven lines and closure. A striking result is the frequency with which several terms coincide at particular positions. This redundancy can be reduced to some extent by doing away with closure, as in a model designed for thirteen lines, but even here much overlapping remains, with as many as four terms for one position. Most serious is that in both versions the terms for D can be employed for persons in the structural position of the W.

If the Omahas were to exhibit a FFMBSSD prescription interpreted as meaning marriage with women of a specific group, identified through the terminology, and the lines in the model were taken to be descent groups (specifically subclans) rather than merely terminological lines, we would expect the combination of Omaha prohibitions to leave only one line from which ego could select a spouse, but in fact women classed as marriageable are found in more than one line. The Omahas give a man the special right to a WZ, WFZ, or WBD, and it is an important defect of the models under consideration that the position of W and WZ coincides with women called by the same term as D. The regulations combined with these prescriptive models do at once too much and too little. They leave women available from more than one line while seeming to exclude those women who are most appropriate. The models combined with the Omaha relationship terminology also fail in another interpretation of prescription—that is, they do not limit choice to a single genealogical kinsman.

A model that sets the prescription back a generation—that is, one based on marriage into the position containing FFMBSSD— arrives at the same results. There seems little point in testing further outlandish hypothetical models of prescriptive marriage. Not only does the Omaha terminology not contain a prescribed category, it does not lead to an implicit prescription. The terminology and rules do not have the effect of prescribing, or even producing a preference for specific descent groups, nor do they produce genealogically defined prescriptions.[2] The only respect in which the idea of preference is relevant is the express Omaha preference that a man's second marriages be in the category $iho^n\acute{g}a$ (WZ, WFZ, WBD, etc.), a fact that has been well known since Dorsey and that was the focus of Kohler's analysis.

10: Dispersed Alliance

Robert McKinley (1971a,b) has elaborated a theory of Crow-Omaha relationship terminologies by reference to what he calls "dispersed affinal alliance." This theory derives from the writings by Lévi-Strauss just reviewed and develops somewhat beyond them. I have published (Barnes 1976) a critique of McKinley's hypothesis from a comparative point of view. We diverge in particular on his assumptions that there is a worldwide class that may be called "Crow-Omaha terminologies" and that the peoples he refers to have a common system deserving the name "dispersed alliance." These comparative matters are less relevant here than the question whether he has succeeded in explaining the Omahas themselves. Since his speculations were formed with reference to that group in particular, it is possible that it works best for them.

The hypothesis states broadly (McKinley 1971b, 411) that, under certain special conditions, Crow or Omaha terminologies provide "some significant ideological advantage." The advantage is that they help resolve a basic contradiction in the structural make-up of the society. McKinley lists the following four elements of the Omaha "complex."

1. Exogamous unilineal descent groups.
2. Dispersed affinal alliance.
3. A strong emphasis on maintaining alliance between groups once linked by marriage.
4. A concept of tribal completeness.

McKinley's minimal definition (1971*b*, 412) of dispersed alliance is as follows: "The pattern which I call dispersed alliance might be expressed by a prohibition against marrying into one's mother's descent group in a patrilineal society, or by a prohibition against marrying into one's father's descent group in a matrilineal society."

The concept of tribal completeness implies that the political organization approximates an independent tribe, district, or region with a number of clans. The clans are well known throughout the community, and the community as a whole, not individual clans, fights wars. McKinley holds the concept of tribal completeness to be important because it provides a context for association between intermarrying descent groups and thus conduces through this association to the establishment of a broad basis of attachment between separate unilineal groups. This basis of attachment conditions the effects of dispersed alliance, for it allows relationships to be extended to the entire lineage or clan. McKinley claims (1971*b*, 414) that "Exogamous unilineal descent groups are an essential precondition because they are the units which would be involved in a system of dispersed alliance." In fact, not all prescriptive societies have lineal descent groups, and they are not a precondition to prescriptive alliance (Barnes 1976, 388). The Omaha descent groups enter into marriage considerations in a variety of ways, so caution should be maintained on this score.

McKinley argues (1971*b*, 413) that his criteria of dispersed alliance and emphasis on maintaining alliance are at odds with each other. The ideology of dispersed alliance prevents the renewal of established alliances and requires the contracting of new ones. The desire to maintain them once they are established entails that they be kept up in one way or another. This situation leads to a discrepancy. Exogamous units are pulled in two directions at once, for they want to initiate as many new bonds as possible and yet retain their old ones as well as they can. Since the device of contracting a new marriage is not available for refreshing standing ties, the descent groups must find new resorts, of which there are two. They may simply introduce extensive ritual and economic links. The second recourse is to be found in the kinship terminology, which, through extensive cross-generational equations in the line of the parent who is not in ego's own group, holds on to the alliance initiated by the marriage of the parents. Generation, McKinley says, is held constant by these equations, and the time dimension frozen; in this way a relationship that is weakened by the passage of time and that is "generationally ephemeral" is kept intact by the deft illusion manufactured by a collective sleight of tongue. The same features of nomenclature also allow complementary filiation to be extended to the entire descent group (pp. 413–14).

McKinley distinguishes two factors in his notion of dispersed alliance: alliance groups will attempt to scatter alliances among a large number of other units; and each unit will "attempt to avoid marriages which repeat alliances that were made in the previous generation" (p. 411). As it happens, there are also societies with prescriptive classifications that nevertheless have subsidiary conventions ensuring that alliances will be well scattered (Barnes 1976, 389). The second matter, that repeated alliances are avoided, is then the essential characteristic of dispersed alliance. The phrasing (McKinley 1971b, 411) "each unit will attempt to avoid" is deceptively weak. What is actually at issue is a rule *absolutely* prohibiting such repetition within a given degree. Of course no such rule is compatible with prescriptive alliance or with a positive form of affinal alliance. Nevertheless, modern studies have shown that in some prescriptive societies—for example, in Sri Lanka, in South India, and among the Karo Bataks and Kédangs—direct repetition is infrequent or, in the latter two instances, actually very unusual (cf. Köbben, Verrips, and Brunt 1974, 221). There may be an ideology favoring repetition, and there may in some cases be certain sanctions encouraging repetition, but the facts prove that individuals in these societies are not forced to do so. If even societies with prescriptive terminologies can get along quite well without repeating alliances, then there is evidently no necessity for societies that do not repeat alliances to adopt Crow-Omaha terminologies. Only unqualified injunctions therefore make McKinley's hypothesis interesting.

In a prescriptive society affinal alliance is to be distinguished from the categorical prescription to which it is in some respects comparable. The latter is a structuring principle linking terminological lines (see Needham 1973b, 174–75, 177, 179). Affinal alliance is an ideologically defined relationship linking collectivities.

These collectivities may or may not have identifiable boundaries, and they may or may not be corporate in some sense. We have come to call such collectivities alliance groups, even though the word "group" invites misunderstanding. The likewise analytic notion of an alliance group may be applied to various kinds of collectivity in different contexts in the same society (see Barnes 1980a, 90–91); all that matters is the various features that make up the definition of alliance in a given society and the different contexts in which various of these features are called into play.

In a prescriptive society, marriage is only one property, if a crucial one, among those that define alliance. It typically involves a somewhat different collection of persons from those who are concerned with the other constitutive factors in the culturally given definition of alliance, such as the giving of bridewealth, the performance of funerals, mutual assistance, and many other obligations or rights. What is of chief importance about marriage is that it initiates a relationship with widespread consequences for a great range of persons. The other duties and privileges entailed by alliances typically continue for several generations, even when marriage is not repeated. There is no particular sense, in these cases, in which one would say that the alliance has weakened or become fictional. It is simply that certain others of its features have come to the fore.

As for the suggested contradiction, everything here turns upon the definition of alliance given by a particular society. In those that do not permit the repetition of marriage, presumably such repetition is not an element in their definition of alliance. This fact does not, though, imply that the other aspects of the alliance must go into abeyance or that the members of such societies are in any way left "to face the problem of how to maintain previous alliances in the absence of renewing marriages" (McKinley 1971b, 413). They may simply maintain them with no sense of problem whatsoever. It is of course possible that in a given society an inherent or explicitly recognized contradiction may exist between the cultural definition of alliance and the desire to hold on to old alliances while establishing new ones, but McKinley has given us no reason to assume in advance that such a contradiction is present. McKinley (pp. 418–19) adduces the familiar evidence showing that the Omahas did, at least within a certain range, cultivate their alliances through gifts, widow remarriage, and special ties, including complementary filiation, with the mother's descent group. He does not, however, show evidence that they felt any sense of contradiction between these activities and the marriage rules. Each of the practices McKinley refers to happens to be in comfortable conformity with the fact that only men of the same generation may repeat marriages. The postulated contradiction seems not to have been a feature of Omaha sociology.

McKinley affirms that the purported contradiction in attitudes toward alliance may be overcome either by establishing extensive ritual and economic ties—which is, then, merely a question of the cultural definition of alliance—or by the use of kinship terminology. The terminology makes a positive ideological contribution by "fabricating an ideal sort of social bond." Members of societies whose rules forbid the repetition of alliance are thus able to deceive themselves into thinking that these alliances are in fact maintained by use of a "convenient fiction" allowing them to ignore the passage of time (1971a, 244–45; 1971b, 414). This fiction is the presence of matrilineal equations in the father's line for a matrilineal terminology or patrilineal equations in the mother's line in a patrilineal one. These equations are said to hold on to the original alliance, to lump together members of different genealogical levels in that line, to hold generation constant, and to freeze the time dimension.

The presumption that time is frozen in these terminologies derives from Lévi-Strauss, who suggested, in two papers originally published in 1953 (1963, 67–80, 277–323; 1953a,b), that Crow-Omaha systems require several different models of time. Lévi-Strauss speaks of an "empty" time in those lines where the same term is retained for members of successive generations, but a progressive time in those lines where there is a new term at each genealogical level and an undulating, cyclical time in those lines where the same term recurs in alternating levels (1963, 301–2). All these different kinds of time are exhibited in the same terminology!

This view of relationship nomenclatures has the drawback that it makes the interpretation of the representations of time directly dependent upon superficial aspects of the categories; analysis is not oriented toward underlying principles or properties and thus is not carried on at a different level from the empirical diversity in terminological equations. Consequently, a small shift in the application of terms requires the recognition of a new variety of time. Since the equations found in a social classification vary not only internally among the different descent lines, but often in at least minor ways from community to community within the same society, Lévi-Strauss's interpretation commits the anthropologist to recognizing an unlimited number of different kinds of time within the same set of collective representations. He has been taken up on this point by J. A. Barnes (1971a, 541; 1971b, 121–22) and criticized because his designations for different kinds of time are analytically redundant. Lévi-Strauss has not shown that there really is any question of different kinds of time; nor has he given us any good reason to suppose that more than one attitude toward time is implied throughout the terminology. In any case, the use of the same word for successive positions in a descent line indicates neither an empty nor a frozen time, as will be evident from the following observations about the recognition of the passing of generations.

In the Omaha nomenclature one term, $iho^{n\prime}$ (when used by the child $i^{n\prime}no^{n}ha$), is applied to all women of the mother's line. Two terms, however, are applied to the men of that line (see Barnes 1975b); for while MB, MBS, MBSS, and their further male descendants are called $ine\prime gi$, MF and MFF are $iti\prime go^{n}$. This last is the same term applied to all men of the second ascending genealogical level and above, including FF and FFF. The crucial line for Mc-Kinley's purposes does not correspond to his hypothesis among the Omahas. We have to go a step further among the Omahas to find a line that does so—that is, to the MM line, where all men and women are referred to by the terms otherwise used for the second ascending genealogical level.

Such equations do not, as a matter of fact, allow, as McKinley asserts (1971b, 412, 414), the extension of complementary filiation to the point where it takes in entire descent groups. The absence of Crow-Omaha equations has never been any obstacle to involving entire lines in, for example, the obligations of marriages, as is shown in a conclusive way by the Jinghpaw system (Leach 1961). Distinct terms are used at each level in the all-important line of the wife-givers, but this situation does not hinder them in any way in maintaining their ties. If the view that their absence is an obstacle were correct, we would then be compelled to acknowledge that among the Omahas complementary filiation is not so extensively found in the mother's line, with its two terms for men, as it is in that of MM, where only one term is used. Complementary filiation would then increase in strength with the distance of the genealogical connection—a very novel use of the idea of filiation. Cross-generational equations neither help nor hinder the recognition of the connection of complementary filiation or of any other kind of ties or obligations other than a principle of lineal descent.

It may be doubted, though, that such equations really do hold generation constant or ignore the passing of generations. The first consideration is that some lines, as just seen, do employ different terms at different genealogical levels, so that they cannot be said to ignore absolutely the passing of generations in McKinley's sense. More significantly, it can be held that cross-generational equations imply a comment about the succession of generations that takes their passage as its premise.

The view that cross-generational equations ignore the succession of generations derives from a failure to distinguish properly between lines in a terminology and empirical lineages. McKinley's theory seems to entail that members of one lineage would continue to call those of another lineage by the same term generation after generation, once a marriage had taken place connecting them, even though no further marriage took place. This situation would occur in some prescriptive societies such as the Kédangs or the Purums, which make not only the appropriate patrilineal equations but also specific affinal equations ensuring that the categorical relationship will be inherited regardless of whether marriage continues with the same lineage. It is precisely the absence of this specific pattern of affinal equations that marks the Crows and the Omahas off from prescriptive societies.

McKinley's position may be interpreted in this way. If ego marries into a lineage, his son and grandson will pretend that they retain the same relation to that lineage, even though they marry elsewhere, and they will call members of that lineage by the same term that ego employs in order to maintain this fiction.

This interpretation implies that men of lineage A in figure 16 use the same term for men of lineage B without a change of generation

A   B

$$\begin{array}{c} \text{Ego} \ \triangle = \bigcirc \quad \triangle \\ \text{S} \ \triangle \qquad\quad \triangle \\ \text{SS} \ \triangle \qquad\quad \triangle \end{array}$$

Figure 16. Marriage between lineages.

in either lineage leading to a change in term. The nature of alliance, however, will change in each case. The psychological meaning of the term will change in each case too. For ego the term will be correct. For his son it will be a fiction. For his son's son it will be a fiction of a fiction.

Among the Omahas, ego would call the men of lineage B in figure 16 *ita´hoⁿ*. McKinley's argument implies that his son and son's son would call them *ita´hoⁿ* as well. Let us see what in fact happens. Figure 17 demonstrates that ego's son ("ego b") calls the three men of lineage B not *ita´hoⁿ* (e.g., brother-in-law) but *ine´gi* (e.g., MB). This is the famous Omaha set of equations (MB = MBS = MBSS). Ego's son's son ("ego c"), on the other hand, calls the same three men *iti´goⁿ*—the same term he uses for FF and MF.

In other words, the terms that lineage A applies to lineage B change at each generation. We can see, then, that the terminological features McKinley hopes to explain cannot possibly be accounted for in the way he has chosen, because generation, as the examples above show, is not held constant. The passing of generations is not ignored; on the contrary, it is emphasized by the use of the terminology. An Omaha could not help noticing that a given set of men or women are addressed differently by various members of his own

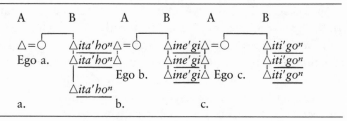

Figure 17. Wife-giving lineages and Omaha categories.

lineage and that this variation in the use of terms corresponds to generation and to the changing nature of the tie instituted by marriage.

Time cannot therefore be said to stand still, and the time dimension is in no way frozen. A different term is actually applied to a given lineage by successive generations, thus implying an affirmation of the passage of time. Consequently the use of the Omaha terminology cannot be said to lend permanence or stability to interlineage relationships; it does not provide a "convenient fiction" for covering up the fact that the nature of the ties entailed by a marriage changes with each generation, nor does it work to prevent groups from drifting apart. Rather, the workings of the Omaha terminology may be said to make it explicit that the relationship between lineages changes with time. If there is a correspondence between terminology and the dispersal of alliance, it is to be found in the fact that a designated lineage is given a different terminological position by successive generations. The illusion that generation is ignored or that time is in any way stopped is the result of the analyst's failure to draw the consequences from the analytic distinction to be made between descent lines in a social classification and empirical descent groups.

McKinley's theory endeavors to explain a set of common terminological features involving cross-cousins, and in his selection of cousin terms he continues an anthropological tradition, if a mistaken one. Omaha equations are found among the Gilyaks, the Purums, and—in a recently reported case—the Kédangs, all of which have asymmetric prescriptions (Barnes 1975b). Lévi-Strauss argued as long ago as 1949, and has since reiterated, that Crow-Omaha systems are not to be identified with prescriptive ones on the mere coincidence of cousin terms (1969, 372; 1966b, 19; Needham 1969, 153–66). If the kind of extensive cross-generation equations McKinley is seeking to explain are frequently and perhaps even typically found in terminologies of asymmetric prescriptive alliance, then those equations cannot be accounted for by dispersed alliance.

The traditional focus on cousin terms was in any case misdirected. Lineal terminologies may make few or no equations at all between genealogical levels. Conversely, some—the terminology of the Omahas is a case in point—exhibit a multitude of such features.

Nomenclatures that in most ways are identical and that are organized according to corresponding principles may be expected to differ from one another in a number of particulars of lesser or greater importance. It is sometimes in precisely those categories including cousins that terminologies of the same sociological character distinguish themselves most strikingly. The Purums and the Kachins both have asymmetric categorical prescriptions; but while the Purums use a single term for all the men of mother's line (thus effecting a series of patrilineal equations of an even greater extent than is made by the Omahas in the corresponding line), the Jinghpaw system reserves a separate term for each level except for the second and third descending. Only in the line of wife-givers of wife-givers does one find among the Kachins a single term for all males. Despite these differences, both systems are ordered by patrilineal descent and asymmetric alliance—two crucial comparative similarities that would be passed over by placing one of them in a category of Omaha societies while excluding the other. On the other hand, systems that coincidentally share the same distribution of cousins among their categories may otherwise be of a radically different nature.

Taken by themselves, so-called cousin terms are no interpretive guide. They provide clues to analysis only when put in the context of a total system; but in that context they constitute no unusually rich source of information. There is no reason to fix on the distribution of a given set of genealogically defined relatives, such as cousins, to the exclusion of the profusion of other diagnostically revealing equations and distinctions to be found in a social classification (Barnes 1975a, 54, 63–65).

11: Conclusion

Other authors have tried to link the Omahas to asymmetric marriage rules in various ways. Faron (1956, 1961) interprets "Omaha" (patrilineal) patterns in Mapuche terminology as coinciding with the introduction of MBD and WBD marriage. The Lanes (1959) claim that Omaha terminologies are associated with matrilateral cross-cousin marriage. They propose, in fact, that Dakota terminology (which is generally symmetric, makes some distinctions compatible with lineage exogamy, and lacks patrilineal or matrilineal equations) is associated with symmetric marriage exchange and transforms itself into Crow or Omaha systems in conjunction with asymmetric first cross-cousin marriages. Eyde and Postal (1961) adopt the Lanes' hypothesis, placing emphasis on the additional fact that in Omaha systems sisters marry into the same lineage. Acknowledging that the Omahas prohibit cross-cousin marriage, they suggest that in advanced forms such marriages eventually become prohibited, at first only for first cousins. They suggest that many societies preventing first cousin marriages prefer marriage with second or third cousins in the same lineage as MBD.

Each of these inferences confuses the important difference between the Omaha and asymmetric alliance systems, but the main objection to them is that there is no evidence whatever that the Omahas ever practiced cross-cousin marriage. The Dakotas also prohibited marriage with first cross-cousins. Indeed, of the ten cultures using languages of the Siouan family for whom the relevant information is available, only one even permits first cross-cousin marriage, the matrilineal Mandans, who prefer marriage with the MBD (see table 20). Murdock (1967) lists the patrilineal Winnebagos as permitting bilateral cross-cousin marriage, apparently on inference from their exogamous moieties. His source, Radin (1923), nowhere says that this is the case, and there is no other evidence for it.

Gifford (1916) attempted to explain the complicated and difficult Miwok ethnography as resulting from a shift from WBD marriage to MBD marriage. Moore (1963) has modified this position, arguing more generally that in a patrilineal Omaha system, if a son takes his father's place in marriage arrangements a preference for WBD can change to an asymmetric cross-cousin marriage rule (see also Lucich 1968). Murdock (1949, 123) and Lévi-Strauss (1969, 361–63) object to explaining terminologies by secondary and therefore infrequent forms of marriage, though Moore's hypothesis, unlike Gifford's, does not attempt to explain terminology. Lévi-Strauss (1963, 64, 66) has also objected to treating the Miwok terminology as though it were in the same class as the Omaha. The relevance of these arguments to the Omahas lies largely in the fact that they reverse the direction of change from that postulated by Eyde and Postal and by the Lanes. Since we have no way of knowing what some future state of Omaha society would have been, we can expect no gain in knowledge about them by further consideration of these speculations. None of these theories explains the actual state of Omaha society at the time the ethnographies of the tribe were made, nor do they relate Omaha society to the actual state of other Siouan societies at the same period.

The time has come to focus more closely upon the ethnological context of Omaha culture, the restricted geographical area of shared historical and ethnological links that Eggan (1954) and Evans-Pritchard (1965) have argued are the most advantageous for controlled comparison. In this case the district of immediate interest comprises the northern Great Plains and the neighboring woodlands of the Middle West, where several of the plains tribes lived before they moved west. The languages represented belong to either the Siouan or the Algonkian family (ignoring Pawnee and other Caddoan-speaking groups on the southern and western periphery). Except the Mandans, all groups for which evidence is available,

Table 20. Siouan Marriage Rules Involving Cousins

Marriage Forbidden with First or Second Cousins	Marriage Forbidden with First Cousins, Evidence Available Only for First Cousins	Matrilateral Cross-Cousin Marriage Permitted
Assiniboins		
	Crows	
	Hidatsas	
		Mandans
Omahas		
	Osages[a]	
	Otos	
	Poncas	
	Santees	
	Tetons	

Source: Murdock (1967).　[a]According to Nett (1952).

irrespective of the nature of descent, prohibit marriages with close cross-relatives. It appears therefore that these prohibitions themselves ought to be treated as a common ethnological set. When they vary, they vary as do other aspects of the culture, in ways that accommodate differences in institutions affected by rules of unilineal descent or by the absence of such rules. In all cases, however, there is a general bilateral distribution of prohibitions, which, where the facts are known, invariably include as a minimum restrictions on marriage between men and women who share a common grandparent.[1] Possibly even second cousins and more remote relatives were always prohibited, though this supposition cannot be proved.

There is little or no evidence in historical times of a shift from prescribed, preferred, or permitted cross-cousin marriage rules to this present pattern within the immediate district of comparison.

One of two conclusions therefore may be reasonably reached. Either the tribes adopted the marriage restrictions by the beginning of the historical period through borrowing from some internal or external source, or else the regulations derive from some ancient ancestral tribal organization.

Eggan (1937b, 93) proposed a classification of Great Plains terminologies, the principal division of which was between those societies that make equations only within each genealogical level, as is the case with the Cheyennes, Kiowa-Apaches, Dakotas or Piegans, and those displaying terminological lines through equations between levels, or in the older jargon those that "override the generation principle." The latter category manifests itself in two forms: the Omaha or patrilineal variety and the Crow or matrilineal kind. Many anthropologists have argued on various grounds that the unilineal arrangements derive from the symmetric "Dakota" form. As indicated by Lowie (1915), the Dakotas made distinctions and equations that would fit exogamous descent groups, though most such peoples lacked corporate unilineages or clans. For this reason Lesser (1930, 571) took the position that if the Crow and Omaha social patterns derived from that of the Dakotas, then the exogamous institutions must have developed later.

Rivers (1914, 49–55) first suggested that the Dakota system itself derives from bilateral cross-cousin marriage. Since the Dakota terminology does not conform to such a rule and the Dakotas actually prohibit cousin marriage, Eggan (1937b, 95; 1955) recast the hypothesis as a theory about some previous stage of Dakota society that has changed. There are some equations in Dakota terminologies (in the medial and first ascending levels) that would be compatible with a symmetric marriage prescription and direct exchange of wives (MB = FZH, FZ = MBW, MBS = FZS, and so on). These indications do not, however, carry through consistently in the level of ego's children. Lesser (1930, 564) writes that his unpublished evidence shows that the Teton Dakota terms for cross-cousins derive from those for brother- and sister-in-law, taking the additional suffix ci (see also Hassrick 1944, 344). Walker (1914, 96) says the suffix indicates that marriage may not take place. In the central three levels, these terminologies lack further equations of the appropriate kind. They preponderantly deviate from the symmetric prescriptive and even the unilineal models. The shape of these terminologies, however, is quite in keeping with the standard that "a man could not marry any girl with whom he had a common grandparent" (Hassrick 1944, 339).

The evidence permits the hypothesis that an ancestral Siouan terminology was, like the Dakota terminology, generally symmetric, compatible with exogamous lineages, but lacking any pronounced bias toward matriliny or patriliny and above all devoid of any explicit marriage prescription. Such a hypothetical form might or might not represent a deterioration of a previous system of marriage prescription and symmetric marriage alliance. As is evident, this hypothesis bears comparison with several of its predecessors, and like them it suffers from the lack of direct proof. In any event, the contrast between the "generational" Dakotas and the "lineal" Crows and Omahas carries through a number of institutions in addition to the classification of relatives. For example, when a Dakota man took additional wives, he married by preference the sisters of his first wife (Hassrick 1944, 339), whereas an Omaha would turn as well to the WFZ and WBD, women within her patrilineal descent group whom the Dakotas would have assigned to different terminological levels. The Omaha marriage prohibitions also display a lineal application lacking among the Dakotas. The hypothesis as stated permits us to regard this sequence of contrasts as representing concomitant transformations presumably occurring simultaneously and pointing in the same direction.[2]

Surveying evidence presented by Strong (1929), Hallowell (1928, 1930), and others, Eggan (1955, 536–51; 1966, 85–111) notes the possibility that northern Algonkian peoples practice cross-cousin marriage. In his interpretation, a range of North American groupings of differing language families once possessed what today would be called symmetric prescriptive systems with bilateral cross-cousin marriage. Several of the Algonkian, Ojibwa, and Dakota groups then adopted rules forbidding marriage with relatives (among the Santees or eastern Dakotas any relative closer than fourth cousins). The social classifications then made distinctions in keeping with the new attitudes. For the Dakota groups, the purpose of these regulations is to ensure that marriage takes place outside of the exogamous, cognatic bands or hamlets. Eggan (1937b, 95) also suggests that an influence in favor of these changes may have been contact with more cognatically organized plains peoples such as the Cheyennes and Arapahos.

A comprehensive demonstration of the existence of symmetric prescriptive marriage systems in North America, as distinct from recorded instances of bilateral first cross-cousin marriage, remains to be made. The early papers by Strong and Hallowell are too incomplete to prove their point. Such systems do not require unilineal descent groups but can be maintained on a basis of cognatic groups, and systems of the appropriate kind are known from South America. Recent studies have shown how easily the symmetric terminologies of Gê tribes can be modulated by the same speaker to express a matrilineal or patrilineal bias (Da Matta 1979, 122; Maybury-Lewis 1979, 239–41). The Dakota system might well be subject to the same flexibility, and Fox (1967, 140) has even argued that "There is absolutely no reason why Crow, generational and many other 'types' of usage should not sit side by side in the same system." Eggan suggests (1966, 65), in fact, that the Crows used their matrilineally biased terminology in reference but shifted to a "generation" or Dakota model in address. Whether or not the Omahas may once have practiced cross-cousin marriage, perhaps in conjunction with exogamous moieties, such a pattern would belong to a remote period. The Omaha structure as we know it requires a different explanation by reference to the nonprescriptive, symmetric Dakota variety. Omaha marriage rules are part of a broadly shared cognatic theme in Siouan sociology (cf. Héritier 1981, 104–5). They coexist with, and in their expression are modified by, the patrilineal Omaha institutions. They do no more than restrict marriage among known, remembered relatives. There is no evidence that they give rise to any implicit prescription, or even any unstated genealogical preference.

The Omahas have attracted anthropological speculation of various kinds as much for their acquired academic fame as for the intrinsic suitability of the ethnography. In consequence, anthropological writing occasionally gives the impression that we know a good deal more about them than we do. The Omahas are associated with unilineal principles. As time has gone by, anthropologists have produced more and generally better studies of unilineal institutions. Some anthropologists have incautiously assumed that our knowledge of the Omahas has correspondingly advanced, perhaps mistakenly taking it for granted that what is true of one unilineal society is true of another. As it happens, earlier writers' speculations about the Omahas frequently are more accurate than those of later authors because they were closer to the ethnographic facts. Another factor perhaps has been a tendency to draw the balance on the basis of published reports alone, inferring that what they do not contain can no longer be discovered.

The place of the Omahas in anthropological theory poses two problems of a kind that appear whenever anthropologists turn from description to comparison. Is the Omaha ethnography good enough to test theories made up about the tribe? Can the anthropologist test these theories without committing himself to becoming at least as expert in Omaha language and culture as the ethnographers? Numerous disagreements between the ethnographers suggest that their reports are inadequate. In many respects, though, this study has shown that the evidence available permits a more conclusive check than might be thought. Though points of fact remain in doubt, in many instances the grounds for disagreement can be discovered. Despite the very plain differences in style and preoccupations of the ethnographers, which sometimes lead to conflicting pictures of Omaha culture, the basic features of that culture nevertheless come through in all reports. The personalities of the ethnographers may act as a filter, but, especially where there are independent reporters, ethnographic facts impose themselves sufficiently to prove that the facts are not merely the imaginative creations of the anthropologist.

Omaha Sociology and *The Omaha Tribe* are classics not just because they appeared at a favorable time. They were drawn into the mainstream of anthropological advancement because of their merits. Whereas *Omaha Sociology* remains of interest primarily because of its description of Omaha terminology and marriage rules, *The Omaha Tribe* excels in the richness of its general coverage. If the latter can be viewed, as some have claimed, as an elaboration of *Omaha Sociology,* then Dorsey's book can also be seen as an elaboration of its predecessors, particularly Morgan and the collection of reports on basic Omaha social organization in James's account of S. H. Long's expedition to the Rocky Mountains. They would, how-

ever, today remain rather lifeless books had they not been extensively supplemented by further writings, both published and
unpublished, by La Flesche, Fletcher, Dorsey, Mead, Fortune, and
others. This study is certainly not the only one that might result
from looking again at the Omaha literature. Understanding of the
place of the Omahas in anthropology would be enhanced by similar
investigations of adjacent, particularly Siouan, peoples. A history of
the Omahas in the nineteenth century is desirable. Perhaps the most
rewarding project would be a reanalysis of Omaha society from the
point of view of Omaha religion.

Further advancement on many Omaha topics probably *will* require working knowledge of Omaha language, though lack of such
capacity should not be accepted as a reason for ignoring what is
already known. More widely conceived comparative studies would
do well to stop taking the Omahas as standing for a representative
type, whether of terminology, descent, or alliance. A more complex
picture doing justice to the systematic differences within a set of
linguistically and ethnologically related peoples of the northern
Great Plains and midwestern woodlands, would be more instructive
for students of similar themes in other regions. *Omaha Sociology*
was published in 1884. It was neither the first nor the last important
Omaha text, yet in this book we have looked back on a hundred
years of analytic progress initiated in large measure in its pages and
associated in anthropological convention with the people it describes. The analytic impact of Dorsey's monograph shows that
Durkheim was right in underlining the revolutionary importance of
ethnography to social anthropological understanding.

Notes

INTRODUCTION

1 National Anthropological Archives, box 30 (4558 [101]), A. C. Fletcher's trip from Omaha to South Dakota, 1881.

2 Preserved in the National Anthropological Archives 4558, item 72, no. 2, Omaha tribal roll and catalog of land ownership.

3 Partch to Lowrie, 13 October 1883, Nebraska State Historical Society, Presbyterian Board of Foreign Missions, film MS2683, roll 1, series 2, Correspondence, 1880–83, Homer W. Partch. Fletcher describes the hardships of her work on the allotment in chapter 11 of *Life among the Omahas*, National Anthropological Archives 4558, item 65. This work is soon to be published by the University of Nebraska Press, edited by Joanna C. Scherer.

4 Francis married Alice Mitchell, daughter of Washu´she or Henry Mitchell of the Black Shoulder Pipe subclan on 26 June 1877 (*Vindicator*, Decatur, Nebraska, vol. 1, no. 1—in the Green Collection, Nebraska State Historical Society). She died in 1878 (Dorsey 1890*a*, 692). He then married Alice La Flesche (Solomon), daughter of Little Prairie Chicken or Horace Cline, Black Bear subclan, On the Left Side clan, in August 1879. He divorced her in 1884 on grounds of infidelity, and she later married Sioux Solomon, brother of Two Crows. Green's confusion of these two women (1969, 178) is understandable. Francis later married and (in 1908) divorced Rosa Bourassa, a half-Chippewa. She later settled on First Street, SE, in Washington, D.C., a few hundred feet from the home of Alice Fletcher and Francis La Flesche (Green 1969, 179–82).

5 Dorsey to La Flesche, 8 June 1894; La Flesche to Dorsey, 8 June 1894;

and Dorsey to La Flesche, 14 June 1894, National Anthropological Archives, 4800 Dorsey Papers, General Correspondence.

6 A treaty of peace and friendship between the United States and the Otoe tribe . . . (26 December 1817), *Nebraska History* 5, 2:26. Letter of 19 May 1840, Jos. V. Hamilton to Joshua Pilcher, National Archives, microcopy M234, roll 215, Council Bluffs Agency, 1836–43.

7 Life of Joseph La Flesche Told by Wajapa, 2 September 1900, National Anthropological Archives, Fletcher, Alice C., and Francis La Flesche 4558, item 69, Omaha ethnography, no. 3.

8 National Archives, microcopy M234, roll 217, Council Bluffs Agency, 1847–51.

9 "Big Elk adopted Jos. with the understanding that Jos. was not to succeed Big Elk if his boy lived, but the lad died." Wajepa, March 1906, National Anthropological Archives, Fletcher, Alice C., and Francis La Flesche, 4556, item 69, no. 5. Notes regarding Wajapa, Joseph La Flesche, Big Elk, and other Omahas. Also Life History of Joseph La Flesche, in the same place, no. 3.

10 Wajepa, Life of Joseph La Flesche, 2 September 1900. Logan was one of several children of Lucien Fontenelle, of a distinguished New Orleans French family. De Smet baptized Lucien's four children and his wife in 1838. De Smet says that Logan's mother was the daughter of the elder Big Elk. He is, however, the only source of this story (Chittenden and Richardson 1905, 4:1532). Gilmore (1919) attempted to prove that Logan had never been a principal chief, but there is contrary evidence that he did not consider; see this volume, chapter 1.

La Flesche family papers relate that Sarpy named Logan head chief at the time the Omaha party went to Washington in 1853 in order to recover through him $10,000 the Omahas owed Sarpy. The ensuing dispute almost resulted in tragedy when Logan approached Joseph with a gun. Joseph's wife disarmed him, and later the two men exchanged horses (Life History of Joseph La Flesche). Oglala Sioux killed Logan in July 1855 while he was picking gooseberries in a ravine of the stream later named Logan Creek after him.

11 Hamilton to Lowrie, 2 September 1856, and Hamilton to Lowrie, 2 February 1857, Nebraska State Historical Society, Presbyterian Board of Foreign Missions, film MS2683, roll 2, series 1, Correspondence and Reports, 1846–86.

12 Furnas to Taylor, 30 December 1865, and Furnas to Taylor, 28 February 1866, National Archives, microcopy M234, roll 605, Letters, Omaha Agency, 1864–70. Furnas to Lowrie 29 July 1866, ibid.

13 Life History of Joseph La Flesche. Story of Joseph La Flesche from Mary, 1 September 1900. National Anthropological Archives, Fletcher, Alice C., and Francis La Flesche 4558, item 69, Omaha ethnography, no. 3. Statement on the Families of Joseph and Mary La Flesche . . . from Dr. Picotte's Journal, Nebraska State Historical Society, Norma Kidd Green Collection, series 6, box 2, folder 1.

14 National Anthropological Archives, 4800 Dorsey Papers, Omaha (3.2.1.1 [206]), Omaha genealogies, arranged by gens and subgens. This contains only part of the tribe, but the rest are found in 4800 Dorsey Papers (3.2.1.2 [212]), Ponca genealogies. This is mislabeled, since only a small part of the genealogies, those of the Wajaje Real Osage and Wajaje Qude subclans, are Ponca. Also of interest is 4800 Dorsey Papers Omaha-Ponca (155), Notes on Dhagiha genealogies; and two letters from George Miller to Dorsey, Omaha Agency, Nebraska, 5 November and 9 December 1889.

Fortune (1932, 14) refers to his own Omaha genealogies and publishes one. In a letter of 12 July 1978 he wrote to me, "I doubt that I have more genealogies than I published. In any case, I have none to hand; and if I collected more I am sure that I might search for months without result." After his death his papers were deposited in the Alexander Turnbull Library (the New Zealand National Library), Wellington, New Zealand. In a letter of 16 April 1982 Dr. Michael E. Hoare, head of Manuscripts Section of the Turnbull Library, wrote, "There is no material specifically on genealogies although there are some notes on vocabulary and some material on Omaha Secret Societies relating to Fortune's published work. The amount of Omaha material in relation to Fortune's other areas of interest is thus disappointingly small." Access to the Fortune collection is at the discretion of the chief librarian with special permission of certain designated anthropological experts in special areas of sensitivity. The Omaha material is one such area. I thank Professor Ralph Bulmer, Fortune's niece Mrs. Ann McLean, and Dr. Hoare for their assistance.

Part 2 of Margaret Mead's study of the Omahas (1932) contains a great deal of information dating from 1930 about Omaha families, unidentified by name or descent group. Her papers have recently been deposited in the Library of Congress, but those relating to the Omahas had not been made available to the public at the time of my visit in 1982. Apparently they contain little genealogical information pertaining to the nineteenth century.

15 Nebraska State Historical Society, roll RG 530. Court of Claims, Gener-

al Archives Division, National Archives, Omaha Tribe of Indians, part 1, docket sect. no. 1, Depositions of Ellis Blackbird, etc.

1. CHIEFTAINSHIP

1 A more elaborate version of this tale may be found in Bradbury (1904–7, 85). Bibaud (1848, 271–74) repeats and much embroiders several of the stories about Blackbird. His account is full of inaccuracies. Washington Irving (1836, 171–76) retails similar stories.

2 Some additional names appear on treaties, but we do not know what order they belonged to, or even whether they were actually chiefs rather than warriors.

3 Letter from Dougherty to Harris, November 1837, National Archives, Letters Received, microcopy M234, roll 215, Council Bluffs Agency, 1836–43. See also Smith 1974, 94.

4 Letter from Miller to Mitchell, 25 January 1844, ibid., 1844–46, microcopy M234, roll 216.

5 Notebooks (2) on Joseph La Flesche and Wajapa, National Anthropological Archives 4558, item 69.

6 Fletcher and La Flesche (1911, 205) mention "the death of the son of old Big Elk, who died of small pox in the early part of the nineteenth century." He was not the second Big Elk and might be the Iron Eye in question.

7 La Flesche family papers give another name, In´gthuⁿhoⁿgasha (Night Thunder), for this son. Life History of Joseph La Flesche. A Joseph Elk attended mission school in 1858. Denvers from Sturgis, 1 January 1858, Nebraska State Historical Society, Presbyterian Board of Foreign Missions, film MS2683, roll 2.

8 Manypenny to Hepner, 8 November 1854, National Archives, Letters Received, microcopy M234, roll 218, Council Bluffs Agency, 1852–57.

9 Hepner to Cummings, 27 December 1854, ibid.

10 Barrow to Mitchell, 15 January 1851, and Barrow to Mitchell, 8 April 1852, ibid., 1847–51 and 1852–57, rolls 217 and 218.

11 Hepner to Cumming, 4 August 1855. In September 1855 Joseph La Flesche gave a speech in council in which he referred to the loss of "our Great Chief Logan Fontenelle." Speeches of the Omaha tribe . . . , Left by Sarpy, recorded by L. B. Kinney, 12 September 1855, ibid., roll 218.

12 "He had been a member, with Joseph [La Flesche], of the last delegation to go to Washington . . . and took Joseph's place as chief until the confused position was abolished in 1880" (Green 1969, 34).

13 O'Shea (1981, 41) attributes a "weakly defined system of hereditary ranking" to the Omahas and says their "petty hierarchy" was reflected in burial practices.

2. THE TRIBAL CIRCLE

1 In their paper of 1903 on primitive classification, when only Dorsey's writings were available, Durkheim and Mauss had written (1963, 57–58) of the Omahas, "Clans and things are oriented, not yet according to the cardinal points, but with reference to the centre of the camp. The divisions do not correspond to the quarters properly speaking, but to ahead and behind, right and left, with respect to this central point." "In order to appreciate how little the orientation of the clans is determined by relation to the cardinal points, it is enough to realize that it changes completely according to whether the route followed by the tribe goes from north to south, or west to east, or the other way." The Omahas did designate the cardinal points by the phrases "toward the cold," "toward the coming of the sun," "toward the heat," and "toward where the sun has gone." They also expressed skyward and earthward (Fletcher and La Flesche 1911, 111). See Needham (1963, xiii–iv).

2 The same is confirmed by Dorsey (1897, 233–34).

3 Mauss (1913, 105) identifies a conflict between Dorsey's translation of Hon´ga as meaning "ancestral" or "foremost" and Fletcher's rendering "leader," but there is no reason why all three English words should not be accurate translations.

4 "We have no record of Omaha ritualism of right and left connected with the moieties" (Fortune 1932, 15).

5 "In mixed society, not in camp circle, women sat to the left, men to the right. But a left side man in terms of the camp circle, belonged to the Sky or male moiety" (Fortune 1932, 15).

6 Compare Lloyd (1966, 162) for observations on two ways contraries may permit intermediates.

7 Needham (1980, 51) has reversed Aristotle's definitions of contradictories and contraries, and he has also asserted that contradictories pertain only to propositions. The correct definitions are given by Lloyd (1966, 162) and Lyons (1977, 272).

8 Dumont's choice of the word "identical" rather than the expectable "equivalent to" or "stands for" raises large issues, but they would lead us astray if we pursued them here.

3. DESCENT GROUPS

1 "An important event always occurs four times in any Omaha record of past events" (Fortune 1932, 38).
2 Notes on Dhegiha genealogies, National Anthropological Archives, 4800 Dorsey Papers, item 155.
3 Another marginal note on the genealogies says that Gashka'wongthe calls Little Buffalo Horns *dadiha* or father, though Little Buffalo Horns was in fact the younger man.

4. PERSONAL NAMES

1 The doctrine originated by J. F. McLennan of an early universal stage of human society in which persons associated in groups bound together through the common worship of a plant or animal (see Goldenweiser 1910; Lévi-Strauss 1962).
2 A Comparative List of Omaha and Ponka Proper Names, Omaha and Ponca Personal Names, National Anthropological Archives, 4800 Dorsey Papers.

5. RELATIONSHIP TERMINOLOGY

1 Dorsey to Lucy Sammis, 6 April 1883, and Lucy La Flesche to Dorsey, 9 April 1883, National Anthropological Archives, 4800 Dorsey Papers. Lucy was married to Gray Cottonwood or Noah, whose English surname shifted from Leaming to Sammis to La Flesche.
2 I agree with Scheffler (1982, 174) that there are practical limits to this predictive potential.

6. TERMINOLOGY AND MARRIAGE

1 Among these twenty-one men only ten were currently married to women in the same subclan (FZ/BD 4; Zs 3; FBDs 1). These figures of course reflect only the information that has chanced to survive in the available documents.
2 Marginal note, Omaha genealogies.
3 Françoise Héritier published through 1968 under the surname Izard, for a time thereafter as Héritier-Izard, and more recently as Héritier.
4 "Meanwhile the old people, depending entirely upon the Indian names and cognizant of each individual genealogy, are still on the alert for

incest which the young people are not properly equipped to avoid" (Mead 1932, 80).

5 Miller to Dorsey, 25 November 1889, and Miller to Dorsey, 9 December 1889, National Anthropological Archives, 4800 Dorsey Papers, item 155. Two letters from George Miller to Dorsey.

7. MARRIAGE, RESIDENCE, AND KINSHIP

1 Painter to Janney, 16 August 1869, 17 December 1869, and 27 December 1871, National Archives, microcopy M234, roll 605, Letters, Omaha Agency, 1864–70.

8. THE PATTERN OF MARRIAGE

1 Héritier (1981, 98) infers, incorrectly as it happens, that Two Crows's daughter and brother both married into the same subclan. Elsewhere (Barnes 1982b, 117) I show that they did not.

9. "OMAHA ALLIANCE"

1 This virtue of Dorsey's chart was pointed out to me by Professor Lévi-Strauss when I showed him that the complete terminology can be put into a two-dimensional figure.

2 Ackerman's (1976) fantastic attempt to discover unilateral marriage among the Omahas depends on forcing the fact that a man is *permitted* to marry into the clans, but *not* subclans, of FM, MM, and FMM into an injunction to do so. There is no basis in the ethnography for this construction. His figures 2 and 4 are drawn for repeated marriage between lines, which the Omahas make impossible by forbidding marriage into M's clan. His figure 3 overlooks the numerous cases of direct exchange among not only clans, but also subclans.

11. CONCLUSION

1 The known exception is the Mandans. Ambiguities in Lowie's evidence leave open the possibility that Crow men were permitted to marry into their father's matriclans, though Lowie seems to have concluded that they were not (see Barnes 1976, 386).

2 On the basis of eastern Dakota ethnography, Howard (1979) speculates that patrilineally organized Siouan peoples may once have had patrilineally biased exogamous villages that later became authentic patrilineal clans consolidated into a single village.

Bibliography

Aberle, D. F. 1974. Historical reconstruction and its explanatory role in comparative ethnology: A study in method. In *Comparative studies by Harold E. Driver and essays in his honor.* New Haven: Human Relations Area Files Press.

Ackerman, Charles. 1976. Omaha and "Omaha." *American Ethnologist* 3, 4:555–72.

Alexander, Hartley B. 1933. Francis La Flesche. *American Anthropologist* 35:328–31.

[Anonymous]. 1912. *Review* of Fletcher and La Flesche, *The Omaha tribe.* *American Historical Review* 17:634–36.

Bangs, S. D. 1887. History of Sarpy County. *Transactions and Reports of the Nebraska State Historical Society* 2:293–306.

Barnes, J. A. 1971a. Time flies like an arrow. *Man* 6:537–52.

——. 1971b. *Three styles in the study of kinship.* London: Tavistock.

Barnes, R. H. 1975a. Editor's introduction to Josef Kohler, *On the prehistory of marriage: Totemism, group marriage, mother right.* Chicago: University of Chicago Press.

——. 1975b. Elementary and complex structures. Letter in *Man* 10:472–73.

——. 1976. Dispersed alliance and the prohibition of marriage: Reconsideration of McKinley's explanation of Crow-Omaha terminologies. *Man* 11:384–99.

——. 1978. Injunction and illusion: Segmentation and choice in prescriptive systems. *Anthropology* 2, 1:19–30.

——. 1980a. Hidatsa personal names: An interpretation. *Plains Anthropologist* 25, 90:311–31.

——. 1980b. Concordance, structure and variation: Considerations of alliance in Kédang. In *The flow of life: Essays on eastern Indonesia*, ed. James J. Fox. Cambridge: Harvard University Press.

———. 1982*a*. Personal names and social classification. In *Semantic anthropology*, ed. David Parkin. Association of Social Anthropologists Monograph 22. London: Academic Press.

———. 1982*b*. Review of Françoise Héritier, *L'exercice de la parenté*. *Culture* 2, 2:113–18.

Bibaud, F. M. Maximilien. 1848. *Biographie des Sagamos illustrés de l'Amérique septentrionale*. Montreal: Lovell and Gibson.

Bowden, Ross D. 1977. *The Kwoma: A study of terminology and marriage alliance in a Sepik River society*. Ph.D. thesis, Monash University, Clayton, Australia.

Bowers, Alfred W. 1950. *Mandan social and ceremonial organization*. Chicago: University of Chicago Press.

———. 1965. *Hidatsa social and ceremonial organization*. Bulletin 194, Bureau of American Ethnology. Washington, D.C.: Government Printing Office.

Bradbury, John. 1904–7. Travels in the interior of America, 1809–1811. In *Early western travels*, ed. Reuben G. Thwaites, vol. 5. Cleveland: Clark (first published London, 1819).

Brooke-Rose, Christine. 1958. *A grammar of metaphor*. London: Secker and Warburg.

Buchler, Ira R. 1966. Measuring the development of kinship terminologies: Scalogram and transformational accounts of Omaha-type systems. *Bijdragen Tot de Taal-, Land- en Volkenkunde* 122, 1:36–63.

Buchler, Ira R., and Henry A. Selby. 1968. *Kinship and social organization*. New York: Macmillan.

Catlin, George. 1841. *The manners, customs and condition of the North American Indian*, vol. 2. London: Egyptian Hall.

Chittenden, Hiram Martin, and Alfred Talbot Richardson. 1905. *Life, letters and travels of Father Pierre-Jean De Smet S.J., 1801–1873*. 4 vols. New York: Harper.

Cooke, P. St. G. 1859. *Scenes and adventures in the army*. Philadelphia: Lindsay and Blakiston.

Coult, A. D. 1962. The determinants of differential cross-cousin marriage. *Man* 62, 47:34–37.

———. 1963. Causality and cross-sex prohibitions. *American Anthropologist* 65, 2:266–77.

———. 1967. Lineage solidarity, transformational analysis and the meaning of kinship terminologies. *Man* 2, 1:26–47.

Da Matta, Roberto. 1979. The Apinayé relationship system: Terminology and ideology. In *Dialectical societies,* ed. David Maybury-Lewis. Cambridge: Harvard University Press.

Deacon, A. B. 1934. *Malekula: A vanishing people in the New Hebrides,* ed. Camilla H. Wedgwood. London: Routledge.

Donaldson, Thomas. 1886. The George Catlin Indian Gallery in the United States National Museum (Smithsonian Institution). *Smithsonian Institution Annual Report for 1885, pt. 2.* Washington, D.C.: Government Printing Office.

Dorsey, James Owen. n.d. Omaha and Ponca personal names [typescript]. National Anthropological Archives, Washington, D.C.

————. 1884. *Omaha sociology.* Third Annual Report of the Bureau of Ethnology (1881–82). Washington, D.C.: Government Printing Office.

————. 1886. Indian personal names. *Proceedings of the American Association for the Advancement of Science* 34:393–99.

————. 1889. Omaha folk-lore notes. *Journal of American Folk-Lore* 2:190.

————. 1890a. *The Çegiha language.* Contributions to North American Ethnology, vol. 6. Washington, D.C.: Government Printing Office.

————. 1890b. Indian personal names. *American Anthropologist* 3:263–68.

————. 1891. *Omaha and Ponka letters.* Bulletin of the Bureau of Ethnology, no. 11. Washington, D.C.: Government Printing Office.

————. 1894. *A study of Siouan cults.* Annual Reports of the Bureau of American Ethnology, vol. 11 (1889–90). Washington, D.C.: Government Printing Office.

————. 1897. *Siouan sociology.* Annual Reports of the Bureau of American Ethnology, vol. 15 (1893–94). Washington, D.C.: Government Printing Office.

Dumont, Louis. 1953. The Dravidian kinship terminology as an expression of marriage. *Man* 53, 54:34–39.

————. 1961. Marriage in India: The present state of the question. *Contributions to Indian Sociology* 5:75–95.

————. 1979. The anthropological community and ideology. *Social Sciences Information* (Sage, London and Beverly Hills) 18, 6:785–817.

————. 1980. *Homo hierarchicus: The caste system and its implications.* Rev. English ed. Chicago: University of Chicago Press.

Durkheim, Emile. 1897. Review of Josef Kohler, *Zur Urgeschichte der Ehe. L'Année Sociologique* 1:306–19.

————. 1913. Review of Alice Fletcher and Francis La Flesche, *The Omaha Tribe. L'Année Sociologique* 12:366–71.

————. 1915. *The elementary forms of the religious life,* trans. J. W. Swain.

London: Allen and Unwin (originally published in French in 1912).

Durkheim, Emile, and Marcel Mauss. 1963. *Primitive classification,* trans. R. Needham. London: Cohen and West (originally published in French in 1903).

Eggan, Fred. 1937a. Historical changes in the Choctaw kinship system. *American Anthropologist* 39:34–52.

––––––. 1937b. The Cheyenne and Arapaho kinship system. In *Social anthropology of North American tribes,* ed. Fred Eggan. Chicago: University of Chicago Press.

––––––. 1954. Social anthropology and the method of controlled analysis. *American Anthropologist* 56, 5:743–63.

––––––. 1955. Social anthropology: Methods and results. In *Social anthropology of North American tribes,* enlarged ed., ed. Fred Eggan. Chicago: University of Chicago Press.

––––––. 1966. *The American Indian: Perspectives for the study of social change.* Chicago: Aldine.

Evans-Pritchard, E. E. 1960. Introduction to Robert Hertz, *Death and the right hand.* Glencoe, Ill.: Free Press.

––––––. 1962. *Essays in social anthropology.* London: Faber and Faber.

––––––. 1965. The comparative method in social anthropology. In *The position of women in primitive societies and other essays in social anthropology.* London: Faber.

––––––. 1973. Fifty years of British anthropology. *Times Literary Supplement* (6 July), 763–64.

Eyde, D. B., and P. M. Postal. 1961. Avunculocality and incest: The development of unilateral cross-cousin marriage and Crow-Omaha kinship systems. *American Anthropologist* 63, 3:747–71.

Faron, L. C. 1956. Araucanian patri-organization and the Omaha system. *American Anthropologist* 58, 3:435–56.

––––––. 1961. The Dakota-Omaha continuum in Mapuche society. *Journal of the Royal Anthropological Institute* 91, 1:11–22.

Firth, Raymond. 1975. An appraisal of modern social anthropology. In *Annual Review of Anthropology,* ed. Bernard J. Siegel, vol. 4. Palo Alto, Calif.: Annual Reviews.

Fletcher, Alice. 1883. Observations on the laws and privileges of the gens in Indian society. *Proceedings of the American Association for the Advancement of Science* 32:395–96.

––––––. 1884a. Observations on the usage, symbolism and influence of the sacred pipes of fellowship among the Omahas. *Proceedings of the American Association for the Advancement of Science* 33:615–17.

———. 1884b. The religious ceremony of the four winds or quarters. *Report of the Peabody Museum* 3, 19 (1881–87):289–95.

———. 1884c. Lands in severalty to Indians: Illustrated by experiences with the Omaha tribe. *Proceedings of the American Association for the Advancement of Science* 33:654–65.

Fletcher, Alice C., and Francis La Flesche. 1911. *The Omaha tribe.* Annual Report of the Bureau of American Ethnology, vol. 27. Washington, D.C.: Government Printing Office.

———. 1912. Communication. *American Historical Review* 17:885–86.

Fontenelle, Henry. 1885. History of the Omaha Indians. *Transactions and Reports of the Nebraska State Historical Society* 1:76–83.

Fortune, Reo. 1932. *Omaha secret societies.* New York: Columbia University Press.

Fox, Robin. 1967. *The Keresan bridge: A problem in Pueblo ethnology.* London: Athlone Press.

Frege, Gottlob. 1891. *Funktion und Begriff: Vorträge gehalten in der Sitzung vom 9. Januar 1891 der Jenaischen Gesellschaft für Medizin und Naturwissenschaft* 2:1–31. Jena: H. Pohle.

———. 1892. Uber Sinn und Bedeutung. *Zeitschr. f. Philos. u. Philos. Kritik,* n.s., 100:25–50.

Gay, E. Jane. 1981. *With the Nez Perces: Alice Fletcher in the Field, 1889–92,* ed. Frederick E. Hoxie and Joan T. Mark. Lincoln: University of Nebraska Press.

Gell, Alfred. 1975. *Metamorphosis of the cassowaries: Umeda society, knowledge and ritual.* London: Athlone Press.

Giffen, Fannie Reed. 1898. *Oo-mah-ha Ta-wa-tha (Omaha City),* with illustrations by Susette La Flesche Tibbles (Bright Eyes). Lincoln, Nebr.: The authors.

Gifford, E. W. 1916. Miwok moieties. *University of California Publications in American Archaeology and Ethnology,* vol. 12, 139–94.

———. 1940. A problem in kinship terminology. *American Anthropologist* 42:190–94.

Gilbert, W. H. 1943. *The eastern Cherokees.* Bulletin of the Bureau of American Ethnology, no. 133, 169–414. Washington, D.C.: Government Printing Office.

Gilmore, Melvin Randolph. 1919. The true Logan Fontenelle. *Publications of the Nebraska State Historical Society* 19:64–71.

Goldenweiser, Alexander. 1910. Totemism: An analytical study. *Journal of American Folk-Lore* 23:179–293.

———. 1913a. On Iroquois work. *Summary Reports of the Geological Survey of Canada,* 365–72.

248

———. 1913b. Remarks on the social organization of the Crow Indians. *American Anthropologist* 15:281–94.

Green, Norma Kidd. 1969. *Iron Eye's family: The children of Joseph La Flesche.* Lincoln, Nebr.: Johnsen.

Hallowell, A. Irving. 1928. Recent changes in the kinship terminology of the St. Francis Abenaki. *International Congress of Americanists* 22:97–145.

———. 1930. Was cross-cousin marriage formerly practiced by the north-central Algonkian? *International Congress of Americanists* 23:519–44.

Hassrick, Royal B. 1944. Teton Dakota kinship system. *American Anthropologist* 46:338–47.

Héritier, Françoise. 1974. Système omaha de parenté et d'alliance: Etude en ordinateur du fonctionnement matrimonial réel d'une société africaine. In *Genealogical mathematics,* ed. Paul A. Ballonoff. The Hague: Mouton.

———. 1975. L'ordinateur et l'étude du fonctionnement matrimonial d'un système omaha. In *Les domaines de la parenté: Filiation, alliance, résidence,* ed. Marc Augé. Paris: Maspero.

———. 1976. Contribution à la théorie de l'alliance: Comment fonctionnent les systèmes d'alliance omaha? *Informatique et Sciences Humaines* 29:10–46.

———. 1981. *L'exercice de la parenté.* Paris: Gallimard.

Hertz, Robert. 1974. The pre-eminence of the right hand: A study in religious polarity. In *Right and left,* ed. Rodney Needham. Chicago: University of Chicago Press (originally published in French in 1909).

Hewitt, J. N. B. 1895. James Owen Dorsey. *American Anthropologist* 8:180–83.

Hinsley, Curtis M. 1981. *Savages and scientists: The Smithsonian Institution and the development of American anthropology, 1846–1910.* Washington, D.C.: Smithsonian Institution Press.

Houck, Louis, 1909. *The Spanish régime in Missouri: A collection of papers and documents relating to Upper Louisiana.* 2 vols. Chicago: Donnelly.

Hough, Walter. 1923. Alice Cunningham Fletcher. *American Anthropologist* 25:254–58.

Howard, James H. 1965. *The Ponca tribe.* Bulletin of the Bureau of American Ethnology, no. 195. Washington, D.C.: Government Printing Office.

———. 1979. Some further thoughts on eastern Dakota "clans." *Ethnohistory* 26, 2:133–40.

Hoxie, Frederick E., and Joan T. Mark. 1981. Introduction to E. Jane Gay, *With the Nez Perces.* Lincoln: University of Nebraska Press.

Irving, Washington. 1836. *Astoria; or, Anecdotes of an enterprise beyond the Rocky Mountains.* 2 vols. Philadelphia: Carey, Lea and Blanchard.

Izard, Françoise. 1968. A propos de l'énoncé des interdits matrimoniaux. *L'Homme* 8, 3:5–21.

James, Edwin. 1905. Account of S. H. Long's expedition, 1819–1820. In *Early western travels,* ed. Reuben G. Thwaites, vols. 14–17. Cleveland: Clark (first published London, 1823).

Köbben, A. J. F., J. Verrips, and L. N. J. Brunt. 1974. Lévi-Strauss and empirical inquiry. *Ethnology* 13:215–23.

Kohler, Josef. 1897. *Zur Urgeschichte der Ehe: Totemismus, Gruppenehe, Mutterrecht.* Stuttgart: Enke.

——. 1975. *On the prehistory of marriage: Totemism, group marriage, mother right,* ed., R. H. Barnes, trans. R. H. Barnes and Ruth Barnes. Classics in Anthropology. Chicago: University of Chicago Press.

Korn, Francis. 1973. *Elementary structures reconsidered: Lévi-Strauss on kinship.* London: Tavistock.

Kroeber, A. L. 1909. Classificatory systems of relationship. *Journal of the Royal Anthropological Institute of Great Britain and Ireland* 39:11–22.

Kurz, Rudolph Friederich. 1937. *Journal of Rudolph Friederich Kurz,* ed. J. N. B. Hewitt, trans. Myrtis Jarell, Bulletin of the Bureau of American Ethnology, no. 115. Washington, D.C.: Government Printing Office.

La Flesche, Francis. 1900. *The middle five: Indian schoolboys of the Omaha tribe.* Boston: Small, Maynard.

——. 1921. *The Osage tribe: Rites of the chiefs, sayings of the ancient men.* Annual Report of the Bureau of American Ethnology, vol. 36 (1914–15). Washington, D.C.: Government Printing Office.

——. 1923. Alice C. Fletcher. *Science,* 17 August 1923, 115.

——. 1925. *The Osage tribe: The rite of vigil.* Annual Report of the Bureau of American Ethnology, vol. 39 (1917–18). Washington, D.C.: Government Printing Office.

——. 1928. *The Osage tribe: Two versions of the child-naming rite.* Annual Report of the Bureau of American Ethnology, vol. 43 (1925–26). Washington, D.C.: Government Printing Office.

——. 1973. Right and left in Osage ceremonies. In *Right and left,* ed. Rodney Needham. Chicago: University of Chicago Press.

Laguna, Frederica de. 1957. Some problems of objectivity in ethnology. *Man* 57, 228:179–82.

Lane, R., and B. Lane. 1959. On the development of Dakota-Iroquois and Crow-Omaha kinship terminologies. *Southwestern Journal of Anthropology* 15, 3:254–65.

Leach, E. R. 1954. *Political systems of highland Burma: A study of Kachin social structure.* London: Bell.

———. 1961. *Rethinking anthropology.* London: Athlone Press.

Lesser, Alexander. 1929. Kinship origins in the light of some distributions. *American Anthropologist* 31, 4:710–30.

———. 1930. Some aspects of Siouan kinship. *Proceedings of the Twenty-third International Congress of Americanists (for 1928)*, 563–71.

———. 1958. *Siouan kinship.* Ph.D. diss., Columbia University. Ann Arbor, Mich.: University Microfilms.

Lévi-Strauss, Claude. 1953a. Social structure. In *Anthropology today*, ed. A. L. Kroeber. Chicago: University of Chicago Press.

———. 1953b. Results of the Conference of Anthropology and Linguistics. *International Journal of American Linguistics,* Supple. 19, 2:1–10.

———. 1956. Les organisations dualistes existent-elles? *Bijdragen Tot de Taal-, Land- en Volkenkunde* 112, 2:99–128.

———. 1960. On manipulated sociological models. *Bijdragen Tot de Taal-, Land- en Volkenkunde* 116, 1:45–54.

———. 1962. *Totemism,* trans. Rodney Needham. Boston: Beacon Press.

———. 1963. *Structural anthropology,* trans. Claire Jacobson and Brooke Grundfest Schoepf. New York: Basic Books.

———. 1966a. *The savage mind.* London: Weidenfeld and Nicolson.

———. 1966b. The future of kinship studies. *Proceedings of the Royal Anthropological Institute of Great Britain and Ireland for 1965.*

———. 1966c. Anthropology: Its achievements and future. *Current Anthropology* 7, 2:124–29.

———. 1967. Préface de la deuxième édition. In *Les structures élémentaires de la parenté.* Paris: Mouton.

———. 1969. Preface to the second edition. In *The elementary structures of kinship,* trans. J. H. Bell, J. R. von Sturmer, and R. Needham. London: Eyre and Spottiswoode.

Lienhardt, Godfrey. 1964. *Social anthropology.* London: Oxford University Press.

Lloyd, G. E. R. 1966. *Polarity and analogy.* Cambridge: Cambridge University Press.

Lounsbury, F. G. 1964. A formal account of the Crow- and Omaha-type kinship terminologies. In *Explorations in cultural anthropology*, ed. W. H. Goodenough. New York: McGraw-Hill.

Lowie, Robert. 1912. *Crow social life.* Anthropological Papers of the American Museum of Natural History 9, 2. New York: American Museum of Natural History.

———. 1915. Exogamy and classificatory systems of relationship. *American Anthropologist* 17, 2:223–39.

———. 1917a. *Culture and ethnology.* New York: Boni and Liveright.

———. 1917b. *Notes on the social organization and customs of the Mandan, Hidatsa and Crow Indians.* Anthropological Papers of the American Museum of Natural History 21, 1. New York: American Museum of Natural History.

———. 1934. The Omaha and Crow kinship terminologies. *Proceedings of the Twenty-fourth International Congress of Americanists (for 1930),* 103–8.

———. 1935. *The Crow Indians.* New York: Farrar and Rinehart.

Lucich, Peter. 1968. *The development of Omaha kinship terminologies in three Australian aboriginal tribes of the Kimberley Division, Western Australia.* Australian Aboriginal Studies, no. 15; Social Anthropology Series, no. 2. Canberra: Australian Institute of Aboriginal Studies.

Ludwickson, John. n.d. Omaha ethnohistory and the "Big Village": 1750–1850. Unpublished manuscript, Nebraska State Historical Society.

Ludwickson, John, Donald Blakeslee, and John O'Shea. 1981. *Missouri National Recreational River: Native American cultural resources.* Denver: Heritage Conservation and Recreation Service, Interagency Archeological Services.

Lurie, Nancy Oestreich. 1966. The lady from Boston and the Omaha Indians. *American West* 3, 4:31–33, 80–85.

Lyons, John. 1977. *Semantics.* 2 vols. Cambridge: Cambridge University Press.

McGee, W. J. 1897. *The Siouan Indians.* Annual Report of the Bureau of American Ethnology, vol. 15 (1893–94). Washington, D.C.: Government Printing Office.

McKenney, Thomas L., and James Hall. 1838. *History of the Indian tribes of North America with biographical sketches and anecdotes of the principal chiefs.* 3 vols. Philadelphia: Greenough.

McKinley, Robert. 1971a. A critique of the reflectionist theory of kinship terminology: The Crow/Omaha case. *Man* 6:228–47.

———. 1971b. Why do Crow and Omaha kinship terminologies exist? A sociology of knowledge interpretation. *Man* 6:408–26.

McLennan, J. F. 1876. *Studies in ancient history comprising a reprint of primitive marriage,* ed. D. McLennan. London: Macmillan.

MacMurphy, J. A. 1893. Some Frenchmen of early days on the Missouri River. *Transactions and Reports of the Nebraska State Historical Society* 5:53–81.

Margry, Pierre, ed. 1876–86. *Découvertes et établissements des français dans l'ouest et dans le sud de l'Amérique septentrionale (1614–1754).* 6 vols. Paris: Jouaust.

Mark, Joan. 1980. *Four anthropologists: An American science in its early years.* New York: Science History Publications.

Matthews, G. H. 1959. Proto-Siouan kinship terminology. *American Anthropologist* 61:252–78.

Mauss, Marcel. 1913. Review of Alice Fletcher and Francis La Flesche, *The Omaha Tribe. L'Année Sociologique* 12:104–11.

Maybury-Lewis, David. 1960. The analysis of dual organizations: A methodological critique. *Bijdragen Tot de Taal-, Land- en Volkenkunde* 116, 1:17–44.

———. 1979. Cultural categories of the central Gê. In *Dialectical societies,* ed. David Maybury-Lewis. Cambridge: Harvard University Press.

Mead, Margaret. 1932. *The changing culture of an Indian tribe.* New York: Columbia University Press.

Mill, John Stuart. 1843. *System of logic.* London: Parker.

Milner, Clyde A. 1982. *With good intentions: Quaker work among the Pawnees, Otos, and Omahas in the 1870s.* Lincoln: University of Nebraska Press.

Minot, George, ed. 1855. *Statutes at large and treaties of the United States of America,* vol. 10. Boston: Little, Brown.

Mooney, James. 1928. *The aboriginal population of America north of Mexico,* ed. John R. Swanton. Smithsonian Miscellaneous Collections, vol. 80, no. 7. Washington, D.C.: Government Printing Office.

Moore, S. F. 1963. Oblique and asymmetrical cross-cousin marriage and Crow-Omaha terminology. *American Anthropologist* 65, 2:296–311.

Morgan, L. H. 1870. *Systems of consanguinity and affinity of the human family.* Smithsonian Contributions to Knowledge, vol. 17. Washington, D.C.: Smithsonian Institution.

———. 1959. *The Indian journals, 1859–62,* ed. Leslie White. Ann Arbor: University of Michigan Press.

Morton, J. Sterling, and Albert Watkins, eds. 1907. *Illustrated history of Nebraska,* vol. 2. Lincoln. Nebr.: North.

Muller, Jean-Claude. 1980. Straight sister-exchange and the transition from elementary to complex structures. *American Ethnologist* 7, 3:518–29.

Murdock, George Peter. 1949. *Social structure.* New York: Macmillan.

———. 1967. Ethnographic atlas: A summary. *Ethnology* 6:109–236.

Nasatir, Abraham P. 1952. *Before Lewis and Clark: Documents illustrat-*

ing the history of the Missouri, 1785–1804. 2 vols. Saint Louis: Saint Louis Historical Documents Foundation.

Needham, Rodney. 1962. *Structure and sentiment*. Chicago: University of Chicago Press.

———. 1963. Introduction to Emile Durkheim and Marcel Mauss, *Primitive classification*. Chicago: University of Chicago Press.

———. 1969. Gurage social classification: Formal notes on an unusual system. *Africa* 39:153–66.

———. 1971. Remarks on the analysis of kinship and marriage. In *Rethinking kinship and marriage*, ed. Rodney Needham. Association of Social Anthropologists Monograph 11. London: Tavistock.

———, ed. 1973a. *Right and left: Essays on dual symbolic classification*. Chicago: University of Chicago Press.

———. 1973b. Prescription. *Oceania* 42:166–81.

———. 1980. *Reconnaissances*. Toronto: University of Toronto Press.

Nett, B. R. 1952. Historical changes in the Osage kinship system. *Southwestern Journal of Anthropology* 8:164–81.

Onvlee, L. 1949. Naar Aanleiding van de Stuwdam in Mangili: Opmerkingen over de Sociale Structuur van Oost-Sumba. *Bijdragen Tot de Taal-, Land- en Volkenkunde* 105:445–59. (Republished 1977 as The construction of the Mangili Dam: Notes on the social organization of eastern Sumba, in *Structural anthrepology in the Netherlands*, ed. P. E. de Josselin de Jong. The Hague: Nijhoff.)

O'Shea, John. 1981. Social configurations and the archaeological study of mortuary practices: A case study. In *The archaeology of death*, ed. Robert Chapman, Ian Kinnes, and Klars Randsbord. Cambridge: Cambridge University Press.

Peters, Richard, ed. 1848. *The public statutes at large of the United States of America*, vol. 7. Boston: Little, Brown.

Powell, J. W. 1894. *Administrative report*. Eleventh Annual Report of the Bureau of Ethnology (1889–90). Washington, D.C.: Government Printing Office.

Putnam, Frederic W. 1887. *Twentieth Report of the Peabody Museum of American Archaeology and Ethnology* (for 1886), 13:7.

Quaife, Milo M., ed. 1916. *The journals of Captain Meriweather Lewis and Sergeant John Ordway*. Publications of the State Historical Society of Wisconsin. Madison: The Society.

Radcliffe-Brown, A. R. 1941. The study of kinship systems. *Journal of the Royal Anthropological Institute* 71, 1:1–18.

———. 1951. The comparative method in social anthropology. *Journal of the Royal Anthropological Institute* 81:15–22.

Radin, Paul. 1923. *The Winnebago tribe.* Annual Report of the Bureau of American Ethnology, vol. 37 (1915–16). Washington, D.C.: Government Printing Office.

Rivers, W. H. R. 1914. *Kinship and social organisation.* London: Constable.

Ruhemann, Barbara. 1967. Purpose and mathematics: A problem in the analysis of classificatory kinship Systems. *Bijdragen Tot de Taal-, Land-en Volkenkunde* 123, 1:83–124.

Sanger, George P., ed. 1868. *Statutes at large . . . , vol. 14. Boston: Little, Brown.*

Sapir, Edward. 1938. Why cultural anthropology needs the psychiatrist. *Psychiatry* 1:7–12.

Scheffler, Harold W. 1982. Theory and method in social anthropology: On the structures of kin classification. *American Ethnologist* 9, 1:167–84.

Service, E. R. 1960. Kinship terminology and evolution. *American Anthropologist* 62, 5:747–63.

Smith, G. Hubert. 1974. *Omaha Indians: Ethnohistorical report on the Omaha people.* New York: Garland.

Speck, F. G. 1939. Eggan's Yuchi kinship interpretations. *American Anthropologist* 41:171–72.

Spier, Leslie. 1925. The distribution of kinship systems in North America. *University of Washington Publications in Anthropology* 1, 2:69–88.

Starcke, C. N. 1889. *The primitive family.* London: Kegan Paul, Tranch.

Strathern, Andrew. 1970. Wiru penthonyms. *Bijdragen Tot de Taal-, Land-, en Volkenkunde* 126, 1:59–74.

Strawson, P. R. 1950. On referring. *Mind* 59:320–44.

Strong, W. D. 1929. Cross-cousin marriage and the culture of the northeast Algonkian. *American Anthropologist* 31:777–88.

Tax, Sol. 1937a. Some problems of social organization. In *Social anthropology of North American tribes,* ed. Fred Eggan. Chicago: University of Chicago Press.

———. 1937b. The social organization of the Fox Indians. In *Social anthropology of North American tribes,* ed. Fred Eggan. Chicago: University of Chicago Press.

Teitelbaum, Michele. 1980. Designation of preferential affinity in the Jokwele Kpelle Omaha-type relationship terminology. *Journal of Anthropological Research* 36, 1:31–48.

Thompson, Basil H. 1895. Concubitancy in the classificatory system of relationship. *Journal of the Anthropological Institute of Great Britain and Ireland* 24:371–87.

Thwaites, Reuben Gold, ed. 1904–5. *Original journals of the Lewis and Clark expedition, 1804–1806,* 8 vols. New York: Dodd, Mead.

Tibbles, Thomas Henry. 1957. *Buckskin and blanket days.* Garden City, N.Y.: Doubleday.

Tonkin, Elizabeth. 1980. Jealousy names, civilised names: Anthroponomy of the Jlao Kru of Liberia. *Man* 15, 4:653–64.

Ubelaker, Douglas H. 1976. The sources and methodology for Mooney's estimates of North American Indian populations. In *The native population of the Americas in 1492,* ed. William M. Denevan. Madison: University of Wisconsin Press.

United States Statutes at Large. 1883. December 1881 to March 1883, Vol. 22. Washington, D.C.: Government Printing Office.

Voegelin, C. F. 1941. Internal relationships of Siouan languages. *American Anthropologist* 43:246–49.

Walker, James R. 1914. Oglala kinship terms. *American Anthropologist* 16:96–109.

Wedel, Mildred M. 1981. The Ioway, Oto, and Omaha Indians in 1700. *Journal of the Iowa Archaeological Society* 28:1–13.

Westermarck, Edward. 1894. *The history of human marriage.* 2d ed. London and New York: Macmillan.

White, Leslie A. 1939. A problem in kinship terminology. *American Anthropologist* 41:566–73.

Wolff, Hans. 1950. Comparative Siouan. *International Journal of American Linguistics* 16, 2:61–66, 113–21, 168–78; 17:197–204.

Subject Index

Name Index